PRAGMATICS:
THEORIES AND APPLICATIONS
语用学——理论及应用

姜望琪　编著

北京大学出版社
2000年·北京

图书在版编目(CIP)数据

语用学——理论及应用：英文/姜望琪著. —北京：北京大学出版社，2000.1

ISBN 978-7-301-04377-6

Ⅰ. 语… Ⅱ. 姜… Ⅲ. 语用学—英文 Ⅳ. H0

中国版本图书馆 CIP 数据核字(2000)第 01151 号

书　　　名：语用学——理论及应用
著作责任者：姜望琪
责 任 编 辑：徐 刚
标 准 书 号：ISBN 978-7-301-04377-6
出　版　者：北京大学出版社
地　　　址：北京市海淀区成府路 205 号　100871
网　　　址：http://cbs.pku.edu.cn/cbs.htm
电　　　话：邮购部 62752015　发行部 62750672　编辑部 62752028
电 子 信 箱：zpup@pup.pku.edu.cn
排　版　者：兴盛达打字服务社　82715400
印　刷　者：北京虎彩文化传播有限公司
发　行　者：北京大学出版社
经　销　者：新华书店
　　　　　　890 毫米×1240 毫米　A5 开本　10.25 印张　251 千字
　　　　　　2000 年 1 月第 1 版　2019 年 8 月第 7 次印刷
定　　　价：16.00 元

未经许可，不得以任何方式复制或抄袭本书之部分或全部内容。
版权所有，翻印必究

献给——

我的老师

序

我是1979年在澳大利亚进修学习时首次接触语用学的。弹指二十年,目睹了语用学研究在我国的迅猛发展。有关语用学的教材、专著、论文、学术会议,在我国频频出台。我本人虽无新的建树,为同行们的每一个成就总感到无比的喜悦。就像攀登华山一样,自己在金锁关前止步不前自愧不已,唯对那些义无反顾继续向中峰、东峰、西峰挺进的勇士们却总是肃然起敬,夸不绝口的。如今,我似乎再现了这种心情。当同仁姜望琪教授将他的语用学手稿交到我手中时,我既感到它的学术分量,也共享作者登临顶峰后的喜悦心情。

《语用学——理论及应用》一书,填补了我国语用学教材,特别是高级教材的贫乏和过时。在市场经济的大潮中,能否编写和出版一部销量有限的学术性专业书籍是对作者、编者和出版社胆识的考验。一瞬间,在我眼前出现的形象不是在海边卷起裤腿的弄潮儿,而是在大海远处波涛中时隐时现的冲浪者。

外语界老前辈许国璋先生在世时曾多次表示,语言学的外语教材既要介绍国外的新动向、新成果、新思路,也要反映我国学者的认识和学术水平。《语用学——理论及应用》一书应该说是我国学者近年来向这个方向努力的一个成果。不能说,作者已经提出了自己的模式,但在本书中,作者不时比较不同观点和发表自己的远见卓识。为了方便读者阅读,作者将大量的讨论放在附注中,供有兴趣者进一步研究思考。由此展开的讨论无疑将推动我国语用学的研究。

《语用学——理论及应用》是用英语写作的。文笔通顺流畅，表达正确。这一方面让我国英语专业学生和语言学研究生有书可读，专业知识和英语水平同步提高；另一方面，必然能让国外学者了解我国语用学研究的现状和水平，推动我国语用学研究与国际接轨，我们不妨拭目以待。

　　最后要指出的是，姜望琪教授是在眼疾不时发作，编写工作时停时缀的困难情况下完成的。在这个意义上，《语用学——理论及应用》可谓他的呕心沥血之作。我总有这样的感觉，即使在他用眼不方便时，作者没有停止思考，本书的字里行间都闪现他深邃的思想火花。愿读者与我共享这一感受。

胡壮麟
1999 年 5 月 1 日于
北京大学畅春园

自　序

语用学是一门新兴学科。五十年代正式面世,六七十年代即成为显学,八九十年代又提出了新的理论。

国内自八十年代以来,不断有文章介绍语用学。许多学校相继开设了语用学课程,教科书也应运而生。本人从 1992 年开始为英语系研究生讲授语用学(中间因眼疾耽搁了不少时日),深感编撰一部有深度、成系统、合国情的教材迫在眉睫,因此不揣冒昧,斗胆一试。

本书不纠缠语用学的定义,而重在其研究的内容,即指称、会话含义、预设、言语行为、会话分析五个方面。其中会话含义是重点,特别是系统介绍了八九十年代提出的关联理论、新格赖斯原则。鉴于国内学者,尤其是研究生,不容易读到国外语用学原著,本书以原原本本介绍理论首创者的思想为宗旨。力求做到忠实、准确,同时尽可能简单明了。

有人以为语用学是**教**人用语言的。既然人人都会说话——运用语言的基本形式,那么语用学毫无用处,就是不证自明的。这其实是一种误解。语用学是**研究**语言运用规律的。人人都会说话不等于人人都明白其中的道理,都懂得其规律。可以毫不夸张地说,迄今为止尚无一人已明白了说话的规律,至少无人能清楚地将其表达出来。因此才有了语用学,才有了这门研究其规律的学科。

可是为什么要明白说话的规律呢?现成的答案是为了更自觉地运用这些规律,把语言运用得更巧妙。但深层次的答案涉及到语言研究的意义,甚至一切学术研究的意义,或曰人生的意义。凡能思考者皆为人生感到疑惑。人是什么？世界是什么？这一切从哪来？又将走向何方？人类几千年文明史,就是孜孜不倦探寻其答案的历史。语言作为人类区别于他类的重要特征,甚至是关键特征,是人类本质的重要外在形式。研究其机制必将加深对人类本质的了解。在某种意义上,弄明白人类是如何运用语言的,是理解人生的第一步(这是乔姆斯基把语言学归于心理学的一个原因)。这种探索是艰难的,但人类终将逼近答案。

　　语用学无用论,或广义说,语言学无用论,还来自它与国计民生无关的看法。这些人忽略了一个简单的事实:倡导抽象思维、探索苹果为什么往下掉的民族成就了工业革命,领导人类飞速进入现代文明;而讲究实际、天天询问"吃了吗？"的民族却遭受了百年屈辱,反而吃不上饭。貌似最远的路却是真正的捷径,这就是辩证法。万丈高楼起自千尺地下,似乎南辕北辙,实际欲擒故纵,反之则欲速不达。人工智能计算机的研制计划数十年前就宣布了,但至今仍无重大突破。为什么？症结不在计算机科学,在语言学。在于我们还不清楚语言机制,更谈不上成功地形式化描写语言,以致计算机无法理解传递人类智慧的工具——自然语言。

　　基于上述考虑,本书以相当篇幅阐述各种语用学理论,讨论各自的解释语言运用的能力。当然,理论是不能脱离实际的。它来自实际,为解决实际问题而提出;它还原实际,以其解决实际问题的能力被取舍。因此本书副标题的第二部分是"应用"。讨论理论时的各种例句都是应用的尝试,但集中讨论应用的是最后一章——会话分析。这是本书照搬莱文森(Levinson 1983),把这一题目包括进来的根本原因。

　　历经数载,终于草就。本人辛苦,自不必说;众人相助,亦不可少。本书是献给我的老师的,没有他们便没有本书。我感谢我的老师,所有的老师,小学的、中学的、大学的,中国的、外国的,教过我的、没教过我的，年长的、年轻的。但在这里，我只能具体提及曾给予本书直接帮助的师友。而且不是全部，只是主要的几位。首先是胡壮麟教授，他是向国内介绍语用学的第一人。当我跟他谈起自己的写作意图时，他欣然答应为我作序，并把自己收集多年的资料全部赠送与我，其中包括奥斯汀的 How to Do Things with Words。他还利用在香港讲学的机会，为我复印了两本最新的外国教材。在我写完后，他又在百忙中拨冗阅读了手稿，提出了许多中肯的意见。钱军博士在哈佛做研究时，抽出宝贵时间为我复印了国内找不到的资料。中文系索振羽教授也在写语用学教材，但他毫无保留地向我讲述了他的写作计划。我们在一起探讨了一些有争议的问题，我从中获益非浅。北外刘润清教授曾帮我从他们学校借书，并赠送了他的新作。北大英语系复印室张连敏老师，资料室蔡润、王志会、张燕敏老师为搜集资料提供了不少方便，在此一并致谢。最后，没有北大出版社胡双宝编审、郭力主任的鼎力相助，本书是不可能出版的。责任编辑徐刚为本书付出了艰辛的劳动。我感谢他们，感谢一切帮助过我的朋友。

Contents

序(胡壮麟) ………………………………………………………… I
自序 ……………………………………………………………… Ⅲ

1 **Introduction** ……………………………………………… (1)
  1.1 An informal definition ……………………………… (1)
  1.2 The origin of pragmatics …………………………… (2)
    1.2.1 The term "pragmatics" …………………… (3)
    1.2.2 Semiotics …………………………………… (4)
    1.2.3 Pragmatism ………………………………… (6)
    1.2.4 Semiotic pragmatics ……………………… (8)
2 **Deixis** …………………………………………………… (11)
  2.1 The egocentricity of deixis ………………………… (12)
  2.2 Different uses ………………………………………… (14)
    2.2.1 Gestural and symbolic uses ……………… (14)
    2.2.2 Deictic and anaphoric uses ……………… (15)
  2.3 Types of deixis ……………………………………… (20)
    2.3.1 Person deixis ……………………………… (20)
    2.3.2 Time deixis ………………………………… (25)
    2.3.3 Place deixis ………………………………… (28)
    2.3.4 Discourse deixis …………………………… (29)

  2.3.5 Social deixis ………………………………… (31)
3 Conversational implicature (I) …………………… (34)
 3.1 The Gricean theory ………………………………… (34)
  3.1.1 The cooperative principle ………………… (35)
  3.1.2 Violation of the maxims ………………… (43)
 3.2 Elaborations on the theory ……………………… (55)
  3.2.1 Characteristics of conversational implicature
    ………………………………………………… (55)
  3.2.2 Entailment …………………………………… (60)
  3.2.3 Conventional implicature ………………… (62)
  3.2.4 Distinctions within conversational implicature
    ………………………………………………… (65)
 3.3 Formalization of implicature ……………………… (71)
  3.3.1 Scalar quantity implicature ……………… (71)
  3.3.2 Clausal quantity implicature …………… (80)
4 Conversational implicature (II) …………………… (86)
 4.1 Relevance theory …………………………………… (86)
  4.1.1 Ostensive-inferential communication ……… (88)
  4.1.2 Relevance …………………………………… (96)
  4.1.3 Differences between the Gricean theory and
    relevance theory ………………………… (103)
 4.2 The Q- and R-principles ………………………… (110)
  4.2.1 Wherefore the principles ………………… (110)
  4.2.2 Evidence for the principles ……………… (117)
 4.3 The Q-, I- and M-principles ……………………… (128)
  4.3.1 A neoclassic interpretation ……………… (129)
  4.3.2 Anaphoric reference ……………………… (136)
  4.3.3 Some alternative approaches …………… (148)

5 Presupposition ·· (161)
- 5.1 The philosophical tradition ···························· (161)
- 5.2 A semantic analysis ······································· (166)
  - 5.2.1 Presupposition vs. focus ······················· (166)
  - 5.2.2 As a type of lexical information ············ (169)
  - 5.2.3 Factive and non-factive ························ (171)
  - 5.2.4 Presupposition-triggers ························ (173)
- 5.3 Problems in the semantic approach ·················· (177)
  - 5.3.1 Defeasibility ·· (177)
  - 5.3.2 The projection problem ······················· (179)
- 5.4 The pragmatic approach ································ (182)
  - 5.4.1 Holes, plugs and filters ························ (182)
  - 5.4.2 Potential and actual presuppositions ······ (187)
  - 5.4.3 A principled account ··························· (190)

6 Speech acts ··· (197)
- 6.1 The performative-constative dichotomy ············ (198)
  - 6.1.1 Early development ······························· (198)
  - 6.1.2 Felicity conditions ······························· (201)
  - 6.1.3 Collapse of the dichotomy ···················· (203)
- 6.2 The theory of illocutionary acts ······················· (206)
  - 6.2.1 Three kinds of speech act ····················· (206)
  - 6.2.2 Some counter-arguments ······················ (209)
- 6.3 Classes of illocutionary acts ···························· (213)
  - 6.3.1 Austin's classification ··························· (213)
  - 6.3.2 Searle's revision ·································· (217)
- 6.4 A semanticist view ·· (224)
  - 6.4.1 The performative hypothesis ·················· (224)
  - 6.4.2 A detailed examination ························· (226)

    6.5   Indirect speech acts .... (239)
            6.5.1   A pragmatic analysis .... (240)
            6.5.2   Idiomatic, but not idioms .... (245)
7 Conversation analysis .... (248)
    7.1   Turn-taking .... (249)
            7.1.1   Rules for turn-taking .... (250)
            7.1.2   The significance of the rules .... (255)
    7.2   Adjacency pairs .... (259)
            7.2.1   Insertion sequences .... (260)
            7.2.2   Three-turn structures .... (263)
    7.3   Preference organization .... (266)
            7.3.1   Preference in repair .... (266)
            7.3.2   Preferred and dispreferred seconds ... (269)
    7.4   A neo-Gricean interpretation .... (277)
            7.4.1   Pre-sequences .... (277)
            7.4.2   Minimization in conversation .... (282)
    7.5   Searle on conversation .... (285)
            7.5.1   The structure of conversation .... (285)
            7.5.2   Turn-taking "rules" .... (290)
            Appendix: transcription conventions .... (294)
Bibliography .... (295)

Chapter 1: Introduction

Pragmatics is a newly arising discipline. Its English name was only invented in 1937 and its first major theory, Speech Act Theory, did not take shape until the 50s. But it has been developing rapidly. By the early 80s, pragmatics had been generally accepted as one of the basic branches of linguistics together with phonetics, phonology, morphology, syntax, and semantics.①

1.1 An informal definition

Pragmatics has been defined in many different ways.② But no at-

---

① It has to be said that this is a moderate view. There are less moderate views on the relation between linguistics and pragmatics. H. Haberland and J. Mey, the first editors of *Journal of Pragmatics*, for instance, in their editorial of the first issue (1977: 9) argue that "linguistics is pragmatic or it is not". "[D]oing pragmatics, in our sense, is simply doing linguistics, and vice versa. The pragmatic 'aspect' can neither be separated from linguistics 'proper', or even postponed, or added on as a new component. Pragmatics, far from being an aspect of the linguist's work, is its very essence." Jef Verschueren, Secretary General of the International Pragmatics Association, also advocates "a radical departure from the established component view which tries to assign to pragmatics its own set of linguistic features in contradistinction with phonology, morphology, syntax and semantics". In his opinion, "pragmatics does not belong to the contrast set of these 'horizontal' components of the study of language, neither does it belong to the contrast set of 'vertical' components such as psycholinguistics, sociolinguistics, etc." "<u>Pragmatics</u> should be defined, rather, as a <u>perspective</u> on whatever phonologists, morphologists, syntacticians, semanticists, psycholinguists, sociolinguists, etc. deal with" (1987: 36).

② There is an extensive survey of them in S. Levinson (1983: 5-35).

tempt at any rigorous definition is made in this book. Instead, I define it in very general terms as the study of language in use, as against the study of language as an abstract system. It does not take an elaborated examination to show that these two studies differ. The following sentence, for example, as a unit in the system is a question concerning the ownership of a pen.

(1) Is this your pen?

In actual situations, however, it may have several different meanings. When it is used in a post office by someone to a stranger beside, it may serve as a request, meaning (2). When it is used by a teacher to a student leaving the classroom after the class, it may function as a reminder, meaning (3). And when it is used by a mother to a child, especially if the pen is on the floor, it may be intended as a command as in (4).

(2) May I use it?

(3) Don't leave it behind.

(4) Pick it up!

As this aspect of meaning is outside of semantics proper, we may also agree with the formula: pragmatics = meaning - semantics.[1]

1.2 The origin of pragmatics[2]

The term "pragmatics" may be used in three senses. First, it may refer to a discipline, as is used in the beginning of this chapter. Secondly, owing to its token-reflexivity[3], the term may refer to itself. In this sense, we usually enclose it in quotation marks, as is done in the

---

[1] Cf. G. Gazdar (1979: x, 2).

[2] For a more detailed account, see 姜望琪 (1997).

[3] This notion will be discussed at some length in section 2.2.2.

first sentence of this paragraph. Thirdly, "pragmatics" may refer to the phenomenon of language use, or that of the regularity in language use. For example, G. Leech (1983: 1) argues that "we cannot really understand the nature of language itself unless we understand pragmatics: how language is used in communication." The pragmatics as a discipline is the study of the pragmatics as a phenomenon. The latter, i.e. the phenomenon of language use, has been in existence ever since language came into being, or even earlier, in the very process of its coming into being. There can be no question about that. What requires some discussion is the pragmatics in the other two senses. The origin of the discipline pragmatics, both important and interesting, deserves a much more extended space than is possibly allowed here.① In this chapter, therefore, we shall concentrate on the term "pragmatics".

1.2.1　The term "pragmatics"

　　The term "pragmatics" was first introduced into the literature by the American philosopher Charles William Morris in 1937, when he collected five of his papers written after 1934 and published them under the title of *Logical Positivism, Pragmatism and Scientific Empiricism*. In its preface, he asserted that "Analysis reveals that linguistic signs sustain three types of relations (to other signs of the language, to objects that are signified, to persons by whom they are used and understood) which define three dimensions of meaning. These dimensions in turn are objects of investigation by syntactics, semantics, and pragmatics, semiotic [now usually called 'semiotics'] being the general science which includes all of these and their interrelations"

---

　　① For example, L. Horn (1988: 116) believes that "the study of pragmatics antedates the term by centuries if not millennia".

(p. 4).

In his *Foundations of the Theory of Signs* published in 1938, Morris expressed this idea again. That is, semiotics has three branches: syntactics, semantics and pragmatics. Syntactics studies "the formal relation of signs to one another", semantics "the relations of signs to the objects to which the signs are applicable", and pragmatics "the relation of signs to interpreters" (1971 [1938]: 21-2). In this book, he also made it known that "The term 'pragmatics' has obviously been coined with reference to the term 'pragmatism'.... The term 'pragmatics' helps to signalize the significance of the achievements of Peirce, James, Dewey, and Mead within the field of semiotic" (ibid.: 43).

1.2.2 Semiotics

Semiotics may be traced back to the ancient Greeks, but semiotics in the modern sense started with the American philosopher Charles Sanders Peirce. Peirce was hailed as the most versatile and original thinker America had ever produced. He graduated from Harvard in 1859, and went to the United States Coast and Geodetic Survey in 1861, where he worked for thirty years. In this only official post he ever held, he did research into such diversified fields as astronomy, metrology, mathematics, thermodynamics, gravitation, optics, but he declared "it has never been in my power to study anything... except as a study of semiotic".[①] It is his conviction that all thought is in signs. In this sense, we can say Peirce studied only one discipline in his whole life, the theory of signs--semiotics.

Peirce gave the sign many definitions in his writings. Some are

---

① From M. Fisch (1978: 54).

more or less the same. Some emphasize one aspect or another of the sign, which, when juxtaposed, may seem to be contradictory to each other. But they have one thing in common, that is, the sign is in a triadic relationship, which relates to its object on the one hand and its interpretant on the other. Thus, in one place he said, "I define a *Sign* as anything which on the one hand is so determined by an Object and on the other hand so determines an idea in a person's mind, that this latter determination, which I term the *Interpretant* of the sign, is thereby mediately determined by that Object" (8. 343). [①]

In consequence of this triadic relationship, Peirce divided semiotics into three sub-branches: grammar, logic and rhetoric. The first studies the nature of the sign, i. e. the conditions under which a sign functions as a sign; the second the relation between a sign and its object; and the third the relation between a sign and its interpretant (cf. 1. 191, 1. 444, 1. 559 and 2. 93).

This shows that there is a strong connection between Morris's theory and that of Peirce's. But the differences between them are also obvious. The names of the sub-branches of semiotics are different. And the greatest difference concerns the content of the third sub-branch. In Peirce's theory, this branch deals with the relation between the sign and the interpretant, an idea in a person's mind. In Morris's, however, it is concerned with the relation between the sign and the interpreter, the person who interprets the sign. Why is there such a change? When explaining the coinage of the term "pragmatics",

---

[①] It is customary to indicate the source of quotations from *Collected Papers of C. S. Peirce* with the numbers of the volume and the paragraph. In other words, 8. 343 means par. 343 of vol. 8.

Morris argued that "It is a plausible view that the permanent significance of pragmatism lies in the fact that it has directed attention more closely to the relation of signs to their users than had previously been done and has assessed more profoundly than ever before the relevance of this relation in understanding intellectual activities" (1971 [1938]: 43). Therefore, we shall turn to pragmatism in the next section.

1.2.3 Pragmatism

This is now generally interpreted as a school of philosophy. But it started as a theory of meaning, and it is the most original contribution made by Peirce.

In the early 70s of last century, C. S. Peirce, William James and some others formed a "metaphysical club", discussing philosophical questions. The ideas of Rene Descartes, the first modern philosopher, were among the topics. Descartes advocated universal doubt, doubting everything. But he admitted that there is one thing one cannot doubt, that is, one's own existence. The very fact that one is doubting proves that one is in existence. That is why he said "I think, therefore I am". As this is a clear and distinct idea, Descartes went on to propose a new criterion of truth, namely, any idea that is clear and distinct is true.

Now Peirce did not agree with Descartes on this point. In a meeting of the club in November 1872, Peirce aired his views, which five years later developed into two papers. The first, published in November 1877, is entitled "The Fixation of Belief", discussing belief in contrast to doubt. And in the second "How to Make Our Ideas Clear", in print January the following year, there is a passage, later known as the pragmatic maxim, which reads

> Consider what effects, that might conceivably have practical

bearings, we conceive the object of our conception to have. Then, our conception of those effects is the whole of our conception of the object. (5. 402)

This means "a *conception*, that is, the rational purport of a word or other expression, lies exclusively in its conceivable bearing upon the conduct of life" (5. 412). For example, when we say "Diamond is harder than glass", we mean diamond will scratch glass but glass will not scratch diamond. So if we want to divide a sheet of glass, and there is no tool except a diamond ring at hand, we may use the diamond ring as a tool. On the other hand, if we do not want a sheet of glass, say, a mirror, to be scratched, we will try to keep the diamond ring away from the mirror. The action to use a diamond ring to divide a sheet of glass, or the desire to keep a diamond ring away from a mirror, comes from our belief that "Diamond is harder than glass" and "hard" means "to be able to scratch something".

However, it was in 1898, 20 years later, in a speech delivered by James that the word "pragmatism" was first publicly used. James was then addressing the members of the Philosophical Union at the University of California in Berkeley. After some opening remarks on philosophers as pathfinders and trail blazers, James said,

> I will seek to define with you merely what seems to be the most likely direction in which to start upon the trail of truth. Years ago this direction was given to me by an American philosopher whose home is in the East, and whose published works, few as they are and scattered in periodicals, are not fit expression of his powers. I refer to Mr. Charles S. Peirce, with whose very existence as a philosopher I dare say many of you are unacquainted. He is one of the most original of contemporary thinkers; and

the principle of practicalism--or pragmatism, as he called it, when I first heard him enunciate it at Cambridge in the early 70's--is the clue or compass by following which I find myself more and more confirmed in believing we may keep our feet upon the proper trail.①

As a result, pragmatism, and Peirce's name together with it, beame widely known to the public. But Peirce was not satisfied with James's interpretation, especially his equation of pragmatism with practicalism. Peirce reasoned that his theory came from the German philosopher Immanuel Kant. In Kantian terms, something practical is established a priori, while something pragmatic is based on experience. And in his theory, the meaning of a concept is closely related to human experience, so it can only be called pragmatism, not practicalism (5. 412). In order to make his position clearer, from 1905 onwards, Peirce called his version of the theory "pragmaticism".

1.2.4 Semiotic pragmatics

The division of semiotics into syntactics, semantics and pragmatics by Morris was immediately accepted by other scholars. The German philosopher Rudolf Carnap, for one, adopted these terms and defined pragmatics as the field of investigation which takes into consideration "the action, state, and environment of a man who speaks or hears" a language in his *Foundations of Logic and Mathematics* (p. 146) of 1939. In 1942 when he wrote his *Introduction to Semantics*, he reformulated the definitions as follows:

> If in an investigation explicit reference is made to the speaker, or to put it in more general terms, to the user of the lan-

---

① From K. L. Ketner and C. J. W. Kloesel (eds.) (1986: 284).

guage, then we assign it to the field of pragmatics. (Whether in this case reference to designata is made or not makes no difference for this classification.) If we abstract from the user of the language and analyze only the expressions and their designata, we are in the field of semantics. And if, finally, we abstract from the designata also and analyze only the relations between the expressions, we are in (logical) syntax. (p. 9)

Morris, however, thought that Carnap's "restriction of semiotic to a study of language must be removed, the study of the structure of languages other than the scientific must be made possible, other modes of signification than the designative must be dealt with in semantics, and this in turn requires some modification of the formulation of pragmatics" (1971 [1946]: 302). And his new definitions in this 1946 book are: "*pragmatics* is that portion of semiotic which deals with the origin, uses, and effects of signs within the behavior in which they occur; *semantics* deals with the signification of signs in all modes of signifying; *syntactics* deals with combinations of signs without regard for their specific significations or their relation to the behavior in which they occur" (ibid.).

J. Lyons maintains in his *Semantics* (p. 119) that "it is arguable that, by now, the origins of the tripartite distinction in Peirce's conception of an overall science of semiotics are more or less irrelevant to the way in which this distinction is currently drawn by either linguists or philosophers. Even less relevant... is the connexion, in Peirce's work, between pragmatics as a subdivision of semiotics and the philosophical movement known as pragmatism". We hope to have shown by our brief retrospective survey that Lyons' denial is at fault. There ARE connections between pragmatics and Peirce's ideas, not only in the days when Morris first proposed the study but also in the present period. For example, G. Leech in his *Principles of Pragmatics* (pp. 5 - 6) holds the view that the difference between semantics and pragmatics "can be traced to two different uses of the verb *to mean* :

[1] What does X mean? [2] What did you mean by X?

Semantics traditionally deals with meaning as a dyadic relation, as in [1], while pragmatics deals with meaning as a triadic relation, as in [2]. Thus meaning in pragmatics is defined relative to a speaker or user of the language, whereas meaning in semantics is defined purely as a property of expressions in a given language, in abstraction from particular situations, speakers, or hearers." And he goes on to state explicitly "This is a rough-and-ready distinction which has been refined, for particular purposes, by philosophers such as Morris (1938, 1946) or Carnap (1942)."

There are, undeniably, differences between the pragmatics advocated by Morris and that practised by linguists today. Morris emphasized the semiotic nature of pragmatics while the pragmaticians[1] nowadays rarely associate their study with semiotics. In this sense, we can call the former semiotic pragmatics and the latter linguistic pragmatics. And after this introduction, we shall say no more about semiotic pragmatics, but concentrate on linguistic pragmatics.

---

[1] There are three terms currently in use for people engaging in pragmatics: pragmatist, pragmaticist, and pragmatician. The present author prefers the last for the simple reason that morphologically speaking "pragmatist" corresponds to "pragmatism", and "pragmaticist" to "pragmaticism", which are both names for the philosophical movement started by Peirce and should be kept apart from pragmatics, especially linguistic pragmatics, even though there are undeniable connections between the two.

Chapter 2: Deixis

Deixis, as defined by J. Lyons (1977: 636),[1] refers "to the function of personal and demonstrative pronouns, of tense and of a variety of other grammatical and lexical features which relate utterances to the spatio-temporal co-ordinates of the act of utterance." That is, deixis is the function of grammatical as well as lexical means relating a piece of language to its context in terms of its users, the time and place of its occurrence, and the people and objects it refers to. The words used in this function are known as deictics, indexicals, or indexical expressions. Typical examples are pronouns, demonstratives, time and place adverbs, and some grammatical categories such as tense.

This is the first area of study in linguistic pragmatics that has caught the attention of scholars. In 1954, the Israeli philosopher Yehoshua Bar-Hillel wrote an article "Indexical Expressions", in which he compared the following three sentences:

(1) Ice floats on water.
(2) It's raining.
(3) I'm hungry.

The first sentence would not cause any difficulty for its interpretation in isolation. Whoever says it at whatever time and place, its

---

[1] Quotations of J. Lyons in this chapter are all from this book, henceforth only page number will be shown.

meaning would not be changed. But the second and third sentences, which contain indexical expressions, depend on the context heavily. "[W]hat (2) is intended to refer to will be fully grasped only by those people who know the place and time of its production, the identification of the intended reference of (3) will require the knowledge of its producer and the time of its production", Bar-Hillel (p. 69) contends. And he speculated that more than 90% of the declarative sentences people produce are indexical in that they involve references to the speaker, addressee, time and place of speaking (p. 76). Since then the study of indexicals, or deictics, has always been one of the central topics in pragmatics.

2.1　The egocentricity of deixis

In general, deixis is used in an egocentric way. That is, unless otherwise stated, "(i) the central person is the speaker, (ii) the central time is the time at which the speaker produces the utterance, (iii) the central place is the speaker's location at utterance time..., (iv) the discourse centre is the point which the speaker is currently at in the production of his utterance, and (v) the social centre is the speaker's social status and rank, to which the status or rank of addressees or referents is relative" (S. Levinson 1983: 64).[①] So the first person pronoun *I*, including *my*, *me*, refers to the speaker, no matter who hears or reads it. Violating this rule would result in comic effects, as is amply illustrated by the example quoted on page 68 of Levinson's *Pragmatics*:

　　　　A melamed [Hebrew teacher] discovering that he had left his

---

　　[①]　Quotations of S. Levinson in this chapter are all from this book, henceforth only page number will be shown.

comfortable slippers back in the house, sent a student after them with a note for his wife. The note read: "Send me your slippers with this boy". When the student asked why he had written "your" slippers, the melamed answered: "Yold [Fool]! If I wrote 'my' slippers, she would read 'my' slippers and would send her slippers. What could I do with her slippers? So I wrote 'your' slippers, she'll read 'your' slippers and send me mine". (Rosten, 1968: 443 – 4)

However, when it is not a face-to-face conversation, when the speaker and the addressee are not in the same place at the time of speaking, then the egocentricity may be violated. Lyons (pp. 578f.) notes when someone in London makes a long-distance telephone-call to his friend in New York, he can either greet with *Good morning*! according to his own time, or *Good afternoon*! according to the addressee's time. The speaker may say both *We are going to New York next week* and *We are coming to New York next week*. That is, the centre of discourse may be shifted to the addressee. As a matter of fact, with the verb *come*, it is even possible to shift the centre in a face-to-face dialogue. Usually, *come* means "movement toward the speaker" and *go* "movement away from the speaker". So we say *come in* and *go away*, *come here* and *go there*. But when someone is calling you a little distance away, you may say *I'm coming*, meaning "I'm moving toward you, the addressee". This phenomenon, the speaker projecting himself into a deictic context centred on the addressee is known as deictic projection. Still, to talk about deictic projection presupposes that deixis is egocentric. In a sense, we can say the study of deixis is to identify this centre, and the relevant time, place, people and objects involved can be determined thereupon.

2.2 Different uses

Deictics are by definition words for pointing, pointing to the people, objects, time and place that are relevant to the interpretation of a piece of language. But finer distinctions among this general use may be made, and the first of them is the distinction between the gestural and the symbolic.

2.2.1 Gestural and symbolic uses

This distinction is made on the basis of the presence or absence of paralinguistic features. By paralinguistic features is meant body movements like eye-gaze, facial expressions, nodding of the head, gestures by the hand, and unusual variations of pitch, loudness and duration of sound. The use of deictic expressions together with paralinguistic features is called the gestural use, and that without the symbolic use. For example, the deictics in (4), (5) and (6) are used in the gestural way, accompanied by paralinguistic features, such as, hand gestures, eye-gaze, facial expressions and unusual pitch and loudness. But in (7), (8) and (9) the deictics are used symbolically, there are no paralinguistic features accompanying them.

(4) *This* one is genuine, but *this* one is a fake. [1]

(5) *You*, *you*, but not *you*, are dismissed.

(6) Don't do it *now*, but *now*.

(7) *This* city is really beautiful.

(8) What did *you* say?

(9) I'm working on a new book *now*.

From these examples we can also see that deictic expressions in

---

[1] Examples in this chapter are mostly borrowed from S. Levinson (1983: 54 – 94), J. Lyons (1977: 636 – 77) and relevant sections in R. Quirk et al (1985).

the gestural use usually have more specific reference, which are in the immediate situation of speech, while those in the symbolic use are general, whose referents are sometimes difficult to point to. So it is usually the proximal deictics like *this*, *now*, *here*, which refer to the things nearby, that is used in the gestural way, though it is possible to use them in the symbolic way as the examples show. The distal deictics, those for distant reference, on the other hand, are more often used in the symbolic way, though they can also be used gesturally for the not too distant reference. For example:

(10) I'd like to have a look at *that*.

(11) Put it *there*.

Levinson (p. 74) cites an example to show that one can point to a 1962 model Chevrolet and even use *then* gesturally:

(12) I was just a kid *then*.

Gestural uses are typically associated with face-to-face communications. In communications where the speaker and the addressee are separated by distance, such as on the telephone, or in letters, deictic words will not be used gesturally, whether proximal or distal.

2.2.2 Deictic and anaphoric uses

To point, or to refer, to things, whether gesturally or symbolically, is no doubt an important function of deictics, but it is not the only one. There is another use of deictics, which is at least as important, if not more, known as anaphoric. In other words, deictics may be used non-deictically.

The use of *he* in (13), like the deictic use, refers to an individual that is relevant to the communication.

(13) John got home late and *he* was very tired.

But it is different from the deictic use in that its referent has already been introduced by another word, in this case *John*. And it is this difference that separates the anaphoric use from the deictic use. That is, a deictic word in its anaphoric use will have an antecedent, and it shares the referent with the antecedent. They are coreferential. In its deictic use, on the other hand, a deictic word does not need any antecedent. It can serve to introduce by itself a new referent, which is in the discourse situation, but not in the text or co-text. So, provisionally, we can say the presence of a coreferential nominal in the vicinity of a pronoun is an indication of an anaphoric use. Thus, the *he* in (14) read in normal intonation, i.e. unstressed, is anaphoric. It is coreferential with *my friend*.

(14) My friend looked up when *he* came in.

Even when the subordinate clause is put before the main clause as in (15), the relation between *he* and *my friend* remains the same.[1]

(15) When *he* came in, my friend looked up.

Our provisional rule, however, does not always hold true. If we change the complex sentence into a compound one as in (16), *he* and *my friend* will no longer be coreferential, and this *he* may be deictic.

(16) *He* came in and my friend looked up.

On the evidence of sentences like these, R. Quirk et al (1985: 351-2)[2] conclude

> The conditions under which a pronoun can have coreference to another constituent can be summarized as follows. The con-

---

[1] This use, i.e. the pronoun preceding the nominal, is called cataphoric. In the literature, however, the term "anaphoric" may be used as a cover term.

[2] All references to Quirk et al are to this work, henceforth only page number will be shown.

stituent to which coreference is made must have precedence over the pronoun in one of two senses:
> (i) It must precede the pronoun, or
>
> (ii) it must have a higher position in the constituent structure of the sentence than the pronoun.

With cataphoric pronouns, the first condition fails, and so the second condition must obtain.

However, these two are only necessary conditions, but not sufficient conditions. Consider (17), where *he* is stressed.

(17) My friend looked up when HE came in.

This *he* is not coreferential with *my friend*, even though Quirk's two conditions are both satisfied. The reason of course has to do with the unusual stress, one of the paralinguistic features which signals a gestural use.

To complicate the matter a little further, we shall mention the distinction between a type of deixis, discourse deixis, and anaphoric use here. In the discourse deictic use, there will also be an antecedent. But the deictic word only refers to the linguistic form—the word itself, not the object the word refers to. In other words, the deictic and the antecedent are not coreferential. Look at the example,

> (18) A: That's a rhinoceros.
>
> B: A what? Spell *it* for me.

This *it* refers to the word *rhinoceros*, not the animal named by it, hence not anaphoric. As this *it* functions to link the two sentences together, it belongs to discourse deixis, which is discussed in section 2.3.4.

These two uses are frequently confused, as pronouns are usually said to pro, i.e. stand for, act for, nouns. They are said to refer to their antecedents. But this is not the anaphoric use. As we have been explaining, deictics in their anaphoric use also refer to the objects in the extra-linguistic world, except that this referent is shared by the deictic and its antecedent.

Now if we change the sentence a little bit as in (19), we will have a special property of language revealed here.

(19) Spell *rhinoceros* for me.

The word *rhinoceros*, like the *it* in the previous example, does not refer to the animal, but the linguistic form, in this case, itself. The property of a linguistic form to refer to itself is a special case of intra-sentential deixis, known as token-reflexivity.

Another question related to the distinction between deictic and anaphoric uses is the use of *it* in sentences like (20).

(20) The man who gave his paycheck to his wife was wiser than the man who gave *it* to his mistress.

This *it* differs from the *it* in (18). It does not refer to a linguistic form. The man was not giving the word to his mistress. This *it* does refer to the object called "his paycheck". But it is not anaphoric either, it is not coreferential with the antecedent. It is a different paycheck, belonging to a different man. A similar example is:

(21) I've never cooked a rat, but Paul has, and *it* tasted terrible.

This *it* is not coreferential with *a rat*, which is not in existence. It refers to the rat cooked by Paul, but there is no linguistic form for it. This kind of *it* is known as pronoun of laziness, or lazy pronoun. Lyons (p. 674) thinks this use "may be seen as a purely stylistic or rhetorical device, which enables the speaker or writer to avoid repetition of the antecedent." It is closer to, if not identical with, grammatical substitution such as the *one* and *do* in the following sentences:

(22) I want the red scarf not the blue *one*.

(23) I will go to the party if you *do*.

Quirk et al (p. 863) also discuss substitution, which they set in opposition to coreference, the notion we call anaphoric use here. In their view, a major test of substitution is whether the antecedent can be copied, without change of meaning, into the position taken by its pro-form substitute. And their example is:

(24) Bill got a first prize this year, and I got *one* last year.

The pronoun *one* is grammatically and semantically equivalent to *a first prize*. They both function as objects and mean the same in the sense of logical, cognitive meaning, not the referential, pragmatic meaning, as *one* does not refer to the same prize as does *a first prize*. But there is no requirement on the morphology of the substitute. It may be a grammatical variant of the antecedent, for example,

(25) The coat is more expensive than the *ones* I saw in the market.

(26) Many buildings were damaged, but *none* was destroyed.

At the end of this discussion, the distinction between deictic and anaphoric uses, however, we have to mention cases in which the deictic and anaphoric interpretations are compatible with each other. A deictic word may serve both functions simultaneously. Look at the sentence,

(27) I was born in London and have lived *here/there* ever since.

The word *here*, or *there*, is at the same time coreferential with *London*, and refers symbolically, a type of deictic, to the place where the speaker is at, or not, at the time of speaking. That is, it is both deictic and anaphoric.

2.3 Types of deixis

Even though there are two basic uses of deictic words, in this chapter we will only discuss their deictic use in some detail. In terms of the semantic content of the deictic words, they may be classified into five types: person deixis, time deixis, place deixis, discourse deixis and social deixis.

2.3.1 Person deixis

Person deictics mainly consist of personal pronouns:

I (me, my, myself, mine)	you (your, yourself, yours)	he (him, his, himself); she (her, herself, hers); it (its, itself)
we (us, our, ourselves, ours)	you (your, yourselves, yours)	they (them, their, themselves, theirs)

There are two dimensions of this paradigm. On the horizontal dimension, there is a distinction of person, which is based on a distinction of participant roles. According to Lyons (p. 638), "The Latin word 'persona' (meaning 'mask') was used to translate the Greek word for 'dramatic character' or 'role'". A language event is seen as a drama in which the principal role, speaking, is played by the first person, the subsidiary, hearing, by the second person, and the others by the third person. As a matter of fact, only the first person and the second person are actually participating in the drama. The third person is defined negatively as neither the first nor the second, and does not correlate with any positive participant role. The speaker and addressee are necessarily present in the speech situation, whereas other persons and things to which reference is made may be absent from the situation, they may be left unidentified. In this sense, there is a fundamental difference between the first person and second person pronouns on the one hand and the third person pronouns on the other.

On the vertical dimension, there is a distinction of number: the singular and the plural. But the first person plural *we* differs from the others in that it does not stand in the same relationship to *I* as *they* to *he/she/it*, or *boys* to *boy*. It is to be interpreted as " I, in addition to one or more other persons" (I + he/she/it), not as "more than one I" (I + I + I ...) (cf. Jespersen 1924:192, 213). There can be only one speaker. It is impossible for many people to say exactly the same thing at the same time. When a speaker uses *we*, what he means is that he is acting as a spokesman, there are others who share his position.

Sometimes this *we* may include the addressee, i. e. I + you, known as the "inclusive *we*". For example,

(28) *We* complemented ourselves too soon, John.

In English the form used typically as "inclusive *we*" is *let's*:

(29) *Let's* have a party.

(30) *Let's* enjoy ourselves.

It is odd to say

(31) * *Let's* go to see you tomorrow.

However, Quirk et al (p. 830) observe that "[i]n very colloquial English, *let's* is sometimes used for a first person singular imperative as well", and their example is:

(32) *Let's* give you a hand.

A teacher wishing to instruct without overtly claiming authority may say to a student:

(33) Now then, *let's* have a look at that project, shall we?

In this use, *let's* is like the "editorial *we*" used in formal writing to avoid being egotistical. In a scholarly article, the author often writes

As we showed a moment ago... rather than *As I showed a moment ago*....

Sometimes *we* may also be used to mean "you", when the speaker, usually in the role of a doctor, or a parent, wants to show his concern and to share the problem with the addressee, i. e. being condescending:

(34) How are *we* feeling today?

On some rare occasions *we* may even be used to refer to a third person. For example, one secretary might say to another with reference to their boss:

(35) *We*'re in a bad mood today.

In modern standard English the second person has the same form for both the singular and plural.① In languages like French, there are two distinct forms. However, in French the plural form *vous* is also used as a polite form for the singular. In German there is a separate polite form *Sie* for both the singular and plural, in addition to the singular *du* and plural *ihr*. The use of polite forms will be discussed in the section on social deixis. What we are concerned here is that there seems to be a tendency for the number distinction of the second person pronouns to become blurred. Having said that, however, we should not be so blind as not to notice the development in the opposite direction. In Southern American English, the singular-plural distinction has been re-introduced through suffixation of the originally plural form: *you-all* (Quirk et al 1985: 344 n [b]).

The pronoun *you* is also used as an indefinite pronoun in informal situations. As such it does not refer to the addressee, as its more typi-

---

① Except for the reflexive: *yourself* vs. *yourselves*.

cal use does, or any other person in particular. But it still retains some of its second person meaning. Quirk et al(p. 354) point out this *you* can suggest that the speaker is appealing to the hearer's experience of life in general, or else of some specific situation, as in (36). And they call it "generic *you*".

(36) This wine makes *you* feel drowsy, doesn't it?

In fact, plural pronouns of all persons can function generically with reference to "people in general":

(37) Science tells *us* that the earth goes round the sun.

(38) *We* live in an age of immense changes.

(39) *They* say it's going to snow today.

(40) *They*'re raising the bus fares again.

(41) *They* don't make decent furniture nowadays.

Like *you*, these *we* and *they* also retain something of their respective person meaning. They are therefore not wholly interchangeable. Potentially, the first personal *we*, *us*, *our* have the widest meaning. They may include reference to speaker, addressee, and third parties. This use may be seen as an extension of the "inclusive *we*" from those involved in the immediate speech situation to the whole human race. On the other hand, the third person pronoun *they* excludes reference to speaker and addressee. Consequently, it tends to designate, in a disparaging way, the authorities, the media, the government, etc.

Apart from pronouns, personal names, titles, kinship terms, and forms for occupations may also be used to refer to the second and third persons. The extent, of course, varies from language to language. Levinson (pp. 70 – 1) notes that in modern standard English *cousin* cannot be used as a vocative. One does not say *Hello, Cousin*! nowadays. And we are all aware of the difference between English and Chinese in addressing the teacher and the student.

Vocatives, terms referring to the addressee, can be divided into two classes: calls/summonses and addresses. Calls are terms to draw the attention of the person or persons addressed, singling them out from others in hearing, so they are usually utterance-initial.

(42) *John*, dinner's ready.

(43) *Hey you*, you just scratched my car with your frisbee.

Addresses on the other hand express the speaker's relationship or attitude to the person concerned, and they occur medially or finally.

(44) The truth is, *Madam*, nothing is as good nowadays.

(45) My back is aching, *doctor*.

These other terms may occasionally be used to refer to the first person as well. For example, a child called Billy may say to his mother: ①

(46) *Billy* wants an ice-cream, Mummy.

Demonstratives like *this*, *that* may also perform the function of person deixis, especially when they are used together with nouns for people. As is mentioned in 2.2.1, *this* is a proximal deictic and usually refers to a person nearby, while *that* is distal and for people far away. Now this distinction of distance sometimes may not be physical, but emotional. The speaker may use *this* for somebody emotionally closer to him, somebody he likes, and *that* for somebody emotionally distant, somebody he dislikes. For example:

(47) I hope she doesn't bring *that* husband of hers.

---

① And a writer may refer to himself as "this author", which is related to the use of demonstratives in this function, discussed in next paragraph.

(48) He's awful, *that* Michael.①

Quirk et al (p. 1481 n [b]) remark, "Perhaps because of the unfavourable values associated with *that*, there is some tendency to address the unseen hearer [e.g. on the telephone] with the question 'Is this X?'"

2.3.2 Time deixis

Time deixis is mainly performed by time adverbials like *now*, *then*, *today*, *tomorrow* and expressions formed by units of time *morning*, *afternoon*, *week*, *month*, or their names *Monday*, *January* together with *this*, *that*, *last*, *next*. But calendar-time expressions like *Sept*. 15th 1998, which locate events in somewhat absolute terms, not relative to the time of speaking, are not generally considered deictic.

Terms like *today*, *tomorrow* are said to be pre-emptive in the sense that when they are applicable, the others like *Monday*, *Tuesday* will not be used. Suppose it is Tuesday today, one would not usually say (49), (50) or (51), as if these positions of time deictics were pre-empted, occupied already, by *yesterday*, *today* and *tomorrow*.②

(49) I went to town Monday.

(50) I'm going to town Tuesday.

---

① *This* or *that* referring to objects may also carry this connotation. The following two sentences may be used in the same situation, depending on the speaker's mood.
(1) Have you seen *this* report on smoking?
(2) Have you seen *that* report on smoking?
But this use is, strictly speaking, "thing deixis", a type which no pragmatician has ever discussed.

② News reports may be an exception, especially in the oral medium. We do hear *Tuesday*, *Wednesday* used instead of *today*, or *tomorrow* on the air.

25

(51) I'll go to town Wednesday.

As a result, *last Monday*, *next Wednesday* uttered on Tuesday mean "the Monday of last week" and "the Wednesday of next week". But *next Thursday*, *Friday* or *Saturday* would be ambiguous. They could refer to "the Thursday, Friday or Saturday of the same week" or "that of the next week". On the other hand, *last Monday*, *Tuesday* or *Wednesday* uttered on Friday would be ambiguous in a similar way.

Levinson (p. 75 n8) says that "this pre-emptive nature of pure deictic words is a general tendency: it takes special conventions to make it appropriate for a speaker to refer to himself by name,① and it would be strange to say *Do it at 10.36* instead of *Do it now*, when now is 10.36." Levinson does not define the term "pure deictic word". Presumably, it refers to words like *I*, *you*, *now*, including *today*, *tomorrow*, the reference of which entirely depends on the speech situation. But Levinson notes *here* seems to be an exception. It should perhaps be regarded as a pure deictic word, yet it does not have the pre-emptive force. "One can say *London* instead of *here* if one is in London" (ibid.).

In languages like English where there is a tense system, tense is also a means of time deixis. But nowadays, linguists make a distinction between "time" and "tense". "Time" is a universal concept, which every language is capable of expressing, while "tense" is a linguistic concept, which varies from language to language. In Levinson's terms, "time" is a metalinguistic tense, M-tense for short, and "tense" is a language tense, L-tense for short. Levinson (p. 78)

---

① Example (46) is perhaps a case in point.

argues

it is sometimes claimed that there are languages without true tenses, for example Chinese or Yoruba, and this is correct in the sense that such languages may lack L-tenses morphologically marked in the verb, or indeed systematically elsewhere (Comrie, 1976: 82ff; Lyons, 1977: 678 – 9). But we can confidently assume that there are no languages where part of an M-tense is not realized somewhere in time-adverbials or the like, not to mention the implicit assumption of M-tense if no further specification is provided (Lyons, 1977: 686).

Linguists nowadays also make a distinction between "tense" and "aspect". Tense is deictic, relating the time of an event to the time of speaking, while aspect is non-deictic, relating the time of an event to the time of another event described in the narrative. These two changes in the treatment of the traditional notion of "tense" have brought drastic changes to the analysis of the English tense system. Traditionally there were sixteen tenses in English as follows:

simple present	present progressive	present perfect	present perfect progressive
simple past	past progressive	past perfect	past perfect progressive
simple future	future progressive	future perfect	future perfect progressive
simple past future	past future progressive	past future perfect	past future perfect progressive

Now grammarians say there are only two tenses in English: past and non-past. The so-called future tense is not marked in the same way as past or non-past, i.e. by morphology. *Will* and *shall* are basically modals like *can* and *may*. And they are by no means the commonest way of expressing future time, the best candidate for which perhaps is the *be going to* construction. In their 1985 grammar Quirk et al, for example, have a section on the "means of expressing future time", which include "*will/shall* + infinitive", "*be going to* + infinitive", "present progressive", "simple present" and "*will/shall* + progressive infinitive", but there is no discussion of future tense. And "progressive" and "perfect" are separated from "tense", known as "aspect".

2.3.3   Place deixis

Typical place deictics are place adverbs *here*, *there*, *in(side)*, *out(side)*, *up(stairs)*, *down(stairs)*, *nearby*, *far away*, *opposite*, *behind*, etc. which specify a location relative to the place of a deictic centre.

Demonstratives *this*, *that* can also function as place deictics, e.g. *Sit by this*, *Stand by that*. But more usually they are used together with place nouns like *side*, *place*, *area*, *city*, *country*. Nouns referring to objects, which may stand for the place they occupy, are also used with *this*, *that* to refer to places:

(52) Stand by *this desk*.

(53) Sit in *that chair*.

When the reference is unique, or clearly identifiable in the immediate situation of discourse, *the* may be used in place of *this* or *that*.

(54) Come to *the* blackboard.

If an object has intrinsic sides, then this use may sometimes cause ambiguity. Compare the two sentences:

(55) John is behind the *tree*.

(56) John is behind the *truck*.

There is only one interpretation of (55), but two of (56). A truck has its intrinsic sides. We know which part is the front and which is the back, which side is the left and which is the right. So *behind the truck* may mean "at the back part of the truck", which is not relative to the position of the speaker, or "the further side of the truck" from the speaker's point of view. In the first interpretation, *behind the truck* is not deictic. In the latter interpretation, the deictic interpretation, the truck is something standing between the speaker and John. If the speaker is at the left side of the truck, then John is at the right side. If the speaker is at the back part of the truck, then John is at the front part.

2.3.4 Discourse deixis

Discourse deixis, also known as textual deixis, is a difficult notion in that its scope is not very clearly identified. There are many borderline cases. Levinson (p. 85) defines it as "the use of expressions within some utterance to refer to some portion of the discourse that contains that utterance (including the utterance itself)". But what exactly is meant by "reference to some portion of the discourse" is not clear. Levinson (ibid.) says that *in the last paragraph*, *in the next Chapter* and *this*, *that* in (57), (58) are all discourse deictic.

(57) I bet you haven't heard *this* story.

(58) *That* was the funniest story I've ever heard.

And the token-reflexive use of deictics like *this* in (59) is a special case of intra-sentential discourse deixis.

(59) *This* sentence is not true.

Following Lyons, however, Levinson (p. 87) makes a distinction between pure and impure textual deixis, and claims that *that* in (60) is a case of impure textual deixis.

(60) A: I've never seen him.
   B: *That's* a lie.

In his words, "the pronoun *that* does not seem to be anaphoric (unless it is held that it refers to the same entity that A's utterance does, i.e. a proposition or a truth value); nor does it quite seem to be discourse-deictic (it refers not to the sentence but, perhaps, to the statement made by uttering that sentence)".

Now there are two problems here. First, there is a misinterpretation of Lyons, whose original text reads

> At one remove from what might be called pure textual deixis, though not as clearly distinct from it as anaphora, is the relationship which holds between a referring expression and a variety of third-order entities, such as facts, propositions and utterance-acts (in the more abstract sense of "utterance-act" noted in 1.6). This may be exemplified by means of the following text: (X says) *I've never seen him* (and Y responds) *That's a lie*. It is clear that "that" does not refer either to the text-sentence uttered by X or to the referent of any expression in it. Some philosophers might say that it refers to the proposition expressed by the sentence uttered by X; others, that it refers to the utterance-act, or speech-act, performed by X. However, under either of these analyses of the reference of "that", its function seems to fall somewhere between anaphora and deixis and to partake of the characteristics of both. (p. 668)

It is not, as Levinson claims, that if the word refers to the proposition, it is anaphoric; and if it refers to the sentence, it is discourse-deictic.

The second problem is that the distinction between pure and impure textual deixis is of no real value. Lyons does not define the notion "pure textual deixis". Presumably, it is the use of deictics like *it* in *Spell it for me*, which refers to the linguistic form only. In contrast, impure textual deixis refers to the content, the proposition, i.e. what is expressed by a linguistic form. If this is the correct interpretation of the distinction, then it is of no value for the simple fact that there are very few cases of pure textual deixis. Is the *this* pure deictic in *This sentence is not true*? Does it refer to the form only? Are we not also talking about the proposition it expresses? Otherwise how can we say whether it is true or not? When we say *this story* and *that* in (57), (58) are deictic, are we not also concerned with what is expressed in the forthcoming or preceding portion of the discourse?

After the definition of discourse deixis we quoted earlier, Levinson (p. 85) proceeds to say "We may also include in discourse deixis a number of other ways in which an utterance signals its relation to surrounding text." In this sense, then, discourse deixis is very similar to what is discussed under the name of cohesion by M. A. K. Halliday.

2.3.5 Social deixis

Social deixis is the use of deictic terms for indicating social status of the participants in a discourse, and their relations determined thereupon. So it is mainly the terms used in person deixis that are used here again, namely, personal pronouns and terms of address.

For example, the "editorial *we*" in scholarly writing is used to avoid any possible tension between the writer and his readers, so as not to appear egotistical, or self-concentrated. When assuming responsibility, however, even these writers are not hesitant to revert to the normal usage. In his preface to *Principles of Pragmatics*, Leech declares "The customary disclaimer that I alone am responsible for the shortcomings of this book is particularly appropriate here."

The pronoun which typically reflects the social relation between the participants is the second person pronoun, which in many languages has a polite form, such as *vous* in French, *Sie* in German and 您 in Chinese.

Vocatives are another area in which the social relations between participants are clearly manifested. Whether you call somebody by the official title, the full name, the first name, or the nickname, reflects directly the social distance between you two.

The formality of a discourse also determines the choice of the terms of address. In the classroom, a student would call the teacher, who is his uncle, by the formal term. Even if the teacher is his father, the student would not call him *Father* in class.

In some cultures, the address terms of individuals and objects related to the participants of a discourse will be strongly coloured by their social relations as well. Chinese exhibits a wealth of special terms in this respect, e.g. 贵姓、令尊、大作、玉照.

A question in this area of study is how to draw a demarcation line between social deixis and sociolinguistics. Levinson (p. 93) suggests that social deixis is "concerned with the meaning and grammar (e.g. the problems of honorific concord) of certain linguistic expressions, while sociolinguistics is also concerned, *inter alia*, with how these items are actually used in concrete social contexts classified with reference to the parameters of the relevant social system (Levinson, 1979). Thus, social deixis can be systematically restricted to the study of facts that lie firmly within the scope of structural studies of linguistic systems, leaving the study of usage to another domain." But this restriction is in conflict with the general view of pragmatics as the study of language in use. In this respect, J. Thomas's opinion will fall on more sympathetic ears. She believes that pragmatics and sociolinguistics overlap in certain aspects, but their emphases are different. "[S]ociolinguistics is mainly concerned with the systematic linguistic correlates of relatively *fixed* and *stable* social variables (such as region of origin, social class, ethnicity, sex, age, etc.) on the way an individual speaks. Pragmatics, on the other hand, is mainly concerned with describing the linguistic correlates of relatively *changeable* features of that same individual (such as relative status, social role) and the way in which the speaker exploits his/her (socio)linguistic repertoire in order to achieve a particular goal" (Thomas 1995: 185).

Chapter 3: Conversational implicature (I)

As is pointed out in the Introduction, a sentence used in actual situations may have some extra meaning, something which is not inherent in the words used. "Is this your pen?", which appears to be a question about the ownership of a pen, may be used as a request to mean "May I use your pen?", or as a reminder meaning "You've left behind your pen", or as an order meaning "Pick it up". How can this be possible? What is the mechanism underlying the use of a sentence to convey extra meaning? Or to use the established wording in pragmatics, how can one mean more than one says?[①] This is the kind of questions to which the theory of conversational implicature attempts to provide tentative answers.

3.1 The Gricean theory

The theory of conversational implicature was originally suggested by Herbert Paul Grice,[②] an Oxford philosopher, who later went to

---

[①] "What one says" can more or less be understood as "what one says explicitly and literally", though as R. Harnish (1991 [1976]: 326-8) has amply demonstrated that a specific categorization of this notion involves something more.

[②] L. Horn (1988: 118) holds that there was something similar in the history of philosophical thinking. "[T]he essential insight can be traced back at least to John Stuart Mill. In his response to the logic of Sir William Hamilton (1860), in which *some* is taken (on the default reading) as equivalent to *some only*, Mill observes: ' No shadow of justification is shown... for adopting into logic a mere *sous-entendu* of common conversation in its most unprecise form. If I say to any one, "I saw some of your children to-day", he might be justified

America. The earliest written reference[①] to this theory was made in his 1961 article "The Causal Theory of Perception", where Grice writes that "One should not make a weaker statement rather than a stronger one unless there is a good reason for so doing." But it was in his William James lectures delivered at Harvard in 1967 that he formally presented this theory to the public. Part of these lectures came out in 1975, entitled "Logic and Conversation". A second part appeared in 1978 with the title of "Further Notes on Logic and Conversation".[②] And these two papers, especially the first one, constitute the main source of our introduction here.

3.1.1 The cooperative principle

In his 1975 paper, Grice first notes that most people believe that formal devices such as $\sim$, $\wedge$, $\vee$, $\supset$ used in logic and their counterparts *not*, *and*, *or*, *if...then* in natural language differ in meaning, though they do not all agree that the natural language expressions are imperfect and should be abolished in favour of the formal ones. He himself, however, wishes to maintain that the common assumption that there are divergences in meaning between these two sets of expressions "is (broadly speaking) a common mistake, and that the mis-

---

in inferring that I did not see them all, not because the words mean it, but because, if I had seen them all, it is most likely that I should have said so; even though this cannot be presumed unless it is presupposed that I must have known whether the children I saw were all or not.' (Mill 1867: 501)"

① Grice had apparently been working on this idea quite early. According to P. Strawson (1952: 179), the former had pointed out to him by then that there is a pragmatic rule in operation, namely, that one does not make the (logically) lesser, when one could truthfully (and with equal or greater linguistic economy) make the greater, claim.

② Judging from the references in recent literature, the lectures were published in full under the title of *Studies in the Way of Words* posthumously in 1989.

take arises from an inadequate attention to the nature and importance of the conditions governing conversation" (p. 43).① So he turns immediately to the question of the general conditions on conversation, which he subtitles "implicature"②, and does not return to the question of logic in this paper.③

Grice begins his discussion of conversation with the following example.

> Suppose that A and B are talking about a mutual friend, C, who is now working in a bank. A asks B how C is getting on in his job, and B replies, *Oh quite well, I think; he likes his colleagues, and he hasn't been to prison yet*. At this point, A might well inquire what B was implying, what he was suggesting, or even what he meant by saying that C had not yet been to prison. The answer might be any one of such things as that C is the sort of person likely to yield to the temptation provided by his occupation, that C's colleagues are really very unpleasant and treacherous people, and so forth. It might, of course, be quite unnecessary for A to make such an inquiry of B, the answer to it being, in the context, clear in advance. I think it is clear that

---

① Quotations of Grice in this section are all from Cole & Morgan (eds.) (1975: 41-58), the specific page numbers will not be indicated each time anew.

② R. Harnish (1991 [1976]: 357) suggests that the introduction of this term frees Grice "from the unwanted 'logical' use of 'implies'", and, we are entitled to add, also the unwanted "logical" use of "implication".

③ As a matter of fact, the theory of implicature is meant to explain the apparent divergences between the logical devices and their language counterparts. That is, these two types of expressions have the same meaning, the additional meanings the linguistic expressions seem to possess in fact are implicatures arising from the way language is used in daily conversations. Grice is especially explicit on this point in his 1978 paper.

whatever B implied, suggested, meant, etc., in this example, is distinct from what B said, which was simply that C had not been to prison yet. I wish to introduce, as terms of art, the verb *implicate* and the related nouns *implicature* (cf. *implying*)[①] and *implicatum* (cf. *what is implied*).

Then he makes a distinction between conventional implicature and nonconventional implicature. Among the nonconventional implicature, there is a subclass--conversational implicature, which he attaches great importance to. And the consideration of this type of implicature forms the major part of this paper.

Grice observes that conversational implicatures are essentially connected with certain general features of discourse. The reason that a hearer of "He hasn't been to prison yet" will derive from it implicatures such as "C is the sort of person likely to yield to monetary temptations" has to do with the way conversations are usually carried out. And his first approximation is:

> Our talk exchanges do not normally consist of a succession of disconnected remarks, and would not be rational if they did. They are characteristically, to some degree at least, cooperative efforts; and each participant recognizes in them, to some extent, a common purpose or set of purposes, or at least a mutually accepted direction.[②] This purpose or direction may be fixed from

---

① In this sense, "implicature" refers to the action, or the phenomenon, to implicate. But most people use it to refer to the entity, i.e. what is implicated, and the term "implicatum" is seldom used.

② This is the technical sense of "cooperative". That is, the two participants in a conversation will have a common purpose. The contributions made by each side will be connected with, or relevant to, each other. On page 48, Grice expands on this point by listing the three features, jointly distinguishing cooperative transactions, that talk exchanges exhibit characteristically:

the start (e. g., by an initial proposal of a question for discussion), or it may evolve during the exchange; it may be fairly definite, or it may be so indefinite as to leave very considerable latitude to the participants (as in a casual conversation). But at each stage, SOME possible conversational moves would be excluded as conversationally unsuitable. We might then formulate a rough general principle which participants will be expected① (ceteris paribus) to observe, namely: Make your conversational contribution such as is required, at the stage at which it occurs, by the accepted purpose or direction of the talk exchange in which you are engaged. One might label this the COOPERATIVE PRINCIPLE.

In order to explain further the cooperative principle, abbreviated as CP, Grice borrows from the German philosopher Immanuel Kant four categories: quantity, quality, relation and manner. That is, the

---

    i   The participants have some common immediate aim, like getting a car mended [This reference is to the example used earlier by Grice, in which one man's car is stranded and another man passing by has come to help.]; their ultimate aims may, of course, be independent and even in conflict—each may want to get the car mended in order to drive off, leaving the other stranded. In characteristic talk exchanges, there is a common aim even if, as in an over-the-wall chat, it is a second-order one, namely, that each party should, for the time being, identify himself with the transitory conversational interests of the other.

    ii   The contributions of the participants should be dovetailed, mutually dependent.

    iii   There is some sort of understanding (which may be explicit but which is often tacit) that, other things being equal, the transaction should continue in appropriate style unless both parties are agreeable that it should terminate. You do not just shove off or start doing something else.

    ①   Grice explains on page 48 that the standard type of conversational practice should not be thought of "merely as something that all or most do IN FACT follow but as something that it is REASONABLE for us to follow, that we SHOULD NOT abandon." This may be the gloss of "expected" here.

CP is specified from these four aspects. And the content of each category is known as maxim.

The category of Quantity, concerned with the quantity of information to be provided, has two maxims:

1. Make your contribution as informative as is required (for the current purposes of the exchange).
2. Do not make your contribution more informative than is required.

Grice has some doubts as to the necessity of the second maxim. First, to be overinformative may not be a transgression of the CP but merely a waste of time. Second, there is a later maxim concerning relevance, which ensures that no excess of information will be given to lead to any side effects or cause any confusion. As we shall see in the next chapter, the second approach is exactly what L. Horn (1984), and D. Sperber & D. Wilson (1986) have proposed to adopt.

In the category of Quality there is a supermaxim:

Try to make your contribution one that is true.

and two specific maxims:

1. Do not say what you believe to be false.
2. Do not say that for which you lack adequate evidence.

Grice does not offer any comment here. After presenting all the maxims, however, he suggests that the observance of the Quality maxims is a matter of greater urgency than is the observance of others. "[A] man who has expressed himself with undue prolixity would, in general, be open to milder comment than would a man who has said something he believes to be false. Indeed, it might be felt that the importance of at least the first maxim of Quality is such that it should not be included in a scheme of the kind I am constructing; other maxims come into operation only on the assumption that this maxim of Quality is satisfied."①

The category of Relation has a single maxim "Be relevant". "Though the maxim itself is terse," Grice goes on, "its formulation conceals a number of problems that exercise me a good deal: questions about what different kinds and focuses of relevance there may be, how these shift in the course of a talk exchange, how to allow for the fact that subjects of conversation are legitimately changed, and so on". ②

The category of Manner, different from others, relates not "to what is said but, rather, to HOW what is said is to be said". There is also a supermaxim "Be perspicuous", and the specific maxims are:

1. Avoid obscurity of expression.
2. Avoid ambiguity.
3. Be brief (avoid unnecessary prolixity).
4. Be orderly.

Grice does not think this list exhausts all the possible maxims. "There are, of course, all sorts of other maxims (aesthetic, social, or

---

① This consideration is perhaps the reason why some writers make Quality the first category in their presentations of the theory. But D. Sperber & D. Wilson (1986) do not think so. They argue "The speaker is presumed to aim at optimal relevance, not at literal truth" (p. 233). Suppose somebody earns £797.32 a month, he would tell his friend over a drink that he earns £800 when asked to, rather than give the exact figure. The question is: Would he say he earns £1000? See section 4.1 for the details of relevance theory.

② This maxim has stimulated heated arguments as to its proper interpretation. R. Harnish (1991 [1976]: 358) argues that Relevance is so central and important that "it is not clear that it belongs on equal footing with the rest." He suspects "that maxims are (at least partially) ordered with respect to weight, etc. and relevance is at the top, controlling most of the others." And D. Sperber & D. Wilson (1986) on the basis of their interpretation established a comprehensive theory years later, which is discussed in section 4.1 as noted above.

moral in character), such as 'Be polite', that are also normally observed by participants in talk exchanges, and these may also generate nonconventional implicatures."①

The fact that the cooperative principle, (and its component maxims), is expressed in the imperative has misled many readers to regard it as prescriptive: telling speakers how they ought to behave; while the truth is the CP is meant to describe what actually happens in conversation. That is, when we speak we generally have something like the CP and its maxims in our mind to guide us, though sub-consciously, or even unconsciously. We will try to say things which are true, rele-

---

① Grice does not proceed to consider these other types of maxims any further, though Leech (1983) has developed the politeness maxim into a principle, comparable to the cooperative principle. But he does indicate that there may be other Manner maxims apart from the four listed. And he actually adds one in 1981 (p. 189), namely, "Frame whatever you say in the form most suitable for any reply that would be regarded as appropriate", or "Facilitate in your form of expression the appropriate reply." J. Searle (1975b) adds another, which is presented in section 6.5. However, R. Harnish (1991 [1976]: 358) finds this passage a bit misleading. "It is easy to see how the maxims given might fall under the cooperative principle, but it is not at all obvious that esthetic, social, or moral maxims need contribute to rational cooperation. Indeed, moral maxims may well preclude obedience to other maxims. (Presumably, one was not obliged to give all necessary information when the Gestapo came calling.)" In my opinion, the Gestapo example lends support to Grice's position rather than weakens it. Maxims are not necessarily compatible with each other. The conversational ones envisaged by Grice may be in conflict with the moral, social ones to be offered, as indeed the conversational ones may be in conflict among themselves. J. Sadock (1991 [1978]: 366) also thinks this passage odd. "I have some trouble understanding exactly why it is that such maxims differ from those that fall under the Cooperative Principle, for, on the one hand, it would be uncooperative to be gratuitously impolite, antisocial, or unpleasant, and, on the other, the requirement that we make our contributions true and that we tell the whole truth could easily be construed as moral principles as well as, or instead of, cooperative principles." His problem, I think, is to have mixed the technical sense of words like *cooperative*, *polite* with their everyday sense.

vant, as well as informative enough, and in a clear manner. Hearers will also try to interpret what is said to them in this way. If there are obvious signs that one, or more, of the maxims is not followed, one will try to find out the reason, as long as the speaker may still be thought to be observing the CP. And it is usually the case that there is some extra meaning intended. In this sense, the CP may be seen as an answer offered by Grice to the question we posed at the beginning of this chapter. In other words, it is because there is such a quasi-contract① as the CP between interlocutors that they manage to mean more than they say. J. Thomas (1995: 62) compares the CP with traffic regulations. "When we drive, we assume that other drivers will operate according to the same set of regulations as we do (or, at the very least, that they know what those regulations are). If we could not make such assumptions the traffic system would rapidly grind to a halt." The trouble is that traffic regulations are explicit while the CP is implicit. What is more, traffic regulations are prescriptive, any violation of which is subject to formal penalty. A better analogy is perhaps the unwritten laws, such as, that women and children are saved first from a sinking ship; that one is not supposed to make *ad hominem* comments at academic conferences; 礼尚往来; 两军对阵, 不斩来使; etc.

As a matter of fact, Grice does compare talk with other types of purposive, rational behavior in terms of the maxims. He says, "If you are assisting me to mend a car, I expect your contribution to be neither more nor less than is required". When "I need four screws, I expect

---

① Grice's term (1975: 48).

you to hand me four, rather than two or six". ① In terms of quality, "I expect your contributions to be genuine and not spurious. If I need sugar as an ingredient in the cake you are assisting me to make, I do not expect you to hand me salt; if I need a spoon, I do not expect a trick spoon made of rubber". In terms of relation, "I expect a partner's contribution to be appropriate to immediate needs at each stage of the transaction; if I am mixing ingredients for a cake, I do not expect to be handed a good book, or even an oven cloth (though this might be an appropriate contribution at a later stage)". And in terms of manner, "I expect a partner to make it clear what contribution he is making, and to execute his performance with reasonable dispatch".

He concludes "it is just a well-recognized empirical fact that people DO behave in these ways; they have learned to do so in childhood and not lost the habit of doing so; and, indeed, it would involve a good deal of effort to make a radical departure from the habit. It is much easier, for example, to tell the truth than to invent lies." However, as we have alluded to already, it is also true that people DO violate these maxims in conversations and people DO tell lies. Grice was fully aware of this, and consequently he devoted the next half of the paper to a discussion of the violations. In a sense, the theory of conversational implicature may be seen as an attempt to explain how communication succeeds in the face of violation of the maxims.

3.1.2 Violation of the maxims

Grice notes that a participant in a talk exchange may fail to fulfill a maxim in four ways:

---

① This is a bit misleading, suggesting as if the quantity of information were comparable to that of material objects, which, as we shall see in section 3.3.1, is not really true.

1. He may quietly and unostentatiously VIOLATE① a maxim; if so, in some cases he will be liable to mislead.
2. He may OPT OUT from the operation both of the maxim and the CP; he may say, indicate, or allow it to become plain that he is unwilling to cooperate in the way the maxim requires. He may say, for example, *I cannot say more*; *my lips are sealed*.
3. He may be faced by a CLASH: he may be unable, for example, to fulfill the first maxim of Quantity (Be as informative as is required) without violating the second maxim of Quality (have adequate evidence for what you say).
4. He may FLOUT a maxim; that is, he may BLATANTLY fail to fulfill it. On the assumption that the speaker is able to fulfill the maxim and to do so without violating another maxim (because of a clash), is not opting out, and is not, in view of the blatancy of his performance, trying to mislead, the hearer is faced with a minor problem; How can his saying what he did say be reconciled with the supposition that he is observing the overall CP? This situation is one that characteristically② gives rise to a conversational implicature; and when a conversational implicature is generated in this way, I shall say that a maxim is being EXPLOITED.

Then he goes on to present detailed examples for the violation of maxims. As no implicature would arise in the first and second ways of

---

① Grice makes a distinction between the violation and flouting (or exploitation) of a maxim here, but most pragmaticians, including Grice himself in some other places, do not.

② Notice the word "characteristically". As we shall see in next paragraph there are also conversational implicatures involving no violation of any maxim. The sub-classification of conversational implicatures will be discussed in detail in 3.2.4.

violation, in which there is no such basis as CP, ① his discussion concentrates on the last two ways of violation. But before doing that he first mentions cases in which no maxim whatsoever is violated. In other words, conversational implicatures may also arise even when all the maxims are observed. And one of his examples is:

A: I am out of petrol.

B: There is a garage round the corner.

Grice comments,

> B would be infringing the maxim 'Be relevant' unless he thinks, or thinks it possible, that the garage is open, and has petrol to sell; so he implicates that this garage is, or at least may be open, etc.

> In this example, unlike the case of the remark *He hasn't been to prison yet*, the unstated connection between B's remark and A's remark is so obvious that, even if one interprets the supermaxim of Manner, "Be perspicuous," as applying not only to the expression of what is said but also the connection of what is said with adjacent remarks, there seems to be no case for regarding that supermaxim as infringed in this example. ②

---

① Grice (1975: 49 – 50) makes it a precondition for the generation of any conversational implicature that the participants should at least observe the CP, in the sense that they have a common purpose, a mutually accepted direction. That is why lies are said to have no conversational implicatures. It does not follow, of course, that lies do not have any extra meanings. A liar does intend his interlocutors to believe what he says, to think that what he says is of value to them. But that is not conversational implicature in the technical sense.

② R. Lakoff (1995: 2) does not agree with Grice's analysis here. She thinks speaker B may be said to have violated the maxim of Quantity, or of Relevance, or both. This shows, as we shall point out at the end of section 3.2.4, that observance, or violation, of maxims is strictly speaking a matter of degree.

45

An example to show there is a clash between two maxims is: when two people are planning a journey in France, A asks "Where does C live?" and B replies "Somewhere in the South of France." Grice glosses "There is no reason to suppose that B is opting out; his answer is, as he well knows, less informative than is required to meet A's needs. This infringement of the first maxim of Quantity can be explained only by the supposition that B is aware that to be more informative would be to say something that infringed the maxim of Quality, 'Don't say what you lack adequate evidence for', so B implicates that he does not know in which town C lives."①

When exemplifying the exploitation of maxims, Grice goes through them one by one② in detail, which is reproduced here in full:

(1a) *A flouting of the first maxim of Quantity*

A is writing a testimonial about a pupil who is a candidate for a philosophy job, and his letter reads as follows: "Dear Sir, Mr.

---

① But why does B choose to violate the first maxim of Quantity instead of the second Quality maxim? Why does he choose to be less informative rather than give groundless information? R. Harnish (1991 [1976]: 331) offers an explanation. That is, there may be an ordering or weighting of the maxims, in which Quality precedes Quantity. Other things being equal, the speaker will choose to be consistent with the maxim of higher weight.

② Grice did not provide any example for the violation of the Manner maxim "Be orderly", which is understandable in that generally a disordered utterance will not convey anything but the fact that the speaker is mentally unsound. "They had a baby and got married" is not a disordered version of "They got married and had a baby". They are both ordered, though, in their own different ways. Gazard (1979: 44 n9) mentions that Herb Clark in personal communication drew his attention to a putative counterexample "John broke his leg. He tripped and fell." He argues against it from the logical point of view, saying "in these cases $\phi \frown \psi$ cannot be replaced by $\psi \frown \phi$". That is, this sentence cannot be replaced by "John broke his leg and he tripped and fell" and imply that John's fall caused his leg to break. But the Chinese example 屡败屡战 may be seen as an instantiation of the exploitation of this maxim.

X's command of English is excellent, and his attendance at tutorials has been regular. Yours, etc." (Gloss: A cannot be opting out, since if he wished to be uncooperative, why write at all? He cannot be unable, through ignorance, to say more, since the man is his pupil; moreover, he knows that more information than this is wanted. He must, therefore, be wishing to impart information that he is reluctant to write down. This supposition is tenable only on the assumption that he thinks Mr. X is no good at philosophy. This, then, is what he is implicating.)[1]

Extreme examples of a flouting of the first maxim of Quantity are provided by utterances of patent tautologies like *Women are women* and *War is war*. I would wish to maintain that at the level of what is said, in my favored sense, such remarks are totally noninformative and so, at that level, cannot but infringe the first maxim of Quantity in any conversational context. They are, of course, informative at the level of what is implicated, and the hearer's identification of their informative content at this level is dependent on his ability to explain the speaker's selection of the PARTICULAR patent tautology.

(1b) *An infringement of the second maxim of Quantity, "Do not give more information than is required", on the assumption that the existence of such a maxim should be admitted*

A wants to know whether p, and B volunteers not only the

---

[1] Some people objected to this example on the ground that no one would actually write a reference letter in this way. But this criticism misses the point. Reference letters may not be of this extreme form, but the principle to refrain from saying explicitly things which are detrimental to the person concerned is generally followed.

information that p, but information to the effect that it is certain that p, and that the evidence for its being the case that p is so-and-so and such-and-such.①

B's volubility may be undesigned, and if it is so regarded by A it may raise in A's mind a doubt as to whether B is as certain as he says he is ("Methinks the lady doth protest too much"). But if it is thought of as designed, it would be an oblique way of conveying that it is to some degree controversial whether or not p. It is, however, arguable that such an implicature could be explained by reference to the maxim of Relation without invoking an alleged second maxim of Quantity.②

(2a) *Examples in which the first maxim of Quality is flouted*

1. *Irony.* X, with whom A has been on close terms until now, has betrayed a secret of A's to a business rival. A and his audience both know this. A says "*X is a fine friend*". (Gloss: It is perfectly obvious to A and his audience that what A has said or has made as if to say is something he does not believe, and the audience knows that A knows that this is obvious to the audience. So, unless A's utterance is entirely pointless, A must be trying to get across some other proposition than the one he purports to be putting forward. This must be some obviously related proposition: the most obviously related proposition is the contradictory of

---

① An example of this type is:
 A: Where is X?
 B: He's gone to the library. He said so when he left.
② As is noted earlier, L. Horn (1984), and D. Sperber & D. Wilson (1986) have opted for exactly this.

the one he purports to be putting forward.)[1]

2. *Metaphor*. Examples like *You are the cream in my coffee* characteristically involve categorial falsity, so the contradictory of what the speaker has made as if to say will, strictly speaking, be a truism; so it cannot be THAT that such a speaker is trying to get across. The most likely supposition is that the speaker is attributing to his audience some feature or features in respect of which the audience resembles (more or less fancifully) the mentioned substance.

It is possible to combine metaphor and irony by imposing on the hearer two stages of interpretation. I say *You are the cream in my coffee*, intending the hearer to reach first the metaphor interpretant "You are my pride and joy" and then the irony interpretant "You are my bane."

3. *Meiosis*. Of a man known to have broken up all the furniture, one says *He was a little intoxicated*.

4. *Hyperbole*. Every nice girl loves a sailor.

(2b) *Examples in which the second maxim of Quality, "Do not say that for which you lack adequate evidence"*, is

---

[1] In his 1978 paper, Grice admits that this treatment of irony is inadequate. The mere fact that the speaker and his audience mutually know that he has said something he does not believe is not enough to induce an ironical understanding. But he rejects the idea that irony is connected with the practice to use one sentence to mean its opposite. It is not the case that any sentence whatsoever can be used ironically in its opposite meaning. In his view, irony is intimately concerned with the expression of a feeling, attitude or evaluation. He also doubts that irony is conveyed by a special tone. D. Sperber and D. Wilson, obviously prompted by Grice's suggestion that irony is concerned with the expression of a feeling, propose a different approach, which will be discussed in section 4.1.3.

flouted [1] are perhaps not easy to find, but the following seems to be a specimen. I say of X's wife, *She is probably deceiving him this evening*. In a suitable context, or with a suitable gesture or tone of voice, it may be clear that I have no adequate reason for supposing this to be the case. My partner, to preserve the assumption that the conversational game is still being played, assumes that I am getting at some related proposition for the acceptance of which I DO have a reasonable basis. The related proposition might well be that she is given to deceiving her husband, or possibly that she is the sort of person who would not stop short of such conduct.

(3) *Examples in which an implicature is achieved by real, as distinct from apparent, violation of the maxim of Relation* are perhaps rare, [2] but the following seems to be a good candidate. At a genteel tea party, A says *Mrs. X is an old bag*. There is a moment of appalled silence, and then B says *The weather has been quite delightful this summer, hasn't it*? B has blatantly refused to make what HE says relevant to A's preceding remark. He thereby implicates that A's remark should not be discussed and, perhaps more specifically, that A has committed a social gaffe.

(4) *Examples in which various maxims falling under the supermaxim "Be perspicuous" are flouted*

---

[1] In the original, these words are not italic. The present form is adopted according to the general format of the paper.

[2] This is advanced as one of the arguments by D. Sperber & D. Wilson (1986: 162) in favour of their relevance theory. That is, "Communicators do not 'follow' the principle of relevance; and they could not violate it even if they wanted to."

1. *Ambiguity*. We must remember that we are concerned only with ambiguity that is deliberate, and that the speaker intends or expects to be recognized by his hearer. The problem the hearer has to solve is why a speaker should, when still playing the conversational game, go out of his way to choose an ambiguous utterance. There are two types of cases:

(a) Examples in which there is no difference, or no striking difference, between two interpretations of an utterance with respect to straightforwardness; neither interpretation is notably more sophisticated, less standard, more recondite or more farfetched than the other. We might consider Blake's lines: "Never seek to tell thy love, Love that never told can be." To avoid the complications introduced by the presence of the imperative mood, I shall consider the related sentence, *I sought to tell my love, love that never told can be*. There may be a double ambiguity here. *My love* may refer to either a state of emotion or an object of emotion, and *love that never told can be* may mean either "Love that cannot be told" or "love that if told cannot continue to exist." Partly because of the sophistication of the poet and partly because of internal evidence (that the ambiguity is kept up), there seems to be no alternative to supposing that the ambiguities are deliberate and that the poet is conveying both what he would be saying if one interpretation were intended rather than the other, and vice versa; though no doubt the poet is not explicitly SAYING any one of these things but only conveying or suggesting them (cf. "Since she [nature]① pricked thee out of women's

---

① Grice's gloss.

pleasure, mine be thy love, and thy love's use their treasure.")

(b) Examples in which one interpretation is notably less straightforward than another. Take the complex example of the British General who captured the town of Sind and sent back the message *Peccavi*. The ambiguity involved ("I have Sind"/"I have sinned") is phonemic, not morphemic; and the expression actually used is unambiguous, but since it is in a language foreign to speaker and hearer, translation is called for, and the ambiguity resides in the standard translation into native English.

Whether or not the straightforward interpretant ("I have sinned") is being conveyed, it seems that the nonstraightforward must be. There might be stylistic reasons for conveying by a sentence merely its nonstraightforward interpretant, but it would be pointless, and perhaps also stylistically objectionable, to go to the trouble of finding an expression that nonstraightforwardly conveys that p, thus imposing on an audience the effort involved in finding this interpretant, if this interpretant were otiose so far as communication was concerned. Whether the straightforward interpretant is also being conveyed seems to depend on whether such a supposition would conflict with other conversational requirements, for example, would it be relevant, would it be something the speaker could be supposed to accept, and so on. If such requirements are not satisfied, then the straightforward interpretant is not being conveyed. If they are, it is. If the author of *Peccavi* could naturally be supposed to think that he had committed some kind of transgression, for example, had disobeyed his orders in capturing Sind, and if reference to such a transgression would be relevant to the presumed interests of the audience, then he would have been conveying both interpretants; otherwise he would be conveying only the nonstraightforward one.

2. *Obscurity*. How do I exploit, for the purposes of communication, a deliberate and overt violation of the requirement that I should avoid obscurity? Obviously, if the Cooperative Principle is to operate, I must intend my partner to understand what I am saying despite the obscurity I import into my utterance. Suppose that A and B are having a conversation in the presence of a third party, for example, a child, then A might be deliberately obscure, though not too obscure, in the hope that B would understand and the third party not.① Furthermore, if A expects B to see that A is being deliberately obscure, it seems reasonable to suppose that, in making his conversational contribution in this way, A is implicating that the contents of his communication should not be imparted to the third party.

3. *Failure to be brief or succinct*. Compare the remarks:
(a) *Miss X sang "Home sweet home."*
(b) *Miss X produced a series of sounds that corresponded closely with the score of "Home sweet home."*

Suppose that a reviewer has chosen to utter (b) rather than (a). (Gloss: Why has he selected that rigmarole in place of the concise and nearly synonymous *sang*? Presumably, to indicate some striking difference between Miss X's performance and those to which the word *singing* is usually applied. The most obvious

---

① Some linguists have proposed the following as an example:
A: Let's get the kids something.
B: Okey, but I veto I-C-E C-R-E-A-M-S.

supposition is that Miss X's performance suffered from some hideous defect. The reviewer knows that this supposition is what is likely to spring to mind, so that is what he is implicating.)

Now there are disagreements over Grice's approach to violation of the maxims. E. O. Keenan (1976) argues that there may be cultural reasons for not following some maxims. On the island of Madagascar, for example, Malagasy speakers regularly provide less information than is required by their conversational partner. The information sought may not be easily available, and the possession of it is seen as a mark of status; or because its release will lead to unpleasant consequences; or because the partner is a stranger, etc. But R. Harnish (1991 [1976]: 357) thinks E. O. Keenan is mistaken here. The maxims are not meant to be observed CATEGORICALLY. "Grice nowhere says, nor would want to say, that all conversations are governed by the cooperative maxims. There are too many garden-variety counterexamples: social talk between enemies, diplomatic encounters, police interrogation of a reluctant suspect, most political speeches, and many presidential news conferences. These are just some of the cases in which the maxims of cooperation are not in effect and are known not to be in effect by the participants." And J. Thomas (1995: 76 – 8) suggests that there is another category of non-observance of the maxims,[①] known as suspending. In her view, "Keenan's example does not falsify Grice's theory if it is seen as a case where the maxim of Quantity is suspended. There is no expectation at all on the part of interactants that speakers will provide precise information about their relatives and

---

① J. Thomas (1995: 64 – 78) insists on distinguishing between different types of violation, and uses "non-observance" as a cover term, of which violation is only one type; even though she admits on page 90 that there are many borderline cases and it is often difficult to determine which type of non-observance is involved in a particular case.

friends, in case they draw the attention of evil spirits to them." Thomas believes that suspension of the maxims is also event-specific. For example, in British theatrical circles, people refer to Shakespeare's *Macbeth* as "The Scottish Play", in order to avoid bad luck. And she holds that "in most cultures the maxim of Quantity appears to be selectively suspended in, for example, courts of law, Committees of Inquiry or indeed in any confrontational situation where it is held to be the job of an 'investigator' to elicit the truth from a witness. The witnesses are not required or expected to volunteer information which may incriminate them, and no inference is drawn on the basis of what they do not say." "We find similar instances of the suspension of the maxim of Quality in the case of funeral orations and ... in the case of obituaries, of the maxim of Manner in the case of poetry, of the maxim of Quantity in the case of telegrams, telexes and some international phone calls and of all three maxims in the case of jokes." L. Horn (1988: 130), however, prefers to view the Madagascar case as an instance of the maxim of Quantity being overruled by some other conversational or non-conversational principles. And I think the other cases mentioned by Thomas may also be seen in this light.

3.2 Elaborations on the theory

The theory of conversational implicature as was expounded in the original form of Grice's is rather crude. There is much room for improvement, therefore pragmaticians have worked on the basis of Grice and introduced some refinements.

3.2.1 Characteristics of conversational implicature

Conversational implicature is a type of extra meaning, or inference,[1] deriving from the words used in interaction with the context. If we are to give it such a prominence as Grice does, we must be able to distinguish it from other extra meanings, other inferences, to show the special properties it possesses. In his "Logic and Conversation", Grice touches upon this topic and mentions six of them. After characterizing the notion of conversational implicature, he argues that "The presence of a conversational implicature must be capable of being worked out; for even if it can in fact be intuitively grasped, unless the intuition is replaceable by an argument, the implicature (if present at all) will not count as a CONVERSATIONAL implicature; it will be a CONVENTIONAL implicature" (p. 50). At the end of the paper, he lists five other features a conversational implicature[2] must possess, which are cancellability, nondetachability, nonconventionality, indeterminacy and the fact that it is not carried by what is said, but by the saying of it[3] (pp. 57 - 8). But Grice was cautious not to make these features "a decisive test to settle the question whether a conversational implicature is present or not" (1978: 114 - 5).

S. Levinson in his *Pragmatics* discusses Grice's suggestions at

---

[1] J. Thomas (ibid.: 58) makes a distinction between "implicature" and "inference", arguing that "To imply is to hint, suggest or convey some meaning indirectly by means of language.... an implicature is generated intentionally by the speaker and may (or may not) be understood by the hearer. To infer is to deduce something from evidence (this evidence may be linguistic, paralinguistic or non-linguistic). An inference is produced by the hearer." However, most people use them interchangeably. That is, both the extra meaning intended by the speaker and that deduced by the hearer may be called "implicature" or "inference".

[2] Though in some places, he seems to be talking about the generalized type only.

[3] Levinson (1983: 114 n14) explains that this means implicatures are not carried by sentences, but by utterances.

some length (pp. 114 – 8), and then explicitly states that conversational implicatures have four major distinguishing properties on page 119. ①

(ⅰ) Cancellability (or defeasibility)

Conversational implicatures are cancellable or defeasible if we add some other premises to the original ones. For example, the implicature "John has only three cows" carried by (1) is cancelled in (2) by "if not more", which in contrast means "John has at least three cows".

(1) John has three cows. ②

(2) John has three cows, if not more.

And the implicature "They were not smoking ordinary cigarettes, but something illegal, such as marijuana" in (3) is cancelled in (4).

(3) The police came in and everyone swallowed their cigarettes. ③

(4) The police came in and everyone swallowed their cigarettes, though they were doing nothing illegal.

A conversational implicature may even be cancelled simply by the situational context. If to have three cows is a condition for anyone to get a subsidy from the government, then when the inspector asks John's neighbour (5), he could very well answer (6), without implicating that "John has only three cows".

(5) Has John really got the requisite number of cows?

(6) Oh sure, he's got three cows all right.

(ⅱ) Non-detachability

The conversational implicature is attached to the semantic content

---

① Levinson is more confident about his four properties "taken together with some additional criteria to be discussed [e.g. reinforceability, universality] as necessary conditions which are...jointly sufficient for an inference to be considered an implicature" (1983: 120).

② The examples in this section are mostly adopted or adapted from Levinson (1983:115 – 7).

③ This example is from Kempson (1977: 70 – 2).

of what is said, not to the linguistic form used. Therefore it is possible to use a synonym and keep the implicature intact. In other words, the implicature will not be detached, separated from the utterance as a whole, even though the specific words may be changed. For example, (7a-e) said ironically will all implicate (8).

 (7) a. John's a genius.
   b. John's a mental prodigy.
   c. John's an exceptionally clever human being.
   d. John's an enormous intellect.
   e. John's a big brain.
 (8) John's an idiot.

In response to "Mrs. X is an old bag", the example Grice used for the violation of the Relation maxim, any utterance which is not directly related to it will generate the implicature "You shouldn't talk about that now". One does not have to say "The weather has been quite delightful this summer, hasn't it?". "What a beautiful dress!" "Your son's very smart!" "The music's great!" will all do.

Conversational implicatures related to the Manner maxims, however, are an exception to this property, as they rely on the form rather than the content. "But I veto I-C-E C-R-E-A-M-S" replaced by "But don't give them ice creams" would give the game away.

 (iii) Calculability①

---

 ① D. Sperber & D. Wilson (1986: 200f.) argue that "we have taken seriously Grice's requirement that implicatures should be calculable; that is, recoverable by an inference process. In Grice's framework, and the framework of most pragmatists, some sort of *ex post facto* justification for the identification of an implicature can be given, but the argument could have worked equally well for quite different assumptions which happen not to be implicated at all." For example, "X is a fine friend" could well mean "Y is a fine friend", instead of "X is not a fine friend" as Grice suggested, since both of them are to some extent opposite to the original sentence. They claim "Relevance theory solves this problem by looking not just at the cognitive effects of an assumption, but also at the processing effort it requires." For the details, see section 4.1.

The conversational implicature of an utterance is different from its literal meaning. There is no direct link between the two. So if it is to succeed as the speaker intends to, there must be ways for the hearer to work it out. In "Logic and Conversation", Grice suggests,

> A general pattern for the working out of a conversational implicature might be given as follows: "He has said that p; there is no reason to suppose that he is not observing the maxims, or at least the CP; he could not be doing this unless he thought that q; he knows (and knows that I know that he knows) that I can see that the supposition that he thinks that q IS required; he has done nothing to stop me thinking that q; he intends me to think, or is at least willing to allow me to think, that q; and so he has implicated that q." (p. 50)

In other words,

> To work out that a particular conversational implicature is present, the hearer will rely on the following data: (1) the conventional meaning of the words used, together with the identity of any references that may be involved; (2) the CP and its maxims; (3) the context, linguistic or otherwise, of the utterance; (4) other items of background knowledge; and (5) the fact (or supposed fact) that all relevant items falling under the previous headings are available to both participants and both participants know or assume this to be the case. (ibid.)

(iv) Non-conventionality[1]

---

[1] J. Sadock (1991 [1978]: 367) notes that this property "is completely circular. Conversational implicata are by definition nonconventional and if it were possible to tell in some intuitive way what is and what is not conventional, then there would be no need for other criteria." And after an almost complete refutation of Grice's characteristics of conversational implicature, Sadock adds "reinforceability ought to be about as good--and about as poor--a test for conversational implicature as cancellability" (p.374).

As has been mentioned, conversational implicature is an extra meaning, not inherent in the words used. One cannot find conversational implicatures listed in the dictionary. To work out the conversational implicature of an utterance, one needs to know its conventional meaning and the context in which it is used. In other words, a conversational implicature is the adding up of the conventional meaning and the context. When the context changes, the implicature will also change. As we have shown, "John has three cows" used in different contexts, either linguistic or situational, will have different implicatures. Similarly, the sentence "Is this your pen?" will have different conversational implicatures in different situational contexts.

In this sense we can also say conversational implicatures are indeterminate, while the conventional meaning is determinate, constant.

3.2.2 Entailment

Conversational implicature is only one type of inference, there are other inferences derivable from an utterance. For example, from (9) one may infer not only (10), but also (11) and (12).

(9) John has three cows.

(10) John has only three cows.

(11) John has some cows.

John has some animals.

John has something.

Somebody has three cows.

Somebody has some cows.

Somebody has some animals.

Somebody has something.

(12) There is a man called John.

The inferences in (11) are known as entailments of (9), and

(12) is a presupposition. Entailment, as a logical relationship, refers to the relation between two sentences① in which the truth of the second necessarily follows from the truth of the first, while the falsity of the first follows from the falsity of the second rather than the other way round. In contrast, presupposition is a relation between two sentences in which the truth of the second is guaranteed whatsoever, even if the first is false. As presupposition is the topic of another chapter, we shall only deal with entailment here.

In last section we discussed the characteristics of conversational implicature. Now the question is whether they apply to entailment. We notice that entailment also has the property of non-detachability. It is also tied to the semantic content of a sentence rather than its form. The three sentences in (13) will all have the same entailments as "John has three cows".

(13) John owns three cows.

John possesses three cows.

There are three cows which belong to John.

But this is the only similarity between conversational implicature and entailment. They differ from each other in all the other three properties. In other words, entailment is not cancellable, not calculable, but conventional. For example, one cannot make an assertion and deny its entailment at the same time:

(14) *John has three cows, but he doesn't have any cows.

---

① In the sense that conversational implicatures are carried by utterances, not sentences, the distinction between conversational implicature and entailment is very clear. However the distinction between sentence and utterance is not itself a clear one. Writers often use these two interchangeably, and J. Austin (1962) is a case in point. So some other criterion is in order.

* John has three cows, but he doesn't have any animals.

* John has three cows, but nobody has anything.

The most important difference between the two is that entailment is conventional, while conversational implicature is not. Entailment is part of the conventional meaning of a linguistic form. Part of the meaning of "cow" is "It refers to an animal". To know the meaning of "John" partly means to know "It is a name of a person", so that it can be replaced by "somebody". If you do not know the entailment of a linguistic form, you simply have to look it up in the dictionary. There is no way to work out an entailment on the basis of the CP and its maxims. Hence entailment is not calculable. Another consequence of its being conventional is that entailment is constant in all contexts. "John has three cows" will always entail "John has some cows" and all the others in example (11). Therefore entailment is determinate as against the indeterminacy of conversational implicature. And this perhaps ultimately explains why entailment is not cancellable.

3.2.3 Conventional implicature

Another inference that has to be distinguished from conversational implicature is known as conventional implicature. In his "Logic and Conversation", Grice makes this distinction soon after the introduction of the term "implicature", when he says,

> In some cases the conventional meaning of the words used will determine what is implicated, besides helping to determine what is said. If I say (smugly), *He is an Englishman; he is, therefore, brave*, I have certainly committed myself, by virtue of the meaning of my words, to its being the case that his being brave is a consequence of (follows from) his being an Englishman. But while I have said that he is an Englishman, and said

that he is brave, I do not want to say that I have SAID (in the favored sense) that it follows from his being an Englishman that he is brave, though I have certainly indicated, and so implicated, that this is so. I do not want to say that my utterance of this sentence would be, STRICTLY SPEAKING, false should the consequence in question fail to hold. So SOME implicatures are conventional, unlike the one① with which I introduced this discussion of implicatures.②(pp. 44-5)

Another instance of conventional implicature provided by Grice concerns the word *but*. In his 1961 paper, Grice points out that *but* has the same truth-conditional meaning as *and*, but it also carries the implicature that there is a contrast between the two conjuncts linked by it. Shakespeare's line "My friends were poor, but honest" is a case in point. And J. Thomas (1995: 57) has found an authentic example, in which the American actress, Kathleen Turner, was discussing perceptions of women in the film industry:

> I get breakdowns from the studios of the scripts that they're developing...and I got one that I sent back furious to the studio that said "The main character was thirty-seven but still attractive." I circled the *but* in red ink and I sent it back and said, "Try again!"

In 1979, L. Karttunen and S. Peters address themselves to this question in their "Conventional Implicature" in some detail. They dis-

---

① The one about someone working in a bank, quoted at the beginning of section 3.1.1.
② Grice (1971 [1968]: 57) says "I would wish to maintain that the semantic function of the word 'therefore' is to enable a speaker to *indicate*, though not to *say*, that a certain consequence holds."

cuss inter alia the word *even*. They argue that in (15) *even* plays no role in determining its truth conditions. This sentence is true when (16) is true and false otherwise. As far as the truth-condition is concerned, (15) is equivalent to (16). They express the same proposition.

 (15) Even Bill likes Mary.
 (16) Bill likes Mary.

The meanings deriving from *even*, as in (17), are subsidiary.

 (17) Other people besides Bill like Mary.
   Of the people under consideration, Bill is the least likely to like Mary.

If it should happen that these meanings are false, the speaker of (15) would be criticized for having said a wrong thing. But such criticism would normally be mild, usually crediting the speaker with saying something that is partially correct. It may be "Well, yes, he does like her; but that is just as one would expect". In contrast, if (16) is false, partial credit would not normally be given, even if the other two meanings were true. One would hardly reply, "Yes, you wouldn't expect Bill to like Mary; as a matter of fact, he doesn't like her". This is because the speaker's principal commitment is not correct. The milder criticism is warranted only when the speaker's error concerns one of his subsidiary commitments.

 This disparity of response indicates that the truth of (15) depends solely on what is SAID, i.e. whether "Bill likes Mary". The other two meanings are only implicated, hence implicatures.

 The distinction between these two aspects of meaning can be brought out more clearly if we consider the complex sentences containing (15). In (18) what the speaker has just noticed is (16), not

(17). And it is only when a speaker is sure of (17) will he be in a position to say (19).

(18) I just noticed that even Bill likes Mary.

(19) If even Bill likes Mary, then all is well.

But these two implicatures are conventional, determined by the conventional meaning of *even*. And they are constant, do not vary with the context. On the other hand if we change the word concerned, the implicatures will disappear. In other words, they do not have the four characteristics of conversational implicature. That is why Levinson defines conventional implicature as "non-truth-conditional inferences that are *not* derived from superordinate pragmatic principles like the maxims, but are simply attached by convention to particular lexical items or expressions" (1983: 127).

Levinson (ibid.: 128-9) also mentions that discourse deictic items like *however*, *moreover*, *besides*, *anyway*, and social deictic items like *sir*, *madam*, *mate*, *your honour* all have conventional implicatures. For example, the difference between (20) and (21) is not truth-conditional. When one is true, the other is also true. But they differ in connotations, or in the Gricean terminology, in implicatures. And this implicature is conventional, determined by a social convention, nobody is able to change it at will. ①

(20) Tu es le professeur.

(21) Vous êtes le professeur.

3.2.4 Distinctions within conversational implicature

---

① But J. Mey (1993: 105) contends that this conventional implicature is cancelled in Quebec, where it is quite all right for a French speaker to use *tu* when asking for a drink in a bar.

Within the category of conversational implicature there are two finer distinctions. One is between the generalized and the particularized. Towards the end of his "Logic and Conversation", Grice says the cases he has been considering might be called particularized conversational implicatures. They are cases in which an implicature is carried by saying something on a particular occasion. But there is another type of implicature, which is normally carried by the use of a certain form of words, in the absence of special circumstances. For example, if A says *X is meeting a woman this evening*, he would normally be regarded as implicating that the person to be met was someone other than X's wife, mother, sister, or perhaps even close platonic friend (p. 56). To show that this is indeed the normal interpretation, Clark & Clark (1977: 122) supply (22) as a possible response from B. Now if A answers (23), B would certainly feel annoyed. He could very well accuse A of deceiving him, though as Leech (1983: 91) says the proposition is true from the logical point of view. X's wife is indeed a woman.

(22) Does his wife know about it?

(23) Of COURSE she does. The woman he is meeting IS his wife.

Grice goes on "Similarly, if I were to say *X went into a house yesterday and found a tortoise inside the front door*, my hearer would normally be surprised if some time later I revealed that the house was X's own" (ibid.). He calls this type of implicature generalized conversational implicature.[1]

---

[1] But Grice has a problem with the exact implicature of expressions like "a woman" and "a house". He notices that the expression "an X" does not necessarily implicate that it is something which is not closely related to the person mentioned. "Sometimes, however, there would

In his *Pragmatics* of 1983, Levinson defines generalized conversational implicatures as "those that arise without any particular context or special scenario being necessary" (p. 126). In an article of 1987, he reformulates the definition as "preferred interpretations in the absence of contextual cues to the contrary" (1987b: 410). And in 1991, he calls them "default interpretations" (p. 127). In other words, generalized conversational implicature is the interpretation one gets when there is no other possible interpretations without invoking a particular context.

The examples we have been considering in this chapter so far are all of the particularized type except one, that is, "John has three cows" implicating "John has only three cows". The others are all particularized conversational implicatures in need of particular contexts. In

---

normally be no such implicature ('I have been sitting in a car all morning') and sometimes a reverse implicature ('I broke a finger yesterday')" (p. 56). Why is it so? Grice did not find a satisfactory answer. Now my suggestion is that the use of an indefinite article indicates that the reference is not definite, i.e. there are many, at least more than one, possible candidates satisfying the description. So if somebody has more than one car, then "a car" may mean "a car of mine", "my car"; otherwise it does not. And as a person has more than one finger, it is perfectly all right for him to use "a finger" to mean "my finger", "a finger of mine". Suppose we are talking about "head" or "nose", one is not entitled to say "I broke a head/nose yesterday", meaning "I broke my head/nose yesterday". A natural response to such an utterance would be "How many heads/noses do you have?" The same principle applies to "a house", as one usually has only one house. The case of "a woman" is a bit more complicated. "Woman" is a more general term, the use of which indicates that the specific terms, such as "mother, wife, sister, girl friend" are not applicable. Hence the use of the word "woman" alone is enough to exclude the other interpretations. In dialects or registers in which "woman" may be used in the sense of "wife" or "girl friend", the use of the expression "a woman" suggests the person mentioned has more than one "woman". It is just like the use of "I ate out with a wife yesterday", meaning "I ate out with my wife/one of my wives", in a country where a man is allowed to have more than one wife.

the reference letter example used by Grice, for instance, if the student is not applying for a lectureship in philosophy but in English, then there will be no such implicature as "He is no good at philosophy".

Another distinction within the category of conversational implicature is the one between the standard and the non-standard. As we have shown, Grice holds that there are also implicatures which arise even when all the maxims are observed. For instance, B's response to A in the following dialogue, which we quoted earlier in 3.1.2 and reproduce here as (24), implicates "the garage is, or at least may be open, etc." (Grice 1975: 51)

(24) A: I am out of petrol.

B: There is a garage round the corner.

But he did not elaborate on this point. It was Levinson who first introduced the term "standard"[1] and discussed this type separately in his *Pragmatics* (pp. 104 - 8), from those which involve the exploitation of maxims (pp. 109 - 12) and might be called non-standard.

This distinction, based on the observance or violation of the maxims, differs quite clearly in principle from the one between the generalized and the particularized, based on the presence or absence of a particular context. Nevertheless there is some overlap between them. The two criteria do not lead to distinctly separated classes of implicatures. The generalized implicatures exemplified by (10), reproduced here as (25), deriving from (26) do not involve any violation of the maxims either.

---

[1] The choice of the term may be due to the fact that Grice time and again referred to the CP and it's maxims as "the standard type of conversational practice" (1975: 48) and "they are standardly (though not invariably) observed by participants in a talk exchange" (1978: 113). And in his 1981 paper (p. 196), Grice used the term "standard conversational implicata" once.

(25) John has only three cows.

(26) John has three cows.

In other words, some generalized implicatures are standard implicatures at the same time. They are a subset of the standard. ① Levinson maintains this subset, i.e. the implicatures that are both derived from observing the maxims and in need of no special context, has a special importance for linguistic theory. "For it is these in particular which will be hard to distinguish from the semantic content of linguistic expressions, because such implicatures will be routinely associated with the relevant expressions in all ordinary contexts" (1983: 127). And his neo-Gricean principles proposed in subsequent years are mainly meant for them.

In closing, one final note must be made. That is, the distinction between generalized and particularized implicatures is not absolute. As is shown in note ①, Levinson thinks that some generalized implicatures work in a RELATIVELY context-independent way. Grice himself also says generalized implicatures are RELATIVELY general

---

① Cf. Levinson 1983: 104 and 126. It is important to take note of Levinson's warning in footnote 6 on page 104 that not all standard implicatures are generalized ones. For example, the standard implicature "You can get petrol there" deriving from "There is a garage round the corner" is a particularized one, which depends on this particular context. If A's utterance is "My car's broken down" or "I have a flat tyre", the implicatures derivable from "There is a garage round the corner" will definitely be different. On the other hand, not all generalized implicatures are standard. Some generalized implicatures also involve violation of the maxims. Levinson (1983: 126 – 7) argues that even though most non-standard implicatures are particularized, in need of particularized contexts, "metaphors like [England is a sinking ship] or tautologies like [War is war] convey what they convey in a relatively context-independent way". That is, metaphors and tautologies have generalized implicatures, though they involve violation of the maxims, and non-standard by that criterion.

(1981: 185). And G. Green (1989: 95) explicitly states that the difference between the generalized and the particularized is only a matter of the degree of dependence on context. This point applies to the distinction between the standard and the non-standard as well. R. Lakoff (1995: 2) argues, as is pointed out in note ②, page 45, that in example (24), speaker B may be said to have violated the maxim of Quantity, or of Relevance, or both. And there is plenty of reference to the relative nature of observance, or violation, of the maxims in Grice's 1975 paper. For instance, on page 50, concerning B's remark "C has not yet been to prison" in his first example, he says "B has apparently violated the maxim 'Be relevant'... given the circumstances, I can regard his irrelevance as only apparent". On page 52, when discussing tautologies like *women are women* and *War is war*, he argues that at the level of what is said "such remarks are totally noninformative and so, at that level, cannot but infringe the first maxim of Quantity", but at the level of what is implicated "They are, of course, informative".

To summarize the classifications concerning implicature, we can draw a figure as follows (adapted from R. Harnish (1991 [1976]: 325), J. Sadock (1991 [1978]: 366-7), S. Levinson (1983: 131) and L. Horn (1988: 121)):

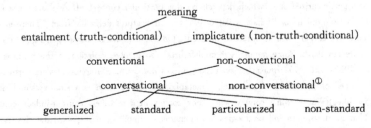

① Many writers have mentioned the existence of this type, though nobody has done any

3.3 Formalization of implicature

Some people have criticized the theory of conversational implicature for being too vague, saying that in its present form one can arrive at almost any conversational implicature one wants. Is there a way to formalize conversational implicatures so that they can be arrived at in a more principled way? Linguists like Laurence Horn, Gerald Gazdar, Jay David Atlas and Stephen Levinson have done some research in this area and produced some promising results. In this section, we shall concentrate on their findings about generalized quantity implicatures, i.e. generalized conversational implicatures having to do with the Quantity maxims. There are two sub-classes: scalar quantity implicatures and clausal quantity implicatures.

3.3.1 Scalar quantity implicatures

L. Horn's Ph.D. dissertation of 1972[①] represents the first attempt in this direction, in which he proposes:

> Given a quantitative scale of n elements $p_1, p_2, \ldots, p_n$ and a speaker uttering a statement S which contains an element p_i on this scale, then
>
> (i) the listener can infer $\sim S^{p_i}_{p_j}$ for all p_j, $p_i (j \neq n)$
>
> (ii) the listener must infer $\sim S^{p_i}_{p_n}$
>
> (iii) if $p_k > p_j > p_i$, then $\sim S^{p_i}_{p_j} \rightarrow \sim S^{p_i}_{p_k}$, where S^a_b denotes

---

detailed work on it. Grice, for example, makes it clear that conversational implicatures are only one subclass of non-conventional implicatures (1975: 45). And L. Horn (1988: 131 n17) suggests, on the basis of Grice's observation that there are also maxims "aesthetic, social, or moral in character", that implicatures having to do with politeness maxims may belong here. But J. Sadock (1991 [1978]: 366) does not agree with this distinction, as we pointed out in footnote ①, page 41.

① I am not in a position to get hold of Horn's original dissertation. The following discussion is based on Gazdar (1979) and Levinson (1983).

the result of substituting *b* for all occurrences of *a* in S.

(from G. Gazdar 1979: 56)

That is, if there is a quantitative scale containing several elements, and a speaker uses one of them, say p_i, in his utterance, then (*i*) the listener can infer that it is not the case that other non-terminal elements, such as p_j, can substitute for p_i; (*ii*) the listener must infer that it is not the case that the last element p_n can substitute for p_i; and (*iii*) if $p_k > p_j > p_i$ are arranged in this order, the fact that p_j cannot substitute for p_i implicates that p_k cannot either.

Some of his quantitative scales are:

<all, most, many, some, few>

<and, or>

<n, ...5, 4, 3, 2, 1>[①]

<excellent, good>

<hot, warm>

<always, often, sometimes>

<succeed in *V*ing, try to *V*, want to *V*>

---

① According to R. Carston (1998: 199 – 200), Horn changed his views about cardinal numbers later. In his 1992 paper, Horn uses examples like the following to show that cardinals behave differently from other scalar expressions:

(i) A: Do you have two children?

　B: No, three./? Yes, (in fact) three.

(ii) A: Are many of your friends linguists?

　B: ? No, all of them are./Yes, (in fact) all of them are.

Horn (1996b: 316) reinforces the point with further examples:

(iii) ?? Neither of us liked the movie – she hated it and I absolutely loved it.

(iv) Neither of us have three kids – she has two and I have four.

And he concludes: "Such paradigms support a mixed theory in which sentences with cardinals may well demand a pragmatic enrichment analysis of what is said, while other scalar predications continue to submit happily to a minimalist treatment on which they are lower-bounded by their literal content and upper-bounded, in default contexts, by quantity implicature."

< necessarily p, p, possibly p >
< certain that p, probable that p, possible that p >
< must, should, may >
< cold, cool >
< love, like >
< none, not all > (from S. Levinson 1983: 134)

Suppose A and B are talking about the students' reception of a new film, and A says (27), then according to Horn, (i) B CAN infer that it is not the case that (28), (29) and (30) can substitute for (27), i.e. the other non-terminal elements of the same scale will not very likely be substitutes for *many*;①(ii) B MUST infer that it is not the case that (31) can substitute for (27), i.e. the terminal element is definitely not a substitute for *many*;② and (iii) since "all > most > many" are arranged in this order, the fact that it is not the case that (29) can substitute for (27) implicates that (28) cannot either.

(27) Many of them went to the film.

---

① As G. Gazdar (1979: 56) points out, L. Horn does not stipulate in (i) and (ii) of his formulation of a quantitative scale that $p_j > p_i$ are arranged in this order, but only $j \neq n$, accordingly *some* will have to be treated differently from *few*. But this is not a right prediction. Since *some* and *few* both come after *many*, they are in the same sense relationship with the latter, which differs from that between *all*, *most* on the one hand and *many* on the other. Sentence (27) entails (30) and (31) in that whenever (27) is true, (30) and (31) will, logically speaking, also be true, but not vice versa. However the relationship between (27) and (28), or that between (27) and (29), is just the opposite, that is, (28), or (29), entails (27), not the other way round.

② As mentioned in the note above, Horn does not stipulate the order of the elements except the last one. So the only thing he can say for sure is about this one, and this is why there is a difference between *can* in (i) and *must* in (ii). But there is a problem here. According to G. Gazdar (ibid.: 56, 58 n22), the scales are of the form: < all, most, many, some, few, ... >, suggesting they are "partial rather than total orderings". In other words, *few* is not necessarily the last element, in which case the inference will not hold.

(28) All of them went to the film.
(29) Most of them went to the film.
(30) Some of them went to the film.
(31) Few of them went to the film.

L. Horn (1972) does not explicitly define the notion "quantitative scale". And G. Gazdar (1979: 57-8) concedes that definition is difficult. First, the items in the scale must be qualitatively similar, but a hard and fast criterion is difficult to come by. For example, we want $<know, believe>$ to be a scale, but not $<regret, know>$, yet we cannot say clearly why. Second, there is some difficulty determining the order of the elements. We may base it on semantic informativeness, but research has shown that the ordering relation is pragmatic.[①] Consequently he contents himself with a (semantically stated) necessary condition borrowed from Caton (1966):

> Let Q be an n-tuple of expressions such that $Q = <\alpha_0, \alpha_1, \ldots \alpha_{n-1}>$ where $n > 1$. Then if Q is a quantitative scale: $[\phi_{\alpha_i}] \subset [\phi_{\alpha_{i+1}}]$ where ϕ_{α_i} and ($\phi_{\alpha_{i+1}}$ are any pair of simple expression alternatives with respect to a_i, $a_{i+1} \in Q$.
>
> (from G. Gazdar 1979: 58)

$[\phi_{\alpha_i}]$ stands for the proposition denoted by the sentence ϕ, which con-

---

[①] For example, R. Harnish (1991 [1976]: 361) notes "To say that some As are B is conversationally taken to mean that some are and some are not; likewise, with saying that some As are not B. It is important to note that this implication is contextually dependent. Consider Fogelin's [1967] case of a prison guard who announces that some of his prisoners have escaped, when they all have. The implication is dependent on the presumption that if more were missing, he would know. Contrast this with another case (due to Merrilee Salmon): I am driving past Jones' house, the light is on, and I say: 'Somebody must be home.' I certainly do not imply that somebody is not; and this is because (I contend) I am not supposed by the hearer to be in any position to know".

tains the expression α_i. The symbol $\subset$ means "is a sub-set of". When the proposition denoted by a sentence is a sub-set of that denoted by another, we say this sentence entails the other. In other words, we may use the entailment relationship as a criterion. If a sentence ϕ containing an expression (or element) α_i, entails but not be entailed by an otherwise identical sentence containing α_{i+1}, then α_i and α_{i+1} form a quantitative scale Q, and α_i precedes α_{i+1}. To put it differently, α_i is stronger, more informative, than α_{i+1}. ①

On this basis, Gazdar defines scalar quantity implicatures as:

$f_s(\psi) = \{X : X = K \sim \phi_{\alpha_i}\}$

for all ϕ_{α_i} such that for some quantitative scale Q, α_i, $\alpha_{i+1} \in Q$

(i) $\psi = X \frown \phi_{\alpha_{i+1}} \frown Y$ where X and Y are any expressions, possibly null

(ii) $[\psi] \subseteq [\phi_{\alpha_{i+1}}]$

where ϕ_{α_i} and $\phi_{\alpha_{i+1}}$ are simple expression alternatives with respect to α_i and α_{i+1}. (ibid: 58 – 9)

"f" stands for "function", "s" for "scalar", and $f_s(\psi)$ means "the function of argument ψ". $\{X : X = K \sim \phi_{\alpha_i}\}$ is a description of the set X. That is, X has the property of not being ϕ_{α_i}, as far as the speaker

---

① G. Gazdar (1979: 58) argues there is another condition, namely, the expressions are not within the scope of any logical functors in the sentences. And not to make any allowance for the scope of other logical expressions in the sentence is a more serious error in Horn's formulation of a quantitative scale. Thus, according to Horn, (1) would implicate (2), and (3) would implicate (4).

(1) It is not the case that Paul ate some of the eggs.
(2) Paul ate all the eggs.
(3) Mary ate some of the bacon and Paul ate some of the eggs.
(4) Either Mary didn't eat all of the bacon or Paul didn't eat all of the eggs. (ibid. : 56)

knows. $\in$ means "is an element of", and $\subseteq$ "is a sub-set of, or identical with". In other words, the whole formula means: if a speaker uses ψ, which contains $\phi_{a_{i+1}}$, and the proposition denoted by ψ, i.e. $[\psi]$, is a sub-set of, or identical with, that denoted by $\phi_{a_{i+1}}$, then it implicates that the speaker knows that it is not the case that ϕ_{a_i}.

J. D. Atlas and S. Levinson on the other hand are more straightforward about the nature of the quantitative scale, which they dub Horn scale. In their 1981 paper, they define it as a set of "equally brief[1] expressions that can be ordered in a...scale of relative informativeness" (p. 38). And they note that there are two ways to define informativeness. One is to identify the informational content with the set of its logical entailments, the more entailments a proposition has the more informative it is. The other is to identify the content with the set of possible falsifiers of a statement, the more states of affairs it falsifies the more informative it is.

In his *Pragmatics* of 1983 (p. 133), Levinson defines a linguistic scale as:

> a set of linguistic alternatives, or contrastive expressions of the same grammatical category, which can be arranged in linear order by degree of *informativeness* or semantic strength. Such a scale will have the general form of an ordered set (indicated by

---

[1] This qualification is expanded on page 44, where they argue "there are natural and independently motivated restrictions to put on Horn scales. First, to constitute a genuine scale for the production of scalar implicatures, each item must be lexicalized to the same degree. Second, to constitute a genuine scale, each item in a position on the scale entails those in positions to its right, and all the items are 'about' the same thing". The motivation for these restrictions will be discussed in section 4.3, when we introduce the neo-Gricean principles proposed by Levinson.

angled brackets) of linguistic expressions or **scalar predicates**, e_1, e_2, $e_3, \cdots e_n$, as in:

$$< e_1, \ e_2, \ e_3, \cdots e_n >$$

where if we substitute e_1, or e_2 etc., in a sentential frame A we obtain the well-formed sentences $A(e_1)$, $A(e_2)$, etc.; and where $A(e_1)$ entails $A(e_2)$, $A(e_2)$ entails $A(e_3)$, etc., but not vice versa.

And in his "Pragmatics and the Grammar of Anaphora" of 1987, Levinson admits the notion of informativeness is fairly intractable. But he thinks, for lack of better alternatives, we may combine the Popperian idea of informativeness-relative-to-falsifiability with the entailment analysis of informativeness, namely:

A proposition A is MORE INFORMATIVE than a proposition B iff the set of entailments of B is properly contained in the set of entailments of A. (p. 404)

This definition of informativeness explains why (32) is more informative than (33).

(32) John has three cows.

(33) John has two cows.[①]

That is, (32) entails (33), but not vice versa; though in the non-technical sense, the greater the number involved does not necessarily mean the more informative.[②]

The entailment requirement prevents strict antonyms[③], such as

---

[①] Notice the numbers are arranged from the bigger to the smaller on the Horn scale.

[②] Grice seems to have blurred the distinction between the two senses of quantity when he extends his maxims to non-verbal behaviour, as we mentioned in note ①, page 43.

[③] In a sense, any pair of words of the same word class may be antonyms. "Man", for ex-ample, may be the antonym of "woman", "boy", "dog" or even "stone". For a fuller discussion of antonyms, see 姜望琪 (1991).

77

"hot : cold", "long : short", "good : bad", "big : small", from being on the same scale. As (34) entails (35), rather than (36).

(34) This soup is hot.

(35) This soup is not cold.

(36) This soup is cold.

In other words, items on the same scale must share the presence or absence of a quality. This is why "hot" and "warm" belong to one scale while "cold" and "cool" another in the list of scales quoted earlier. And zero is not included on the scale of numerals.

To summarize, linguistic items capable of being arranged in terms of informativeness or semantic strength[1] are said to form a Horn scale. That is, the items on the same scale are in a relationship of entailment, sentences using the strong ones entail those using the weak ones. But they are also in a relationship of implicature in that the use of a weaker one implicates that the stronger ones do not obtain. And this type of implicature is known as scalar implicature. As implicatures they exhibit the important property of being cancellable. So it is perfectly all right for one to say (37). In contrast, (38) and (39) are generally[2]

---

[1] As has been pointed out in note ①, page 76, there are also other restrictions. For the time being, however, this one is enough.

[2] This qualification is necessary in that scalar quantity implicatures are of the generalized type. They are the normal, usual interpretations in the absence of contextual cues to the contrary. In some special situations, for example, when we are discussing the bad reception of a film, we could very well say "Some of them went to the film, in fact few." As the presupposition here is that "not many" people went to the film. Similarly, if we are talking about the fewness of the cows John has, then "John has three cows, if not fewer" will also be acceptable. But the principle remains intact, since in these special cases, the order of semantic strength is, as it were, reversed, which becomes $<$few, some, many, all$>$ and $<1, 2, 3, \ldots n>$ respectively. In other words, the entailment relationship has somehow become an implicature relationship, hence the interpretation cancellable.

not acceptable.

(37) Many of them went to the film, in fact all.①

(38) *Some of them went to the film, in fact few.

(39) *John has three cows, if not fewer.

This suggests that a scalar item is two sided, which has two bounds. The lower bound generates the "at least" interpretation and the upper bound the "at most" interpretation. The "at least" interpretation is an entailment and not cancellable, while the "at most" interpretation is an implicature and cancellable. So (40) usually has a two-sided reading (41):

(40) John has three cows.

(41) John has exactly (both "at least" and "at most") three cows.

And the entailment, "John has at least three cows" in this case, is not cancellable. But the implicature "John has at most three cows" will be cancelled in some particular contexts, such as the situational context of responding to an inspector's inquiry whether John is entitled to the government's subsidy or the linguistic context with the addition of "if not more".

If, however, even the weak term does not obtain, then it goes without saying that the strong terms will not either. For example, (42) is generally interpreted as (43).

(42) John doesn't have three cows.

(43) John has fewer than three cows.

It is in this sense that O. Jespersen (1924: 325f) once said negation is equivalent to "less than" rather than "more than". If one wants

---

① The utterance "John has three cows, if not more" used to exemplify the cancellability of implicatures in 3.2.1 is in fact also concerned with scalar implicatures.

to use negation to mean "more than", some abnormal means will have to be employed. For example, the relevant word such as "three" may have to be stressed.

(44) John doesn't have THREE cows, he has FOUR.

The sentences (45), (46) and (47) can also be explained in this way.

(45) Harry doesn't LIKE Martha, he LOVES her.

(46) The wine isn't GOOD, it's EXCELLENT.

(47) You didn't eat SOME of the cookies, you ate ALL of them.

This kind of negation is known as metalinguistic negation, external negation, or implicatural negation. What is negated here is not the truth-conditional meaning, the "at least" interpretation. It is not that the description is not true, but not enough, not up to the right degree. In other words, it is the "at most" interpretation, the implicature, that is negated.

3.3.2 Clausal quantity implicature

G. Gazdar (1979) first[1] notices that there are quantity implicatures in compound sentences[2] as well. When a speaker says (48), he implicates (49). That is, he does not know whether (50) or (51) will

---

[1] G. Gazdar (1979: 61-2), however, has credited H. Sacks (1968) with the discovery of this type of implicature, "who gives the following example (which I have abbreviated) from a newspaper report (*New York Times* 11 February 1967).

David Searles returned to the street with his girl and found the car was missing. At first he thought it had been stolen. Then he realized it had been towed away by the police.

Sacks comments that '*he realized* stands in opposition to *he thought*, by reference to the fact that *thought* would be used were it the case that it turned out he was wrong.'"

[2] There is a systematic ambiguity in Gazdar's use of "compound" and "complex". Sometimes one is used to cover the other and sometimes not.

be true.

(48) If John sees me then he will tell Margaret.
(49) I don't know whether John will see me.
(50) John will see me.
(51) John won't see me.

Similarly, when someone says (52), he implicates (53) or (54).

(52) My sister is either in the bathroom or in the kitchen.
(53) I don't know whether my sister is in the bathroom or in the kitchen.
(54) I don't know that my sister is in the bathroom and I don't know that she's in the kitchen.

Gazdar (1979: 59) calls this type of implicature clausal quantity implicature and defines it as

$$f_c(\phi) = \{X : X \in \{P\psi, P\sim\psi\}\}$$

for all sentences ψ such that

(i) $\phi = X\smallfrown\psi\smallfrown Y$ where X and Y are any expressions, possibly null
(ii) $[\phi] \not\subseteq [\psi]$
(iii) $[\phi] \not\subseteq [\sim\psi]$
(iv) ϕ has some expression alternative ϕ_a with respect to ψ and α where α is an arbitrary sentence such that
  (a) $\alpha \neq \psi$
  (b) $K\alpha \not\in f_p(\phi_a)$
  (c) $K\sim\alpha \not\in f_p(\phi_a)$ (ibid.:60)

The subscripts c and p stand for "clausal" and "presupposition", and $\not\subseteq$ and $\not\in$ are negatives of $\subseteq$ and $\in$ respectively. This formula means: if a speaker uses ϕ, of which ψ is a part, but the proposition denoted by ϕ, i.e. $[\phi]$, is not a sub-set of, nor identical with, that denoted by ψ, nor that by $\sim\psi$ (that is, ϕ does not entail ψ, or $\sim\psi$),

81

then it implicates that the speaker does not know whether it is ψ, or $\sim\psi$. But there is a further condition, (iv), that is, ϕ has an alternative ϕ_a, whose component α is not identical wit ψ (so that neither α, nor $\sim$α is an entailment of ϕ), and the speaker knows that neither α, nor $\sim$α, is an element of the presupposition of ϕ_a. For example, (55) does not presuppose "John will see me", so it implicates (49). In contrast, (56) presupposes "John will see me", and it does not implicate (49).

(55) If John sees me he will regret seeing me.

(56) If John tells Margaret he will regret seeing me.

Levinson (1983: 136) simplifies Gazdar's formulation of clausal implicatures as

> If S asserts some complex expression p which (i) contains an embedded sentence q, and (ii) p neither entails nor presupposes q and (iii) there's an alternative expression r of roughly equal brevity[①] which contains q such that r *does* entail or presuppose q; *then*, by asserting p rather than r, S implicates that he doesn't know whether q is true or false, i.e. he implicates Pq & P$\sim q$.

And he lists the following as examples of pairs of stronger and weaker forms and the implicatures the weaker forms generate:

(a) *stronger form*	(b) *weaker form*	(c) *implicatures of* (b)
"p and q"	"p or q"	{Pp, P $\sim p$, Pq, P $\sim q$}
"since p, q"	"if p then q"	{Pp, P $\sim p$, Pq, P $\sim q$}
"a knows p"	"a believes p"	{Pp, P $\sim p$}

---

① This is the corresponding condition of equal brevity on scalar items, which may be seen as a development of Gazdar's "ceteris paribus" condition.

"*a* realized *p*"	"*a* thought *p*"	{P*p*, P ~ *p*}
"*a* revealed *p*"	"*a* said *p*"	{P*p*, P ~ *p*}
"necessarily *p*"	"possibly *p*"	{P*p*, P ~ *p*} (ibid.: 137)

Levinson notes items with scalar implicatures "could reappear here with additional and slightly different clausal implicatures. For example, the utterance of *possibly p* carries the scalar implicature 'not necessarily p', but since *possibly p* in contrast to *necessarily p* does not entail *p*, there will also be a clausal implicature from the utterance of *possibly p* to the effect that the speaker does not know whether *p* is or is not the case (i.e. the set of implicatures {P*p*, P ~ *p*} will arise). Or again, utterances of the form *p or q* will have the scalar implicature K~(*p* & *q*) and the clausal implicature {P*p*, P~ *p*, P*q*, P ~*q*}" (ibid.).

With these two types of implicatures, we can better account for the use of some words. For example, the word *or* may be used in two different senses. In general it means that one of the two parts linked by it, and only one of them, is the case as is described. Thus (57) means the person referred to is either in the bathroom or in the kitchen. One of them must be true and only one of them can be true, she can't be in both. But in (58), *or* is used in a different sense. Somebody who has both a first-class degree and some teaching experience will definitely also qualify as an applicant, and perhaps more so. This *or* does not mean that one of the two parts must be true and only one of them can be true, but that both of the two parts may be true.

(57) She is in the bathroom or in the kitchen.

(58) The applicant for the job must have a first-class degree or some teaching experience.

These two senses are respectively referred to as "the exclusive *or*" embodying the strict "either...or" sense and "the inclusive *or*" embodying the "both...and" sense. ①

In truth-conditional semantics, *or* is said to be ambiguous between the two senses, which however would lead to wrong predictions. For example, (59) generally means (60). That is, the *or* is inclusive in that the positive is (61). Now if the *or* is also exclusive, then there would, logically speaking, be another interpretation—(62), as the positive would be (63).

(59) He isn't a movie star or a politician.
(60) He is neither a movie star nor a politician.
(61) He is a movie star, or a politician, or both.
(62) He is not a movie star and not a politician, but both.
(63) He is a movie star, or a politician, but not both.

Now one might argue, we do use (59) to mean "He is both". But the point we are making here is that the normal, usual interpretation of (59) is (60). If one intends otherwise, he shall have to stress *or*, just as the stress on *three* and *like* in (44) and (45) above. And the meaning negated here is the implicature, the upper bound interpretation. In other words, when we use *or*, we usually mean "at least one is true" and implicate "not both". So the normal negation, which negates the lower bound only, is "less than", i.e. "neither is true". Only when *or* is stressed, which is a metalinguistic, external or implicatural negation, will the implicature, the upper bound interpretation

---

① Notice when the inclusive *or* is intended, the two parts linked by it must be compatible with each other, such as "The book is red or crimson" (an example used by Levinson (1983: 139)), in which the *or* can be paraphrased by "or rather". If it is "The book is red or green", this *or* is exclusive. Something cannot be red or/and green at the same time.

"not both" be negated.

To summarize, in the pragmatic approach, the word *or* is said to have only one truth-conditional sense—the inclusive sense. The exclusive sense is an implicature, which may be calculated on the basis of the scale $<$ and, or $>$. That is, the use of *or* generally means *and* does not obtain, unless it is otherwise indicated, such as the abnormal stress on *or*. The exclusive interpretation may be arrived at through clausal implicature, too. The use of "p or q", when there is an alternative, equally brief, form "p and q", implicates that the speaker does not know whether p or q is true, in other words, as far as he knows it's not the case that both are true.

Scalar implicatures and clausal implicatures, however, are not always consistent with each other. When there is a conflict, it is the clausal implicature which takes precedence over the scalar implicature. Levinson (1983: 144) has (64) as an example, which has the scalar implicature (65 i) and other four clausal implicatures. But the scalar implicature is in conflict with the clausal implicature (65 ii), and consequently is cancelled by the latter.

(64) Some of the Elgin Marbles are fakes, and either the rest of them are too, or they're inferior originals.

(65) (i) K $\sim$ (all of the Elgin Marbles are fakes)
  (ii) P(the rest of the Elgin Marbles are fakes too)
  (iii) P $\sim$ (the rest of the Elgin Marbles are fakes too)
  (iv) P(the rest of the Elgin Marbles are inferior originals)
  (v) P $\sim$ (the rest of the Elgin Marbles are inferior originals)

Chapter 4: Conversational implicature (II)

Apart from the developments on the basis of Grice's cooperative principle and its component maxims, there have also been attempts to challenge the validity of this basis and suggest some other principles in their stead. On L. Horn's (1988: 130 – 1) account, the Gricean framework is at best incomplete and at worst inadequate beyond repair to the task of predicting non-logical inferences in conversation. It is both internally redundant and inconsistent. The inconsistency between Grice's maxims is to be expected, since conversational implicatures are inherently indeterminate, and different cultures may value different maxims as the research of E. O. Keenan (1976) and others suggests, which we noted in last chapter. The redundancy of the maxims, however, has provided more problems, or at least more challenges, for post-Gricean theorists. They have sought to boil down the maxims to a set of principles which are truly indispensable, and do not overlap at the same time. In this chapter, we shall discuss three such suggestions.

4.1 Relevance theory

Of the three theories to be introduced, this is the most reductionist, reducing all Gricean maxims to a single all-encompassing principle--the principle of relevance. It was formally proclaimed by Dan Sperber and Deirdre Wilson in their book *Relevance: Communication and Cognition* in 1986.① This project started in 1975, when "Deirdre Wilson published *Presuppositions and Non-Truth-Conditional Semantics* and Dan Sperber published 'Rudiments de rhétorique cognitive', a sequel to his *Rethinking Symbolism* " (Sperber & Wilson 1986: vii).② They planned to write a joint essay in a few months. However, the work turned out to be so involved that the months became years. Meanwhile, they made use of every opportunity to try out their new ideas in the papers written separately or jointly in the intervening years. As a result, the principle of relevance had been around informally even before the publication of *Relevance*.

For example, Wilson in her book co-authored with Neil Smith *Modern Linguistics: The Results of Chomsky's Revolution* of 1979③ emphasizes the crucial role played by judgements of relevance in the interpretation of utterances. She argues that in (1) B's reply suggests that A's chocolates were gone.

(1) A: Where's my box of chocolates?

B: Where are the snows of yesteryear?

"However, it will not convey this suggestion unless it is construed as a relevant response to A. If it is construed as irrelevant—for example as the start of a poetry reading, a genuine inquiry in its own right, or a

---

① The second edition of this book appeared in 1995. Judging from the references in D. Wilson (1998), they did not introduce much revision in the new edition, except making explicit in the postface that there are two relevance-based principles, which will be noted in due course.

② The quotations of Sperber and Wilson in this section are all from this book unless specified otherwise.

③ D. Wilson (1998: 59 n3) acknowledges that this is the earliest publication in relevance theory.

rhetorical response to a quite different question—then no such suggestion will arise" (Smith & Wilson 1979: 175). Similarly, if B's response is (2), it will suggest that the children may have eaten his chocolates, or may know where they are, on the condition that it is construed as a relevant answer to A's question.

(2) B: The children were in your room this morning.

If it is not construed as relevant, but as an attempt to change the subject or to dismiss A's question for some other reason, no such suggestion will arise either. And their definition of relevance then is

> A remark P is relevant to another remark Q if P and Q, together with background knowledge, yield new information not derivable from either P or Q, together with background knowledge, alone. [1] (ibid.: 177)

4.1.1 Ostensive-inferential communication

What is new in their 1986 book is that the authors have tried to justify their theory by appealing to a different view of communication and cognition. In what follows, we shall mainly introduce their idea about what communication involves. [2] In their opinion, there are two

---

[1] D. Wilson (ibid.: 66 n10) notes that this definition is inadequate in that it fails to distinguish remarks which contribute to relevance and those whose presence in the context is merely incidental. For instance, Mary is telling Peter something about Bill, when Peter, who is clearing out a kitchen cupboard, holds up a bottle of 1967 French wine with a questioning look. Consequently, Mary utters "Bill, who has thalassemia, is getting married to Susan, and 1967 was a great year for French wines." The second segment, contributing nothing to the relevance of Mary's account of Bill, is there incidentally.

[2] There are four chapters in their book: Communication, Inference, Relevance, and Aspects of verbal communication. We shall spend three sections discussing the first, third and fourth chapters respectively, leaving out the second, which is more cognitive and more speculative.

models of communication: the code model and the inferential model. The former is more traditional, in which communication is seen as the encoding and decoding of messages. The latter, the name they apply to the approach initiated by Grice, in contrast, is of recent origin, which views communication as essentially the recognition of the speaker's intention by the audience. They take Grice's "Meaning" of 1957 as the starting point of this approach. In it, Grice proposes to make a distinction between two senses of *mean*, which are exemplified respectively by (3) and (4).

(3) Those spots mean measles.

(4) That remark, "Smith couldn't get on without his trouble and strife", meant that Smith found his wife indispensable.

He calls the first sense natural and the second nonnatural (abbreviated as $mean_{NN}$) in that there is a natural connection between the sign in (3) and its meaning while there is no such a connection in (4). However, the notion $mean_{NN}$ has been extensively elaborated, in the end Grice declares:

"A $meant_{NN}$ something by x" is (roughly) equivalent to "A intended the utterance of x to produce some effect[①] in an audience

---

[①] By *effect*, Grice meant here *belief that something is as stated* in response to a statement and *action as is requested* in response to a request. In his 1968 article, he changed his wording. The intended effect in response to a statement is rephrased as *belief that speaker believes what is stated* and that in the case of a request is *intention to act as is requested*. J. Searle (ed.) (1971: 8) thinks that Grice's account of meaning, as well as P. Strawson's interpretation, suffers from "a failure to appreciate adequately Austin's distinction between illocutionary uptake (i.e. understanding the utterance) and perlocutionary *effect*". And he argues that "the intended effect of meaning something is that the hearer should know the illocutionary force and propositional content of the utterance, not that he should respond or behave in such and such ways".

by means of the recognition of this intention" (Grice 1971 [1957]: 442).

In 1964, P. Strawson further specifies this idea by separating the intention into three sub-intentions:

S intends (i_1) to produce by uttering x a certain response ① r in an audience A and intends (i_2) that A shall recognize S's intention (i_1) and intends (i_3) that this recognition on the part of A of S's intention (i_1) shall function as A's reason, or a part of his reason, for his response r. (Strawson 1971 [1964]: 28)

But he thinks Grice's analysis is not complex enough for his purpose. There may be situations in which Grice's three conditions are all satisfied by a speaker S, yet S could not be said to mean something in the favoured sense of *mean*, or to communicate with an audience A. And the counterexample he thought up is: In order to induce in A the belief that p, S arranges some convincing-looking "evidence" in a place where A is bound to see it. ② In this case, S obviously has the first intention. And he also intends A to recognize his first intention, otherwise the "evidence" may not necessarily cause A to have the intended response. And thirdly, he intends this recognition to constitute A's reason for the response. But it is difficult to say S means$_{NN}$ by his arrangement, since he has not done any other things to "tell" A that p

---

① Strawson notes "The word 'response', though more convenient in some ways than Grice's 'effect', is not ideal. It is intended to cover cognitive and affective states or attitudes as well as actions."

② The example Sperber & Wilson (1986: 30) provide for the same point is: Mary wants Peter to mend her broken hair-drier, but does not want to ask him openly. So she begins to take her hair-drier to pieces and leaves them lying around as if she were in the process of mending it.

is the case. To exclude situations of this kind, Strawson suggests

> we must add to Grice's conditions the further condition that S should have the further intention (i_4) that A should recognize his intention (i_2). (ibid.: 29)

In other words, he maintains that true communication must be WHOLLY OVERT.

Sperber and Wilson are in favour of the inferential approach. They argue "Communication is successful not when hearers recognise the linguistic meaning of the utterance, but when they infer the speaker's 'meaning' from it" (p. 23). "Verbal communication is a complex form of communication. Linguistic coding and decoding is involved, but the linguistic meaning of an uttered sentence falls short of encoding what the speaker means: it merely helps the audience infer what she[1] means. The output of decoding is correctly treated by the audience as a piece of evidence about the communicator's[2] intentions. In other words, a coding-decoding process is subservient to a Gricean inferential process" (p. 27). But to their mind, Grice's conditions are not only too loose as Strawson points out, but also too restrictive. That is, the first and third conditions are not necessary. Communication may succeed without the fulfilment of intentions (i_1) and (i_3). Suppose Mary utters (5) to Peter, intending (i_1) to produce in Peter the belief that she had a sore throat on the previous Christmas Eve.

---

[1] The authors assume in this book that the communicator is female and the audience male.

[2] The authors are considering communication in the broadest sense, which may be realized by all kinds of means, not just linguistic. It is for this reason that they opt for terms "communicator" and "audience". When "speaker" and "hearer" are used, then only verbal communication is meant.

(5) I had a sore throat on Christmas Eve.
And Peter recognises Mary's intention, but does not believe that she really had a sore throat on that date. Then only Mary's intention (i_2) that he should recognise her first intention is fulfilled. Her intention (i_1) that he believes that she had a sore throat then and intention (i_3) that the recognition of intention (i_1) constitutes the reason for the belief are not. Nonetheless, Mary has succeeded in communicating to Peter what she meant although she has failed to convince him. "Since communication can succeed without intention (i_1) being fulfilled", they reason, "intention (i_1) is not an intention to communicate at all. It is better described as an intention to inform, or as we will call it, an *informative intention*. The true *communicative intention* is intention (i_2): that is, the intention to have one's informative intention recognised" (p. 29).

They are not satisfied with Strawson's way of restricting Gricean conditions either. They point out, as Strawson himself was aware, the requirement to have the second intention recognized is not enough. There may be the further need to have the fourth intention recognized. And "in principle, for any n th-order intention of this type, you need an $n + 1$ th-order intention to the effect that the n th-order intention be recognised" (p. 31). A way out is to make the overt intentions part of the mutual knowledge, part of the necessary background information, of the speaker and the hearer.

But the mutual-knowledge hypothesis is just the other popular idea they rise against. Some authors hold that for an act of communication to succeed, the speaker and hearer must mutually know that they have the same background knowledge.[①] In Sperber and Wilson's view,

---

[①] Strictly speaking, the mutual-knowledge hypothesis is of the form:

however, this "is a philosopher's construct with no close counterpart in reality" (p. 38). They invite us to consider an example in which Mary and Peter are looking at a landscape where she has noticed a distant church. Now she may very well say (6) to him, without first wondering whether he has noticed the building, and whether he assumes she noticed, and assumes she has noticed he has noticed, and so on, or whether he has assumed it is a church, and assumes she assumes it is, and so on.

(6) I've been inside that church.

That is, there is no need for it to become mutual knowledge that both of them have noticed the distant building and assume it is a church before Mary uttered (6). "All she needs is reasonable confidence that he will be able to identify the building as a church when required to: in other words, that a certain assumption will manifest in his cognitive environment at the right time. He need not have accessed this assumption before she spoke. In fact, until she spoke he might have thought the building was a castle: it might be only on the strength of her utterance that it becomes manifest to him that the building is a church" (p. 44).

The notion of manifestness is of central importance in their argument. They explain, to be manifest is "to be perceptible or inferable" (p. 39).

A fact is *manifest* to an individual at given time if and only if he

> A knows that p.
> B knows that p.
> A knows that B knows that p.
> B knows that A knows that p.
> A knows that B knows that A knows that p.
> and ... so on, *ad infinitum*.

is capable at that time of representing it mentally and accepting its representation as true or probably true. (ibid.)

Something can be manifest without actually known or assumed. They cite a car passing audibly in the street as an example. "You have not paid any attention to it, so you have no knowledge of it, no assumptions about it, even in the weakest sense of 'knowledge' and 'assumption'. But the fact that a car is passing in the street is manifest to you" (p. 41).

On this line of thinking, the informative and communicative intentions are reformulated as:

Informative intention: to make manifest or more manifest to the audience a set of assumptions $\{I\}$. (p. 58)

Communicative intention: to make it mutually manifest to audience and communicator that the communicator has this informative intention. (p. 61)

In other words, communication succeeds as soon as the communicator's communicative intention becomes mutually manifest, i.e. he intends to make manifest or more manifest some assumptions. Mutual manifestness, then, is essentially the solution they offer in place of mutual-knowledge hypothesis.

Another consequence of the introduction of the notion manifestness is that it brings into focus the other side of communication: the communicator's attempt to draw the audience's attention to the fact that he has something to inform, which is technically known as ostension.[1] In fact, inferential communication and ostension are one and

---

[1] On page 49, they call "such behaviour—behaviour which makes manifest an intention to make something manifest—ostensive behaviour or simply *ostension*". On page 155, they again argue "To succeed, an act of ostensive communication must attract the audience's attention. In that sense, an act of ostension is a request for attention".

the same thing seen from two angles. From the communicator's point of view, it is ostension, showing, or making manifest his informative intention; and from that of the audience it is inference, inferring from the evidence presented the communicator's intentions. Hence, a complete characterization of communication, by adding these two sides together, is that it is ostensive-inferential. In this sense, "inferential communication", or "ostension", is simply a shorthand. And they define ostensive-inferential communication as follows:

Ostensive-inferential communication: the communicator produces a stimulus which makes it mutually manifest to communicator and audience that the communicator intends, by means of this stimulus, to make manifest or more manifest to the audience a set of assumptions $\{I\}$. (p. 63)

The question, however, remains: how to determine which particular assumptions are meant to be made manifest by the communicator, since, as is defined, there may be a number of things manifest, perceptible or inferable at a given moment. It is at this point that the principle of relevance comes in. They claim "just as an assertion comes with a tacit guarantee of truth, so ostension comes with a tacit guarantee of relevance" (p. 49). In other words, if one person makes manifest to another that he has an informative intention, i.e. intends to make manifest some assumptions to the other, then these assumptions must be relevant enough to the latter to be worth his attention. The audience's effort in processing these assumptions will definitely be paid off.

Suppose, Mary and Peter are sitting on a park bench, when Peter deliberately leans back. Now Mary may regard Peter's movement as a way of communication. That is, he wants to show her something.

The question is what it is. Say, as a result of Peter's leaning back Mary can see three people in particular: an ice-cream vendor, an ordinary stroller, and their acquaintance William. To determine who is the man Peter intends her to see, Mary has to combine the information concerning them with the context. The ice-cream vendor is not new information. She had already noticed him when she sat down. The unknown stroller is new information, but since there is no other information about him, little or nothing follows from it. But William is different, who is known to them as a dreadful bore. This assumption may lead on to a number of other new assumptions, so he must be the one Peter intends her to notice by his leaning back. Then for the first time in this book, they define the principle of relevance as "an act of ostension carries a guarantee of relevance" (p. 50).

4.1.2 Relevance

After a discussion of the human inferential abilities, Sperber and Wilson in Chapter Three address themselves to the question of relevance in detail. They define it in relation to a context, an individual and a phenomenon successively. And the first definition of relevance is:

> An assumption is relevant in a context if and only if it has some contextual effect in that context. (p. 122)

But relevance is also, and more importantly, a comparative concept. Some assumptions may be more relevant than others. What is more, "The assessment of relevance, like the assessment of productivity, is a matter of balancing output against input" (p. 125). It does not only depend on the effect produced by it but also on the effort required to process it. So they have improved on the previous definition by adopting an extent-conditions format:

Extent condition 1: an assumption is relevant in a context to the extent that its contextual effects in this context are large.

Extent condition 2: an assumption is relevant in a context to the extent that the effort required to process it in this context is small. (ibid.)

Then they consider at length the question of what exactly context means. They start with the hypothesis "that the context for the comprehension of a given utterance is the set of assumptions explicitly expressed by preceding utterances in the same dialogue or discourse" (p. 133). In exchange (7), thus, Mary's utterance is relevant in that it has the contextual effect (8), which is not derivable from either Peter's remark or Mary's alone.

(7) *Peter*: I'm tired.

　　Mary: If you're tired, I'll make the meal.

(8) Mary will make the meal.

But this hypothesis will not explain the relevance of Mary's utterance in (9), unless the implicitly expressed assumption (10) in Peter's remark is considered as part of the context.

(9) *Peter*: I'm tired.

　　Mary: I'll make the meal.

(10) Peter wishes Mary would make the meal.

So their second hypothesis is "the context for comprehension contains not only all the assumptions explicitly expressed by preceding utterances in the discourse, but also all the implicatures of these utterances" (p. 133).

However, if Mary's utterance is as in (11), the context would have to be expanded again to include the premise (12), to make it relevant.

(11) *Peter*: I'm tired.

Mary: The dessert is ready. I'll make the main course.

(12) A meal consists of at least a main course and a dessert.

In other words, "the context for comprehension consists not only of the assumptions expressed or implicated by preceding utterances, but also of the encyclopaedic entries attached to any concepts used in these assumptions" (p. 134).

Now Sperber and Wilson argue even this third hypothesis is not adequate enough. In the cases of (13) and (14), assumptions (15) and (16) would have to be included in the context as well.

(13) *Peter*: I'm tired.

Mary: The dessert is ready. I'll make an osso-bucco.

(14) *Peter*: I'm tired.

Mary: The dessert is ready. I'll make the speciality of the Capri restaurant.

(15) An osso-bucco is a main course.

(16) The speciality of the Capri restaurant is osso-bucco.

And their fourth and fifth hypotheses are respectively:

The context for the comprehension of an utterance consists of the assumptions expressed and implicated by preceding utterances, plus the encyclopaedic entries attached to any concept used in any of these assumptions, plus the encyclopaedic entries attached to any concept used in the new utterance. (p. 135)

The context for the comprehension of an utterance consists of the assumptions expressed and implicated by preceding utterances, plus the encyclopaedic entries attached to any concepts used in these assumptions and in the utterance itself, plus the encyclopaedic entries attached to any concepts used in the assumptions contained in the encyclopaedic entries already added to the context. (p. 136)

In this way they hope to have demonstrated that this line of speculation is hopelessly inadequate. With the last two hypotheses, the context is already filled with a huge amount of encyclopaedic information. Most, and sometimes all, of that information will be of no use for the increase of the contextual effects of the new information being processed. For instance, in (17) below the information that the speciality of the Capri restaurant is osso-bucco, which according to the fifth hypothesis should be included in the context, is of no use at all. And the information that an osso-bucco is a main course, which according to the fifth hypothesis should be included in the context, is of no use either. In fact these two pieces of information are distractions in understanding where John lives.

(17) *Peter*: Where does John live?

Mary: John lives next to the Capri restaurant.

On the other hand, if the dialogue between Peter and Mary is (18), then the encyclopaedic entry for John (and the information that he lives next to the Capri restaurant) would be added to the context, which would cause the entry for the Capri restaurant (and the information that its speciality is osso-bucco) to be added. And the hearer would still need the information that an osso-bucco is a main course, and that information is to be found in the entry for osso-bucco. To ensure that the entry for osso-bucco is part of a uniquely determined context, three layers of encyclopaedic information would have to be automatically added.

(18) *Peter*: I'm tired.

Mary: The dessert is ready. I'll make the speciality of that restaurant next to where John lives.

If we go on in this direction, then the context would soon be shown to consist of the whole of encyclopaedic memory. Therefore, they propose to abandon the notion of a given context for that of a chosen context. "It is not that first the context is determined, and then relevance is assessed. On the contrary, people hope that the assumption being processed is relevant (or else they would not bother to process it at all), and they try to select a context which will justify that hope: a context which will maximise relevance. In verbal comprehension in particular, it is relevance which is treated as given, and context which is treated as a variable" (p. 142).

As a result, relevance can no longer be seen as the relation between an assumption and a context. So they define it in relation to an individual:

> An assumption is relevant to an individual at a given time if and only if it is relevant in one or more of the contexts accessible to that individual at that time. (p. 144)

And a comparative definition is:

> *Extent condition* 1: an assumption is relevant to an individual to the extent that the contextual effects achieved when it is optimally processed[1] are large.
>
> *Extent condition* 2: an assumption is relevant to an individual to the extent that the effort required to process it optimally is small. (p. 145)

The last definition of relevance they offer involves the characterization of relevance "not just as a property of assumptions in the mind, but also as a property of phenomena (stimuli, e.g. utterances) in the

---

[1] "Optimally processed" is a new term for "the best possible balance of effort against effect".

environment which lead to the construction of assumptions" (pp. 150
-1). They argue a communicator cannot directly present an audience
with an assumption. All a speaker, or a writer, can do is present a
stimulus in the form of a sound, or a written mark. The presentation
of this stimulus changes the cognitive environment of the audience,
making certain facts manifest, or more manifest. As a result, the audience can mentally represent these facts as strong or stronger assumptions, and even use them to derive further assumptions. The notion of
relevance thus extended becomes:

> A phenomenon is relevant to an individual if and only if one
> or more of the assumptions it makes manifest is relevant to him.
> (p. 152)

A comparative definition is:

> *Extent condition* 1: a phenomenon is relevant to an individual to
> the extent that the contextual effects achieved when it is optimally
> processed are large.
>
> *Extent condition* 2: a phenomenon is relevant to an individual to
> the extent that the effort required to process it optimally is small.
> (p. 153)

Having clarified the notion relevance, the authors come to the
principle of relevance again, defining it as:

> Every act of ostensive communication communicates the presumption of its own optimal relevance.①(p. 158)

---

① D. Wilson (1998: 59) notes there are two relevance-based principles, one governing cognition and the other communication. In the first edition, however, only the second was named, though both were present. Therefore, in the postface to the second edition, they explicitly defined Cognitive Principle of Relevance as: Human cognition tends to be geared to the maximisation of relevance; and renamed the principle defined here as Communicative Principle of Relevance. Judging from Wilson & Sperber (1998:11), the word "ostensive" in this principle has been Changed to "overt".

By presumption of optimal relevance[①] is meant:
> (a) The set of assumptions {*I*} which the communicator intends to make manifest to the addressee is relevant enough to make it worth the addressee's while to process the ostensive stimulus.
>
> (b) The ostensive stimulus is the most relevant one the communicator could have used to communicate {*I*}. (ibid.)

That is, in terms of verbal communication, every utterance comes with a presumption of the best balance of effort against effect. On the one hand, the effects achievable will never be less than is needed to make it worth processing. In other words, there will be enough effects to balance against the effort. On the other hand, the effort required will never be more than is needed to achieve these effects. In comparison to the effects achieved, the effort needed is always the smallest. This amounts to saying "of all the interpretations of the stimulus which confirm the presumption, it is the first interpretation to occur to the addressee that is the one the communicator intended to convey" (pp. 168 – 9). For instance, the first interpretation of (19) to occur to the hearer will usually be that George has a big *domestic* cat.

(19) George has a big cat.

As the word *cat* is ambiguous in that it may also refer to other animals

---

[①] According to R. Carston (1998:211 – 3), in their postface to the second edition of *Relevance*, Sperber and Wilson revised the presumption of optimal relevance as follows:
> (a) The ostensive stimulus is relevant enough for it to be worth the addressee's effort to process it.
>
> (b) The ostensive stimulus is the most relevant one compatible with the communicator's abilities and preferences.

of the species "felid", in some situations, (19) may be used to mean (20).

(20) George has a tiger, a lion, a jaguar, etc.

But Sperber and Wilson argue that even if interpretation (20) is correct, thus verifying the first part of the presumption of relevance—(20) is relevant enough; the second part would invariably be falsified—(20) will not be the most relevant on account of the increased processing effort involved. In other words, if (20) were the intended interpretation, the speaker should have, instead, used something like (21), or, if he lacked the necessary information, something like (22) or (23):

(21) George has a tiger.

(22) George has a tiger or a lion, I'm not sure which.

(23) George has a felid.

These utterances would have saved the hearer the effort of first accessing and considering interpretation (19), then accessing interpretation (20), and then having to compare the two. Hence, they assure the hearer that he need not bother. The first interpretation consistent with the principle of relevance is the best hypothesis. All other interpretations would manifestly falsify the second part of the presumption of relevance. (p. 168)

4.1.3 Differences between the Gricean theory and relevance theory

In the fourth chapter, Sperber and Wilson come to verbal communication proper, presenting in some depth the way relevance theory accounts for language use. Here we shall concentrate on some of the differences between the Gricean theory and relevance theory.

Relevance theory purports to make a paradigm change in pragmatics, reducing the cooperative principle and its component maxims to a single cognitive principle, but Sperber and Wilson have not given any substantial justification for it in the book. There is no detailed exposition as to why and how the Gricean maxims should be replaced by the single principle of relevance. The only place where this point has been touched upon is their 1981 paper "On Grice's Theory of Conversation". In it they define the principle of relevance as "The speaker has done his best to be maximally relevant" (Wilson & Sperber 1998 [1981]: 361) and argue briefly that the Gricean maxims may all be subsumed by it. For example, "[i]f the speaker holds back some information which, together with [initial assumptions], would yield pragmatic implications, he is violating both the principle of relevance and [the first Quantity maxim]. If he gives information which yields no pragmatic implications, he is violating both the principle of relevance and [the second Quantity maxim]" (ibid.: 362). They cite in support of their position Grice's own suggestion that the effect of the second Quantity maxim may be secured by the maxim of Relevance. And they contend the effect of the first Quantity maxim should be equally secured by a principle of maximal relevance as they have formulated there. Hence, in their framework "both maxims of quantity are redundant" (ibid.). In their view, the principle of relevance accounts for language use more succinctly and more explicitly than the Gricean framework. But the most important difference, they maintain, is that the principle of relevance is meant to explain ostensive-inferential communication as a whole, both explicit and implicit; while the Gricean theory is only concerned with the implicit side (pp. 162−3). They argue that the goal of pragmatics is not just to explain the hearer's ability to derive the so-called implicatures, but also his ability to complete and enrich utterances into propositional forms,① a process involving disambiguation, reference assignment, and other developments from logical forms②(p.179). And in line with the idea that relevance is also a property of phenomena—stimuli such as sounds, written marks, etc., the very first task of a hearer is in fact the identification of the assumptions made manifest by a stimulus. While the Gricean framework has nothing to offer for these interpretations,③ the principle of relevance, they claim, is at work in every step of this complicated process.

For instance, when there is a complex sound uttered by Mary, transcribed in (24),

(24) [ɪtlgetˈkəʊld]④

among the assumptions made manifest are those given below:

(25) (a) Someone has made a sound.

---

① To be exact, the hearer should also identify the propositional attitude of the speaker, e.g. whether he intends the utterance to be an assertion, question, request, etc.

② In their theory, a logical form is a well-formed formula, a structured set of constituents, which undergoes formal logical operations determined by its structure, such as contradiction, implication. Logical forms are of two types: the semantically complete ones, capable of being true or false, are propositional, and the others are non-propositional. "She carried it in her hand" is a psychological example of a non-propositional logical form. It is neither true or false, since *she* and *it* do not correspond to definite concepts. But it is capable of implying or contradicting others. For instance, it implies "She held something in her hand", which is equally non-propositional; and it contradicts "No one ever carried anything", which is, or can be understood as, propositional. (pp. 72 – 3)

③ Grice (1981: 186) does consider cases of enriching *and* into *and then*, and there are other cases of enrichment proposed, as will be discussed in sections 4.2 and 4.3. But these are all treated as cases of generalized implicature, which Sperber and Wilson think is a misnomer and would rather call explicature, a notion to be explained later.

④ The original transcription on page 176 is [ɪtl̩getkəʊld], which is inadequate in my view on three accounts. First, l̩ and g are not symbols authorized by the International Phonetic Association. Second, they are not consistent in showing the phonetic details. The dot underneath l is meant to show some secondary articulation, but the fact that the [t] before [k] is usually unexploded is not shown. Third, they did not show the stress.

(b) There is someone in the house.
(c) Mary is at home.
(d) Mary has spoken.
(e) Mary has a sore throat.

(26) Mary has uttered the sentence "It will get cold."

However, according to the principle of relevance, Peter can easily decide that only (26) is the one intended to be made manifest, since to make manifest assumptions (25a – e), there are more economical means, such as a clearing of the throat by Mary, which renders the production of (24) a waste of time.

When it comes to the determination of the sense and reference of "It will get cold", they suggest Peter "should first consider the immediate context, see if any of the concepts of a non-human entity represented in this context, when substituted for 'It', yields a propositional form consistent with the principle of relevance; if not he should extend the context and repeat the procedure" (p. 187). Given the principle of relevance, one of the conditions for the use of a stimulus, linguistic or otherwise, is that it involves the least effort to process it relative to the effect it induces. In other words, it should be easy for Peter to recover the referent, otherwise Mary would not have used it in the first place. One of the possible situations in which (24) will be used is that Mary had told Peter a couple of minutes before "Dinner is ready". In this situation then Peter could determine without much difficulty that "It" refers to "the dinner prepared by Mary", and "will" means "will very soon", "get" "be, become", and "cold" "at a temperature lower than the one suitable for it to be eaten". In other words, one of the assumptions made manifest by (24) would be (27).

(27) The dinner prepared by Mary will be at a temperature un-

suitable for eating very soon.

In the terminology of Sperber and Wilson, this assumption is called the propositional form developed from (24).① This assumption differs in a fundamental way from assumptions like (28), known as implicature, in that it is the development of a logical form encoded by utterance (24),② while the latter is constructed on the basis of contextual information, and information from encyclopaedic memory in particular.

(28) Mary wants Peter to come and eat dinner at once.

They see this as a difference between explicit and implicit communication, and define "explicit" as:

> An assumption communicated by an utterance U is *explicit* if and only if it is a development of a logical form encoded by U. (p. 182)

On the analogy of "implicature", they propose to call an explicitly communicated assumption explicature (ibid.). And in ordinary assertions, the propositional form of the utterance is itself an explicature (p. 183).

Within the realm of implicature, there are also differences between the Gricean approach and that of Sperber and Wilson. Suppose in response to Peter's question (29), Mary says (30), the implicature of which, according to Grice, would be (31).

(29) Would you drive a Mercedes?

(30) I wouldn't drive ANY expensive car.

(31) I wouldn't drive a Mercedes.

---

① But the propositional form of (24) provided by Sperber and Wilson in the book is "The dinner will get cold very soon", which in my view is not rich enough.

② Though contextual information is also used here.

Now in Sperber and Wilson's view, (31) is only an implicated conclusion, there is an implicated premise (32) as well.

(32) Mercedes is an expensive car.

And this information is also relevant. If Peter did not know (32) originally, then Mary's answer could almost be regarded as an explicit statement that Mercedes is an expensive car. Even if Peter knew it beforehand, Mary's indirect answer supplied the reason. So the extra effort needed to process (30) would not be wasted.

But Sperber and Wilson argue that (31) and (32), including other assumptions derivable from them, are not ALL the assumptions Mary expects Peter to have, otherwise (30) cannot be regarded as optimally relevant (p. 196). They suggest that Mary may also encourage Peter to have premises like (33) and (34), from which to derive conclusions (35) and (36). And even premises like (37) and conclusions like (38).

(33) A Rolls Royce is an expensive car.
(34) A Cadillac is an expensive car.
(35) Mary wouldn't drive a Rolls Royce.
(36) Mary wouldn't drive a Cadillac.
(37) People who refuse to drive expensive cars disapprove of displays of wealth.
(38) Mary disapproves of displays of wealth.

Now these are weakly implicated assumptions, for which Mary could not be held to have full responsibility. Then there will be a point at which Mary's responsibility for an assumption is so weak that she could not be thought to be responsible at all. For example,

(39) People who would not drive an expensive car would not go on a cruise either.

(40) Mary would not go on a cruise.

Lastly, we introduce their account of irony in the light of relevance theory. They first proposed this approach to irony in the paper "Irony and the Use-Mention Distinction" of 1981. Based on the distinction between use and mention of expressions, they classified ironical utterances as cases of mention. Now in this book, they have abandoned the term "mention" in favour of a more general term "interpretation", but the basic treatment has not substantially changed. That is, "irony is echoic, and is primarily designed to ridicule the opinion echoed" (p. 241).

As we have mentioned, Grice used to treat irony as a case of saying one thing but meaning its opposite. Sperber and Wilson contend that Grice's treatment is not satisfactory. Suppose Mary and Peter are out for a drive. Before joining the main road, Peter stops to look both ways. As the road is clear, he is going to drive on, when Mary says (41).

(41) There's something coming.
Under the circumstances, Peter would take (41) seriously rather than ironically, meaning (42).

(42) There's nothing coming.
But if Peter is an over-cautious driver, constantly on the alert for danger, who NEVER pulls into a main road in front of oncoming traffic, however far away; then (41) may very well mean (42). That is, Mary is simply echoing the sort of opinion Peter is constantly expressing and she disapproves of it. "Thus, all that is needed to make (41) ironical is an echoic element and an associated attitude of mockery or disapproval" (ibid.). What is more, (42) cannot be said to be the implicature of (41), as Grice would like to claim. In Sperber and

Wilson's view, (42) is at most an implicated premise. The main point of (41) is to express Mary's attitude to the sort of opinion Peter is constantly expressing. And the implicature is that Peter is being overcautious, and he is making a fool of himself by worrying too much, and so on.

4.2 The Q- and R- principles

This is a less reductionist, bipartite model. These two principles, developed by Laurence Horn, were first proposed in his "Toward a New Taxonomy for Pragmatic Inference: Q-Based and R-Based Implicature" of 1984, and further elaborated in his "Pragmatic Theory" of 1988 and *A Natural History of Negation* of 1989. The Q-principle is intended to invoke the first sub-maxim of Grice's Quantity, i.e. to provide enough information, and the R-principle the Relation maxim, but the new principles are more extensive than the Gricean maxims.

4.2.1 Wherefore the principles

In his 1984 paper, Horn begins with some ideas of George Kingsley Zipf, who attempted to explain everything in terms of an overarching Principle of Least Effort.

In the linguistic realm, however, Zipf (1949: 20ff.) acknowledged two basic and competing forces. The Force of Unification, or Speaker's Economy, is a direct least effort correlate, a drive toward simplification which, operating unchecked, would result in the evolution of exactly one totally unmarked infinitely ambiguous vocable (presumably *uhhhh*). The antithetical Force of Diversification, or Auditor's Economy, is an anti-ambiguity principle leading toward the establishment of as many different expressions as there are messages to communicate. Given m meanings, the speaker's economy will tend toward 'a vocabulary of one word which will refer to all the m distinct meanings', while the hearer's economy will tend toward 'a vocabulary of m different words with one distinct meaning for each word'. (Horn 1984: 11)①

Zipf was not alone in this opinion, A. Martinet (1962: 139), for example, said something similar:

In order to understand how and why a language changes, the linguist must keep in mind two ever-present and antinomic factors: first, the requirements of communication, the need for the speaker to convey his message, and second, the principle of least effort, which makes him restrict his output of energy, both mental and physical, to the minimum compatible with achieving his ends. (from Horn 1984: 11)

In Horn's view, these two competing forces are largely responsible for generating Grice's conversational maxims and the implicatures derived therefrom. The first Quantity maxim, concerned with the speaker's need to convey his message fully, is essentially Zipf's Auditor's Economy. Most, if not all,② of the other maxims respond to the Speaker's Economy, e. g. the Relation maxim, the Brevity sub-maxim. The second Quantity maxim, he argues, is especially akin to Relation. He asks "what would make a contribution more informative than required, except the inclusion of material not strictly relevant to and needed for the matter at hand?" (p. 12).③ So Horn proposes to reduce all the Grice's maxims, except the Maxim of Quality, to two

---

① All the quotations of Horn in this section are from this paper except otherwise indicated.

② Horn (1988: 132) assigns the "Avoid ambiguity" and "Avoid obscurity" sub-maxims of Manner together with the first Quantity maxim.

③ Levinson does not agree with this interpretation of the maxim of Relation, which we shall discuss in section 4.3.1.

principles: the Q-principle and the R-principle:

The Q Principle (Hearer-based):
MAKE YOUR CONTRIBUTION SUFFICIENT (cf. Quantity$_1$)
SAY AS MUCH AS YOU CAN (given R)
Lower-bounding principle, inducing upper-bounding implicata[1]

The R Principle (Speaker-based):
MAKE YOUR CONTRIBUTION NECESSARY (cf. Relation, Quantity$_2$, Manner)
SAY NO MORE THAN YOU MUST (given Q)
Upper-bounding principle, inducing lower-bounding implicata

(p.13)

The hearer-based Q-principle is a sufficiency condition in the sense that the information conveyed is the most the speaker can provide. Now Horn also calls it a lower-bounding principle, indicating that the information supplied in line with this principle has satisfied the lower limit. The situation described is at least as such. This side of meaning in fact is asserted. If this "at least" interpretation does not hold, then the speaker may be accused of lying. In contrast, the "at most" interpretation is an implicature, which may be cancelled, as we pointed out in last chapter. For example, if somebody says (43), then he asserts (44) and implicates (45).

(43) Some of my friends are linguists.
(44) At least some of my friends are linguists.
(45) Not all of my friends are linguists.

---

[1] Horn sticks to Grice's original usage and prefers "implicatum" to "implicature". But we shall, as always, follow the general practice.

In other words, scalar quantity implicatures, discussed in section 3.3.1, may all be attributed to this principle.

Following the terminology of Aristotle, Horn calls the assertion, the lower bound "at least" interpretation, "one-sided" reading. The meaning arrived at by combining the assertion and the implicature (the upper bound "at most" interpretation) is known as "two-sided" reading. His examples showing these two types of reading are:

(46) He ate three carrots
 1-sided: "at least three"
 2-sided: "exactly three"

(47) You ate some of the cookies
 1-sided: "some if not all"
 2-sided: "some but not all"

(48) It's possible she'll win
 1-sided: "possible if not certain"
 2-sided: "possible but not certain"

(49) Maggie is patriotic or quixotic
 1-sided = inclusive *or*
 2-sided = exclusive *or*

(50) I'm happy
 1-sided: "happy if not ecstatic"
 2-sided: "happy but not ecstatic"

(51) It's warm
 1-sided: "at least warm"
 2-sided: "warm but not hot" (p. 14)

The R-principle, in contrast, encourages the hearer to infer that more is meant, while also asserting that the situation described is at least so. Typical examples are indirect speech acts like "Can you pass the salt?" Horn (p. 14) says, "if I ask you whether you can pass me the salt, in a context where your abilities to do so are not in doubt, I license you to infer that I am doing something more than asking you whether you can pass the salt—I am in fact asking you to do it. (If I know for a fact that you can pass me the salt, the yes-no question is pointless; the assumption that I am obeying the Relation maxim allows you to infer that I mean something more than what I say.)" To contrast the R-principle with the Q-principle, he calls it an upper bounding principle, and the implicature that more is meant is known as a lower bound interpretation.

In his 1988 article (p. 132), Horn describes the Q-principle as "a hearer-based economy for the maximization of informational content, akin to Grice's (first) maxim of quantity", and the R-principle as "a speaker-based economy for the minimization of form,① akin to Zipf's (1949) 'principle of least effort'". In other words, the Q-principle is concerned with the content. The speaker who follows this principle supplies the sufficient information. The R-principle, on the other hand, is concerned with the form. The speaker who employs this principle uses the minimal form, so that the hearer is entitled to infer that the speaker means more than he says.

Horn (p. 15) recalls in delineating the operation of quantity to generate upper-bounding scalar implicatures in his thesis (Horn 1972: Chapters 1 and 2), he was puzzled by the difference between (52a) and (52b).

(52a) It is possible that John solved the problem →

(For all S knows) John didn't solve the problem

(52b) John was able to solve the problem →

John solved the problem

Now that we have the Q- and R-principles, he suggests this puzzle can be solved. We can say in (52a) it is the Q-principle that is in force while in (52b) it is the R-principle that is in force. And an application of the Q-principle in (52b) would generate the opposite implicature,

---

① Levinson (1987b) thinks that Horn has mixed two kinds of minimization here, which we shall come to in detail in section 4.3.1.

i.e. "John didn't solve the problem". ① Similarly, the problem Grice has with the interpretation of "an X" expression exemplified by (53a) and (53b) can also be explained in this way.

(53a) X is meeting a woman this evening →
    The woman in question is not X's wife, sister, or close platonic friend
(53b) I broke a finger yesterday →
    The finger is mine ②

That is, in (53a) the Q-principle leads to an upper bound on the information communicated, while in (53b) the R-principle renders the indefinite more informative than its logical form suggests. ③

Horn (p. 15) observes "Like the antinomic economies from which they derive, the Q-based and R-based principles just outlined often directly collide. A speaker obeying only Q would tend to say everything she knows on the off-chance that it might prove informative, while a speaker obeying only R would probably, to be on the safe side, not open her mouth. In fact, many of the maxim clashes Grice and others

---

① There is in fact a condition on this interpretation, which we shall mention in next section.

② Horn adds later that this is a normal interpretation, which will not obtain if "I knew you knew that I was an enforcer for the mob" (p.20).

③ R. Carston (1998:196) borrows from J.F.Richardson & A.W.Richardson (1990) the example "I found a finger", implicating "The finger is not mine", in place of (53a), and argues that it is wrong to assume that two different principles are at work here. "In both cases pragmatic inference results in a proposition which is stronger than (entails) the ownership-neutral linguistic content of the utterance." What is different is the background knowledge that is used in the pragmatic process of strengthening, which she thinks is driven by a single principle of relevance. As I commented in note ① on page 66, the implicature derivable from "a woman" is different from that of "a finger". "Woman" is a more general term, the use of which indicates that the specific terms, such as "mother, wife, sister, girl friend" are not applicable. In this sense, I agree with Carston's argument, but I do not endorse a relevance-theoretic account. For the details, see section 4.3.3.

have discussed do involve Quantity$_1$ vs. Relation". ①But he maintains "it is perhaps in the resolution of the conflict between them that they play their major role" (p. 22). And he suggests this resolution comes from a division of pragmatic labor② as follows:

> The use of a marked (relatively complex and/or prolix) expression when a corresponding unmarked (simpler, less "effortful") alternate expression is available tends to be interpreted as conveying a marked message (one which the unmarked alternative would not or could not have conveyed). (ibid.)

Specifically, this means

(a) The speaker used marked expression E' containing "extra" material (or otherwise less basic in form or distribution) when a corresponding unmarked expression E, essentially coextensive with it, was available.

(b) Either (i) the "extra" material was irrelevant and unnecessary, or (ii) it was necessary (i.e. E could not have been ap-

---

① Horn holds that the three way classification of maxims, i.e. the maxim of quality plus the two principles, can also account for the effects of different types of maxim violation. "Grice notes that a speaker may 'quietly and unostentatiously violate a maxim' as well as exploit it to generate an implicature. Clark and Haviland (1977: 2) have suggested that intentional covert maxim violations result in lies, while unintentional violations are simply misleading. In fact, what is crucial is just which sort of maxim or pragmatic principle is violated: intentional quality violations result in lies (another reason for the special status of quality; cf. Coleman and Kay 1981 for additional factors in defining *lie*), intentional violations of the Q-based sufficiency principle result in a speaker's misleading the addressee, and intentional violation of the R-based least effort principle are often simply unhelpful or perverse. A courtroom witness must swear to tell the whole truth and nothing but the truth, i.e. to obey quantity and quality, while violations of relevance lead only to a possible lawyer's objection or judge's scolding" (p. 14).

② There is a comment on this notion in Levinson (1987b: 409), which we shall quote in section 4.3.1.

propriately used).
(c) (i) is in conflict with the R Principle and is thus (ceteris paribus) to be rejected.
(d) Therefore, (b(ii)), from (b) and (c) by modus tollendo ponens.
(e) The unmarked alternative E tends to become associated (by use or—through conventionalization—by meaning) with unmarked situation s, representing stereotype or salient member of extension of E/E'. (R-based inference)
(f) The marked alternative E' tends to become associated with the complement of s with respect to the original extension of E/E'. (Q-based inference) (ibid.)

In short, "unmarked forms tend to be used for unmarked situations (via R) and marked forms for marked situations (via Q)" (p.26).

4.2.2 Evidence for the principles

To show that the two principles are really valid, Horn surveyed "a wide range of linguistic phenomena, both synchronic and diachronic, both lexical and syntactic, both 'parole'-based and 'langue'-based, from conversation implicature and politeness strategies to the interpretation of pronouns and gaps, from blocking and distributional constraints on lexical items to indirect speech acts, from lexical change to case marking" (p.38). In this section we shall mainly introduce his observations on negation as implicature-canceller, pronoun avoidance, synonym avoidance, and indirect speech acts.

First, Horn has found that Q-based implicatures can be readily cancelled by metalinguistic negation, which does not affect what is said, but R-based implicatures cannot be cancelled by negation at all.①

---

① There are apparent counterexamples, which will be discussed later in this section.

And he illustrates it with the following two sets of sentences (54a-f) and (55a-d).

(54a) He didn't eat *three*①carrots—he ate *four* of them.

(54b) You didn't eat *some* of the cookies—you ate *all* of them.

(54c) It isn't *possible* she'll win—it's *certain* she will.

(54d) She isn't patriotic *or* quixotic—she's both patriotic *and* quixotic.

(54e) I'm not *happy*—I'm *ecstatic*.

(54f) It isn't *warm*—it's downright *hot*.

(55a) She wasn't able to solve the problem.

(≠She was able to solve it, but didn't)

(55b) He wasn't clever enough to figure out the answer.

(≠He was clever enough to do it, but he didn't)

(55c) I didn't break a finger yesterday.

(≠I broke a finger, but it wasn't one of mine)

(55d) I don't believe the Yankees will win the pennant.

(≠I believe they'll win the pennant, but I'm not [weakly] asserting that they will) (p.20)

Why is there such a difference in cancellability? Horn's answer is that it has to do with the different logics of Q-based and R-based inferences.

Let S represent a given (stronger) proposition, and W the weaker proposition which it unilaterally entails and from which the relevant implicata are to be drawn. In the case of Q-based implicata, the assertion of "W" Q-implicates $\sim$ S. Where W is a

---

① In the original, Horn did not show the abnormal stress by the italics. The modifications, especially the one in (54d), are introduced on the basis of Horn (1988: 128).

scalar predicate truth-conditionally defined by its lower bound, the ordinary negation of W negates that lower bound, i. e. as "less than W", and is hence incompatible with S; the assertion that he did not eat three carrots would be taken to amount to the assertion that he ate less than three (and hence not four, five, or more). But "not W" uttered in a context where S is affirmed (as in (54a-f)) self-destructs on the unmarked "less than W" understanding and must therefore be sent back through, in effect—whence the marked, metalinguistic quality of this variety of negation.

In the case of R-based implicata, the assertion of "W" R-implicates not $\sim$S but S: the proposition that she solved the problem unilaterally entails the proposition that she was able to solve it (S entails W), but the assertion that she was able to solve it may implicate that she in fact solved it ("W" R-implicates S). Once again, "not W" signifies "less than W" and hence licenses the inference of $\sim$S (via modus tollens from the original S $\Vdash$ W entailment). But crucially, there are no circumstances under which the implicatum S is cancelled and "not W" cannot be interpreted consistently, as an ordinary descriptive negation. The negation in (55a – d) thus never gets sent back through to be interpreted metalinguistically, as an implicatum-canceller. Schematically, the situation we have is [as follows:]

Q-based implicata:	R-based implicata:
S entails W;	S entails W;
"W" Q-implicates $\sim$S;	"W" R-implicates S;
normally, "not W" = "less than W", incompatible with S;	normally, "not W" = "less than W"; "not W" $\Vdash$ $\sim$S (modus tollens);

| "not W", asserted where S is given, reinterpreted as metalinguistic negation | "not W" never gets reinterpreted, since it's always compatible with ~S (the denial of W's implicatum) |

(pp. 20-1)

In Horn's view, R-based implicatures can be cancelled simply by assigning the contradiction contour and stressing the implicature-inducing element. For example,

(56a) She was *able*① to solve the problem (but she didn't solve it).②

(56b) I *believe* the Yankees will win the pennant (but I'm not saying they will).

(56c) I broke *a* finger today (but not one of mine). (p.21)

But there are counterexamples. For instance, "predicate expressions which denote various personal relationships may take on a narrowed symmetric sense (cf. *X and Y are* {*married/friends/lovers/in love*}) but need not (cf. *X and Y are spouses*). When the symmetric sense of these predicates is intended, negation may leave the more general sense unaffected" (ibid.). That is, (57a) is equivalent to (57b), but the marital status and other personal relationships of X are not affected by (57a), X may still be married/friends/in love with Z.

(57a) X and Y aren't {married/friends/in love}.

(57b) X and Y aren't {married/friends/in love} with each other.

---

① The italics in these three examples are mine, adapted in accordance with the theme in Horn's text.

② This example clarifies the point noted earlier that "John was able to solve the problem" could both R-implicate "John solved the problem" and Q-implicate "John didn't solve the problem".

Now Horn argues this exception is more apparent than real. The implicature in question has, in fact, become conventionalized as part of literal meaning. To confirm the claim that only conventionalized R-based implicature can be cancelled by negation, Horn reconsiders (58a) and (58b) from Atlas and Levinson (1981: 41).

(58a) John had a drink. → John had an alcoholic drink.

(58b) The secretary smiled. → The female secretary smiled.

The implicature of (58a) can be cancelled by negation, so (59a) is acceptable. But that of (58b) cannot, and (59b) is not acceptable.

(59a) John didn't have a drink—that was a Shirley Temple.

(59b) *My secretary didn't smile—I have a male secretary. ①

The reason is that "Both speakers' intuition and lexicographers' practice suggest that the implicatum associated with *drink* ('alcoholic drink') has become fossilized into conventional meaning, while the implicatum associated with *secretary* ('female secretary') has not" (p.22). In other words, the cases in which a so-called R-implicature is cancelled by negation in fact involve conventional meaning, literal meaning, or entailment. The interpretation of "drink" in the sense of "alcoholic drink" has become conventionalized, i.e. it is no longer the upper bound interpretation, but has become the lower bound interpretation.

Secondly, Horn has examined the question of pronoun avoidance. He starts the discussion with Chomsky's principle of Avoid Pronoun "interpreted as imposing a choice of PRO over an overt pronoun where possible" (Chomsky 1981: 65). Chomsky uses (60a−b) to substantiate his claim.

---

① Horn does not mark it as unacceptable in his paper, which I think is a slip.

(60a) John would much prefer [his going to the movie]

(60b) John would much prefer [his (own) book]

In (60a), PRO①may be used in place of the pronoun (cf. *John would much prefer going to the movie*), so *his* is taken here as non-coreferential with *John*; in contrast, as PRO cannot appear in (60b), the pronoun *his* may be (and with *own* present must be) taken as coreferential with *John*.

Horn notes, however, this principle may be violated when one needs to avoid ambiguity. Thus, in (61a), coreference is ruled out totally in accordance with Chomsky's principle. But in (61b), it is possible to use the pronoun *me* and for it to be coreferential with *I*, if the speaker wants to make the meaning explicitly clear. The case of (61c) is a bit different. "Technically, Avoid Pronoun should be activated in (61c), since one can be speaking to different addressees within a single sentence, distinguishing them by pointing or eye gaze. This situation, however, is too marginal to trigger the ambiguity avoidance condition on Avoid Pronoun, and the second person case thus works like the first person case in (61b)" (p.24). That is, the two *yous* may be coreferential.

(61a) * He$_i$ wants him$_i$ to win. (no coreference possible)

---

① PRO is one of the four empty categories in the Chomskyan theory, referring to the phonetically unrealized element as in "John tried [PRO to win the race]." The other three are NP-trace, pro and variable. NP-trace refers to the empty category in constructions like the English passive, where an object in the active becomes the subject and moves away, leaving in its original place a trace. The empty category pro refers to the null-subject in pro-drop languages like Italian. And variables are found in wh-interrogatives, where the wh-element is thought to be moved from another place to the initial position, and the trace it leaves behind is called a variable.

(61b) (?)I_i want me to win. (coreference possible in contrastive contexts)

(61c) (?) You_i want you_i to win.

The consideration of these cases leads naturally to the question of reflexives, which, in Horn's view, offers further grist for a suitably upgraded Avoid Pronoun mill. There is a generally accepted rule that a nonreflexive pronoun can usually be interpreted as coreferential with a given antecedent when used in a position where a reflexive (bound by that antecedent) could not have appeared. For example,

(62a) He_i likes {himself_i/ * him_i}. ①

(62b) He_i said that she likes { * himself_i/him_i}.

But ambiguity avoidance is also relevant here in the determination of the occasion when coreference is possible.

(63a) He's voting for him. (no coreference possible)

(63b) I'm voting for me. (coreference possible contrastively)

"In fact", he concludes, "while Avoid Pronoun, or whatever more general principle ultimately includes it, is basically a least effort correlate, the division of labor we ultimately arrive at (in which abstract pronouns, i. e. PROs, are interpreted one way and real pronouns another) requires reference to both R and Q Principles" (p. 25).

The third phenomenon which Horn thinks lends support to his two principles is what I would call synonym avoidance. Aronoff (1976: 43ff.) on the basis of examples like (64a-b) asserts that the existence of a simple abstract nominal underlying a given *-ous* adjective

---

① This explains the reason why *him* in (61a) is not coreferential. That is, this is a position where *himself* may appear.

blocks or prevents the formation of an -*ity* nominalization based on that adjective, and more generally the existence of a simple lexical item can block the formation of an otherwise expected affixally derived form synonymous with it.

(64a) fury   furious   * furiosity
   * cury   curious   curiosity
(64b) fallacy   fallacious   * fallacity
   * tenacy   tenacious   tenacity

But Kiparsky (1982) has found examples like *gloriousness*, *furiousness* alongside *glory* and *fury*, and more generally pairs of words like *refrigerant/refrigerator*, *informant/informer*, *contestant/contester*. And he holds that "blocking can be partial in that the special [less productive] affix occurs in some restricted meaning and the general [more productive] affix picks up the remaining meaning". Only when there is no meaning "left over" for the more productive form to pick up will full blocking result, e. g. * *borer/bore$_N$*, * *inhabiter/inhabitant*.

Thus, Kiparsky formulates a general condition known as Avoid Synonymy:

The output of a lexical rule may not be synonymous with an existing lexical item.

Working independently of the Aronoff-Kiparsky line, McCawley (1978) collects a number of examples from English, Japanese, and other languages to show that a relatively productive process (including syntactic formations) is restricted by the existence of a more "lexicalized" alternative. His first example was originally noticed by Householder (1971: 75). That is, there are many terms formed with the adjective *pale* and colour words like *pale green*, *pale blue*, *pale yel-*

low, but *pale red* sounds odd. For some people, there is simply no such a term. For others its use is very limited. This oddity may be attributed to the existence of the word *pink*. Unless one wants to designate a colour which is paler than red, but not yet as pale as pink, the term *pale red* would not be used. In other words, because of the existence of *pink* the use of *pale red* is limited in a way that *pale blue* and *pale green* are not.

One other example Horn cites from McCawley concerns the causatives as in (65a – b).

(65a) Black Bart killed the sheriff.

(65b) Black Bart caused the sheriff to die.

Lexical causatives like (65a) tend to be used in the stereotypic causative situation: direct, unmediated causation through physical action, while the use of a productive causative as in (65b) tends to indicate an indirect causation. Bart may have caused the sheriff's gun to backfire by stuffing it with cotton, or arranged for scorpions to be placed in the room of the sheriff who is known to have a weak heart, etc. Similarly, the use of the unmarked lexical causative in (66a) implicates that the action was brought about in an unmarked way (presumably by stepping on the brake pedal), while the choice of the morphologically more complex periphrastic (66b) correspondingly implicates that some unusual method was employed (pulling the emergency brake, telekinesis, etc.).

(66a) Lee stopped the car.

(66b) Lee got the car to stop. (Lee made the car stop.)[1]

---

[1] Another instance which in my view is more closely related to the question of synonyms but Horn discusses together with indirect speech acts is double negation. That is, the two negatives of the form *not-(not-p)* do not cancel out functionally even when they do

Horn maintains that though there is still room for improvement in Aronoff, McCawley and Kiparsky's accounts, the insight behind them is real, and "it is essentially a single insight: the unmarked form is used for a stereotypical, unmarked situation (via R-implicature) and the marked counterpart for the situations 'left over' (via Q-implicature)" (p. 29).

Lastly, Horn considers the implication of the Q- and R-principles for indirect speech acts. He finds that modal auxiliaries which can be associated with indirect speech acts tend to become conventionally associated with them. Thus (67a - b) are conventionally used to convey the request in (68), while (67c - e)—which may (very indirectly) convey that request—are not conventionally used to do so.

(67a) Can you (please)① close the window?

(67b) Could you (please) close the window?

(67c) Are you able to (? please) close the window?

(67d) Do you have the ability to (* please) close the window?

---

semantically: they convey a positive which is characteristically weaker than the corresponding simple affirmative. In Jespersen's (1924: 332) words,

> The two negatives [in *not uncommon*, *not infrequently*, *not without some fear*]... do not exactly cancel one another in such a way that the result is identical with the simple *common*, *frequent*, *with some fear*; the longer expression is always weaker: "this is not unknown to me" or "I am not ignorant of this" means "I am to some extent aware of it", etc. The psychological reason for this is that the *détour* through the two mutually destructive negatives weakens the mental energy of the listener and implies on the part of the speaker a certain hesitation which is absent from the blunt, outspoken *common* or *known*.

"Rather than appealing, with Jespersen, to the metaphysical (and somewhat Victorian) notion of double negation sapping the listener's mental energy," Horn (p. 31) argues, "we can more plausibly ascribe the weakening effect to the same general tendency we have already observed: the use of a marked expression when there is a shorter and less 'effortful' alternative available signals that the speaker felt s/he was not in a position to employ the simpler version felicitously".

① In Horn's view, whether *please* can be inserted is an indication of the conventionalness of the utterance.

(67e) It's (* * please) cold in here.

(68) (Please) close the window. (ibid.)

As a mater of fact, the periphrastic counterparts of modal auxiliaries tend to be interpreted literally. For example,

(69a) Can you pass the salt? (request)

(69b) Are you able to pass the salt? (literal question)

(70a) Here, I can help you with that. (offer)

(70b) (? Here,) I am {able/allowed} to help you with that. (not an offer)

(71a) Will you join us? (invitation)

(71b) Are you going to join us? (literal question)

(72a) I will marry you. (promise)

(72b) I am {going to/willing to} marry you. (only very indirect promise) (p. 30)

It is for this reason that Searle (1975b: 76) suggests a new maxim of Manner--"Speak idiomatically unless there is some special reason not to". "In general, if one speaks unidiomatically, hearers assume that there must be a special reason for it, and in consequence, ... the normal conversational assumptions on which the possibility of indirect speech acts rests are in large part suspended".

Horn (pp. 30 – 1) comments, "The pattern discerned here by Searle responds not only to our division of pragmatic labor, but also to the set of statistical correlations at the core of Zipf's analysis of the Principle of Least Effort and its linguistic reflexes (Zipf 1949). Zipf's law of Abbreviation posits an inverse relation between the length of a word and the frequency of its tokens in an arbitrary text. His Principle of Economic Versatility stipulates a direct correlation between a word's frequency and its semantic versatility (i.e. the number of discrete senses or meanings it allows). The Principle of Economic Specialization states that the age of lexical item in the language correlates inversely with its size and directly with its frequency. By these measures, the relative simplicity of (67a), (67b) as against (67c) is directly confirmed: *can* and *could* are historically older than their periphrastic counterparts, phonologically simpler and shorter, more frequent in text tokens, and certainly more versatile semantically, as the contrasts in (73a – c) make clear."

(73a) I {can/am able to} stand on my nose.

This knife {can/? is able to} cut the salami. (cf. .... is capable of cutting it)

The salami {can be cut/ * is able to be cut/is capable of being cut} by the knife.

(73b) Can it really be raining out? /Is it possible that it's raining out?

(73c) Can Billy come out and play? /Is Billy permitted to come out and play?

And he repeats "The corresponding periphrastic forms, stylistically less natural, longer and more complex, are restricted (via Q-implicature) to those situations outside the stereotype, for which the unmarked expression would have been inappropriate" (p. 31).

4.3 The Q-, I- and M-principles

This tripartite model has been suggested by Stephen Levinson. He first began to formulate his ideas along this line in 1981, when writing collaboratively with Jay David Atlas "*It*-Clefts, Informativeness and Logical Form: Radical Pragmatics". But it was in the two articles published in 1987--"Minimization and Conversational Inference" and "Pragmatics and the Grammar of Anaphora: A Partial Pragmatic

Reduction of Binding and Control Phenomena"--that he formally suggested these three principles. And the present introduction is mainly based on the second article of 1987.

4.3.1 A neoclassic interpretation

In essence, Levinson says, the Q-, I- and M- principles are Grice's two maxims of Quantity and a maxim of Manner reinterpreted neoclassically(1987b: 400).① And the maxim of Quality, as is the case in Horn's theory, is kept intact.

When presenting the second maxim of Quantity "Do not make your contribution more informative than is required", Grice raised the doubt whether it was actually required, since its effects might be achieved by the maxim of Relation, i.e. more information than necessary is irrelevant. In Sperber and Wilson's approach and that of Horn's, it is exactly adopted what Grice had anticipated—to use the principle of relevance to subsume the second maxim of Quantity. Now Levinson believes that is mistaken. In his view, the maxims of Quantity have to do with the quantity of information, while the maxim of Relation is "a measure of timely helpfulness with respect to interactional goals" (p. 401), and "is largely about the satisfaction of others' goals in interaction, and the satisfaction of topical and sequencing constraints in discourse, as in the expectation that an answer will follow a question" (Levinson 1989: 467). It is not, at least not primarily, about information. So he renames the second maxim of Quantity the Principle of Informativeness, I-principle for short; and the first maxim of Quantity the Principle of Quantity, or Q-principle. Specifically,

Q-principle

---

① The references in this section are all to this paper, if not otherwise indicated.

Speaker's Maxim: Do not provide a statement that is informationally weaker than your knowledge of the world allows, unless providing a stronger statement would contravene the I-principle.

Recipient's Corollary: Take it that the speaker made the strongest statement consistent with what he knows, and therefore that:

(a) if the speaker asserted $A(W)$, and $<S, W>$ form a Horn scale (such that $A(S) \Vdash^{①}(A(W))$), then one can infer $K \sim (A(S))$, i.e. that the speaker knows that the stronger statement would be false;[②]

(b) if the speaker asserted $A(W)$ and $A(W)$ fails to entail an embedded sentence Q, which a stronger statement $A(S)$ would entail, and $\{S, W\}$ form a contrast set, then one can infer $\sim K(Q)$, i.e. the speaker does not know whether Q obtains or not.[③] (p. 401)

In other words, Q-implicatures enrich utterance meaning just by inducing the negation of a stronger possible proposition.

I-principle

Speaker's Maxim: the Maxim of Minimization

[①] This sign means "entail". But Levinson himself used ⊢, which is more usually used for assertion.

[②] For example, (a) implicates (b) since *all* and *some* form a Horn scale. And this is the type of generalized scalar quantity implicature discussed in section 3.3.1.

(a) Some of my friends are linguists.

(b) Not all of my friends are linguists.

[③] For example, (a) implicates (b) as *know* and *believe* do not form a Horn scale, but only a loose contrast set. This is the generalized clausal quantity implicature discussed in 3.3.2.

(a) John believes there is life on Mars.

(b) John doesn't know that there is life on Mars.

"Say as little as necessary", i.e. produce the minimal linguistic information sufficient to achieve your communicational ends (bearing the Q-principle in mind).

Recipient's Corollary: the Enrichment Rule

Amplify the informational content of the speaker's utterance, by finding the most SPECIFIC interpretation, up to what you judge to be the speaker's m-intended① point. ②

Specifically:

(a) Assume that stereotypical relations obtain between referents or events, UNLESS (i) this is inconsistent with what is taken for granted, (ii) the speaker has broken the maxim of Minimization by choosing a prolix expression.

(b) Assume the existence or actuality of what a sentence is "about" if that is consistent with what is taken for granted.

(c) Avoid interpretation that multiply entities referred to (assume referential parsimony); specifically, prefer coreferential readings of reduced NP's (pronouns or zeros).

The I-principle has the following obvious but far-reaching consequence: a speaker's maxim of MINIMIZATION ("say as little as necessary") has as immediate corollary an addressee's

---

① This term was introduced into the literature by Grice in his article "Utterer's Meaning, Sentence-Meaning, and Word-Meaning", where he used "U [utterer] m-intends to produce in A [audience] effect E" as an abbreviation of "U intends to produce in A effect E by means of A's recognition of that intention". "M" stands for "meaning". (Grice 1971 [1968]: 58)

② R. Carston(1998:186) challenges Levinson's use of this condition here. She thinks there is something important missing, that is, the criterion for deciding the speaker's m-intended point. In her view, this criterion cannot be anything but relevance. It is relevance that controls the application of Levinson's principles.

maxim of INFERENTIAL MAXIMIZATION. Thus there arises a potential paradox, in slogan form "the less you say, the more you mean". In practice, this amounts to a preference for the maximally rich interpretation of minimal, informationally reduced, forms. (p. 402)

Levinson has the following as evidence for the existence of the I-principle, where the (a) utterances will tend to implicate the (b) propositions:

(74) "Conjunction buttressing" (Atlas & Levinson 1981)

 (a) John turned the key and the engine started.

 (b) p and then q (temporal sequence)

  p therefore q (causal connectedness)

  A did X in order to cause q (teleology, intentionality)

(75) "Conditional perfection" (Geis & Zwicky 1971)

 (a) If you mow the lawn, I'll give you $ 5.

 (b) If and only if you mow the lawn, will I give you $ 5.

(76) "Bridging" (Clark & Haviland 1977)

 (a) John unpacked the picnic. The beer was warm.

 (b) The beer was part of the picnic.

(77) "Inference to stereotype" (Atlas & Levinson 1981)

 (a) John said "Hello" to the secretary and then he smiled.

 (b) John said "Hello" to the female secretary and then he John [sic] smiled.

(78) "Mirror maxim" (Harnish 1976: 359)

 (a) Harry and Sue bought a piano.

 (b) They bought it together, not one each.

(79) Preferred Co-reference

 (a) John came in and he sat down.

(b) John₁ came in and he₁ sat down. (p. 403)

He thinks these inferences, though involving a different detailed mechanism in each case, share some important properties. And they are:

(a) the inferences are more informative than the utterances that give rise to them—the implicated propositions entail the sentences that give rise to them but not vice-versa; (b) the implicated propositions are more precise or specific than the corresponding sentences (not more informative, e.g. merely by the conjunction of unrelated propositions); they take one from a semantically general meaning to a pragmatically specific or precise interpretation; (c) these I-inferences differ from Q-inferences which also increase the informativeness of utterances in that the latter do so only by the negation of a stronger proposition that might have been directly expressed but was not. (p. 404)

To avoid possible clashes between the Q- and I-principles, Levinson proposes to restrict the scope of the Q-principle so that it operates only on clearly defined contrast sets, of which the Horn scale is prototypical, and to set the following constraints on Horn scales:

For <S, W> to form a Horn scale

(i) A(S) must entail A(W) for some arbitrary sentence frame A;

(ii) S and W must be EQUALLY LEXICALIZED (hence no Horn scale < *iff*, *if* > to block "conditional perfection");

(iii) S and W must be "ABOUT" THE SAME SEMANTIC RELATIONS, or from the same semantic field (hence no scale < *since*, *and* > to block "conjunction buttressing"). [1] (p. 407)

---

[1] Levinson notes "I have to confess to some doubts that these conditions are sufficient; they may also not be necessary, as they may be somewhat too strong, but the constraints seem to be along the right lines" (p. 407 n37).

On the other hand, implicatures are by definition cancellable in the face of inconsistent assumptions. "If the door is locked I have a key in my pocket" will not undergo "conditional perfection" to "If and only if..." because this would be inconsistent with our assumption that keys do not automatically move to pockets when doors are locked. However, when there is a genuine clash, then Q-implicatures appear to override I-implicatures.

Now let's turn to the M-principle. In his 1987 articles, Levinson does not give a specific formulation of it, he mixes the presentation of his own ideas with the criticism of Horn's principles. He accuses Horn of failing to draw a distinction between two kinds of minimization: a semantic minimization and an expression minimization. The semantic, or content, minimization is equivalent to semantic generality, i.e. the more general terms are more minimal in meaning, having more restricted connotation (in contrast to its more extended denotation); and the less general, the more specific, are less minimal, more maximal on the other hand. For example, *ship* is more general than *ferry*, *flower* than *rose*, *animal* than *tiger*, and the indefinite *a* than the definite *the*. The choice of the former instead of the latter is a process toward minimization. On the other hand, the expression, or form, minimization is some measure of surface length and complexity. It is concerned with the phonetic and morphological make-up of a term. Thus the normally stressed terms are more minimal than their abnormally stressed counterparts. The shorter terms, those consisting of fewer constituents, are more minimal than longer ones, those consisting of more constituents, provided they are commeasurable in meaning, i.e. synonymous, such as *frequent* and *not infrequent*, *to stop a car* and *to cause a car to stop*. (cf. p.402)①

In Levinson's view, only the first type of minimization has to do with the I-principle, the second type, in contrast, is the domain of the principle of manner, as it concerns the form of expression, the way to express something rather than what is to be expressed, or how much is to be expressed. He also criticizes Horn's division of pragmatic labor in this regard. "[T]he contrast involved in the Hornian division of labour is a contrast between marked and unmarked expressions, and more exactly a contrast between usual vs. unusual, or brief vs. prolix expressions. This distinction has nothing to do with quantity of information, the paired expressions being assumed to be synonymous; rather it has to do with surface form, and these implicatures are thus properly attributed to the maxim of Manner" (p. 409).②

According to Huang Yan (1991: 306), the principle of manner, or M-principle, is as follows:③

M-principle

Speaker's Maxim: Do not use a prolix, obscure or marked

---

① Levinson admits that a Zipfian argument can be made to the effect that these two minimizations will tend to conflate. "The argument is simple enough: the first premise is Zipf's Law of Abbreviation ('the more use, the shorter'); the second premise is his Principle of Economic Versatility ('the more semantically general, the more use'); the conclusion is 'the more semantically general, the shorter'" (p. 403 n30). And he uses as an example the three types of NP realization: zero anaphor, pronoun and lexical NP. The first is both semantically and phonetically more minimal than the second, and the second than the third. But he presents them in a reversed order as: Lexical NP > Pronoun > Zero Anaphor. (p. 403)

② However, at this time Levinson thought "there is some reasoning from informational content [too]: since the unmarked expression of such a pair I-implicates a richer, stereotypical interpretation, the use of the marked member Q-implicates the negation of the richer interpretation". And he designates these implicatures Q/M-implicatures rather than simple M-implicatures. (p. 409)

③ I have introduced some modification in format to bring it in line with Levinson's own formulation of the previous two principles.

expression without reason.

Recipient's Corollary: If the speaker used a prolix or marked expression M, he did not mean the same as he would have had he used the unmarked expression U—specifically he was trying to avoid the stereotypical associations and I-implicatures of U.

Clearly, Levinson remarks, such cross-cutting principles would make for interpretive mayhem unless there is a system governing their interaction. And the order of precedence of application he suggests is:

Interaction of the I-, Q- and Q/M-implicatures[①]

(ⅰ) Genuine Q-implicatures from tight contrast sets of equally brief, equally lexicalized linguistic expressions "about" the same semantic relations, take precedence over I-implicatures;

(ⅱ) in all other cases the I-principle induces stereotypical specific interpretations, UNLESS:

(ⅲ) there are two (or more) available expressions of the same sense, one of which is unmarked and the other marked in form. In that case, the unmarked form carries the I-implicatures as usual, but the use of the marked form Q/M-implicates the non-applicability of the pertinent I-implicatures. (p. 409)

4.3.2 Anaphoric reference

Now the point of Levinson's 1987 papers is not just to outline the three principles, it is also, to an extent more, concerned with the pattern of anaphoric reference, seen as an instantiation of the general principles.

[①] Read it as "M-implicatures", and the same below.

In April 1979, Chomsky delivered a series of lectures in Pisa, Italy, in which he expounded the theory of government and binding for the first time. A very important part of this theory is the three binding conditions:

Binding Theory

A. An anaphor is bound in its governing category.

B. A pronominal is free in its governing category.

C. An r-expression is free. (Chomsky 1981: 188)

The term "anaphor" is used in a narrow sense to include only reflexives like *myself* and reciprocals like *each other*. "To be bound" means "to be co-referential with an NP". "A governing category"①, at the risk of over-simplification, refers to the lowest S or NP node in a tree diagram, under which an anaphor or a pronoun appears. And "an r-expression" as the abbreviation of "a referential-expression" covers all the other r-expressions except anaphors and pronouns, e. g. *John*, *Bill*, *the man*. Thus, in (80), (81) and (82), the anaphors *himself*, *each other* are bound, i. e. co-referential with an NP, in their governing categories *John likes himself*, *They hit each other*, and *Bill's criticism of himself* respectively. In (83), the pronoun is free in its governing category, it is not co-referential with *John*. In (84), the pronoun is, as in (83), not locally bound, i. e. not co-referential with *Bill*; but it may be co-referential with *John*. And in (85), the r-expression *the man* is not co-referential with either *Bill* or *John*; it is free in both domains.

(80) John$_1$ likes himself$_1$.

(81) They$_1$ hit each other$_1$.

---

① Also known as "local domain", "binding domain".

(82) John$_1$ doesn't like Bill's$_2$ criticism of himself$_2$.
(83) John$_1$ likes him$_2$.
(84) John$_1$ says Bill$_2$ likes him$_1$.
(85) John$_1$ says Bill$_2$ likes the man$_3$.

But Levinson thinks Chomsky has over-grammaticalized things here. Anaphora is perhaps primarily a semantic and pragmatic matter—and especially a pragmatic matter. And pragmatic principles could better account for the favoured interpretations of certain NP-gaps (cf. pp. 379 – 80). Specifically, Levinson suggests there is a pragmatic apparatus for anaphora generated by the Q-, I- and M-principles as follows:

- (a) Where the syntax permits a direct encoding of co-referentiality, e.g. by the use of a reflexive, the use of an informationally weaker expression, e.g. a non-reflexive pronoun, will Q-implicate a non-coreferential interpretation.
- (b) Otherwise semantically general, minimally informative expressions (pronouns and gaps) will favour a coreferential interpretation by the I-principle, UNLESS:
- (c) the use of a marked form, a lexical NP where a pronoun might have been used, or a pronoun where a zero might have occurred, will Q/M-implicate a non-co-referential interpretation. (p. 410)

And if we accept Binding Condition A as a basic rule of grammar, then Conditions B and C can be partially reduced to pragmatics by the use of the above apparatus. In other words, armed with Levinson's three principles, Chomsky would only need Condition A to explain cases like (80), in which *John* and *himself* are coreferential. There is no need for Conditions B and C any more, since a reflexive and a cognate pronoun form a Horn scale, such as $<himself, him>$. Whenever a reflexive is syntactically possible, the use of a pronoun will Q-implicate a non-coreferential interpretation,① as exemplified by (83), which is what exactly Condition B says. And in terms of both semantic content and surface form, an r-expression like *John, the man* is more specific, less general, less minimal and fuller than a pronoun, and a pronoun than a zero, i.e. there is a semantic and formal hierarchy:②

Lexical NP > Pronoun > Zero

Accordingly the use of a general, minimal, or reduced form would I-implicate a stereotypical, unmarked interpretation, i.e. co-referential; and the use of a specific, maximal, full form, on the other hand, would M-implicate that the stereotypical, unmarked interpretation does not obtain, hence non-co-referential. That is why *him* and *the man* in (84) and (85) are interpreted as non-co-referential locally, a fact partly explained by Condition C. For more examples, we may have a look at the following:

(86) $John_1$ came in and $\emptyset_1$ sat down in the front row immediately.

(87) $John_1$ came in and he_1 sat down in the front row immediately.

---

① More exactly it is a LOCALLY non-coreferential interpretation as is the case in (84). Example (84) also shows that the different interpretations of a reflexive and its cognate pronoun are better said to be complementary. That is, not only when a reflexive is coreferential with a local subject, its counterpart pronoun is non-coreferential; but also when a reflexive is non-coreferential with a matrix subject, the pronoun will on the other hand BE coreferential with it.

② Levinson does not say so clearly and Huang (1991) represents it as a semantic hierarchy only, but see note ① on page 135.

(88) *John₁ came in and himself₁ sat down in the front row immediately.

(89) John₁ came in and the man₂ sat down in the front row immediately.

The zero being a minimal form is naturally interpreted in the co-referential way in (86). The pronoun in (87) is in a position where the reflexive is impossible as (88) shows, so it is also understood in a co-referential way.① *The man* in (89) as that in (85), on the other hand, is a maximal, full form and gets interpreted in a marked way. Incidentally the M-principle also explains the marked interpretation in (90), where *he* is abnormally stressed.

(90) John₁ came in and HE₂ sat down in the front row immediately.

However there are problems in this approach. First, there are cases in which a reflexive and a pronoun are not in contrast, namely, it is not the case that one is interpreted co-referentially and the other not. For example,

(91) (a) John pulled the blanket towards himself.

(b) John pulled the blanket towards him.

(92) (a) John found a snake near himself.

(b) John found a snake near him.

And there are even cases in which we find reflexives when we should expect pronouns according to Binding Condition A.

(93) (a) John thought that Mary knew that paper had been writ-

---

① A problem with (87) is that according to part (c) of Levinson's apparatus, the use of a pronoun where a zero might have occurred will Q/M-implicate a non-coreferential interpretation, but Levinson does not explain why it does not do so here.

ten by Ann and himself.[1]

(b) John thought that Mary knew that paper had been written by Ann and him.

(94) (a) John thought that Mary criticized everyone but himself.[2]

(b) John thought that Mary criticized everyone but him.

These sentences of course also pose problems for Chomsky, so there are amendments to his theory on Chomsky's side as well. Here, however, we shall only discuss Levinson's solutions to them. In 1991, Levinson wrote "Pragmatic Reduction of the Binding Conditions Revisited", in which he mainly adopts Susumu Kuno's (1987) proposal. That is, the reflexive and the pronoun in these sentences are not really interchangeable. There is a subtle meaning difference between them, which concerns the point of view one takes, i.e. whether one looks at the event from the protagonist's view or not. If one does, then one will use the reflexive, otherwise, the pronoun will be used.[3] So Levinson says his theory is still valid. There is still a contrast between a reflexive and a pronoun, though not in reference. And the contrast between the reflexive and the ordinary pronoun now becomes:

    self   *he/she/it*

  + logophoric   ± logophoric[4]

---

[1] This type of reflexive, whose antecedent is the matrix subject rather than the local subject, is known as long-range reflexive.

[2] Cf. John says Bill likes himself.

[3] This difference in point of view has come to be known as logophoricity in the literature.

[4] On page 145, Levinson represents this contrast as:

        <Reflexive,   Pronoun>
        + Co-reference   unmarked
        + logophoric   unmarked

+ locally co-referential   ± referential dependency
(Levinson 1991: 124)

A more serious problem is that there are languages in which there is no true reflexive, in which case Condition A is simply not applicable, and consequently the whole apparatus built on it would collapse. This point was brought to the notice of linguists by Levinson himself. He came upon an Australian language—Guugu Yimidhirr and did some field work on it from June to October 1982. As a matter of fact his original idea to tackle the question of anaphora from the pragmatic point of view results from his exposure to this language in the first place (Levinson 1987b: 380f.). He notices that zero NPs are frequently used in Guugu Yimidhirr, and there seems to be no grammatical constraint on them. In English, for example, a zero NP occurs within the same sentence as its antecedent and is usually in the subject position, of which (86) above may serve as an example. In Guugu Yimidhirr, however, a zero NP could occur quite freely, in subject position, object position, even determiner position;[①] and it could occur either within the same sentence or across sentence boundaries. Hence Levinson began to look for pragmatic explanations. In his 1987 article, Levinson tried to bring Guugu Yimidhirr in line with languages like English, and interpreted a type of zero NP as a reflexive pronoun. He discussed sentences like (95),

(95) bama   gudhirra   guuda-dhi

[①] Guugu Yimidhirr is an ergative language. The terms of "subject" "object" are used here in order to make it easier to compare it with English. By "determiner position", which is my term, is meant the position where a determiner in English usually occurs, such as *his* in *his pocket*.

people-ABS[①]　　two-ABS　　　　hit-ANTIP （pp. 387f）
which can mean either "The two people hit themselves/each other" or "Someone (unidentified) hit the two of them (accidentally)". But he claimed then that the reflexive/reciprocal function is central, which may be supported by the possibility of adding the emphatic suffix -*gu* to the subject, meaning something like "They themselves hit".

In 1991, however, Levinson changed his mind and said in his paper "this special verb-form does not directly encode reflexivity, but only indicate directly that one argument is missing" (p. 132). The reflexive interpretation is a pragmatic inference, and only when the emphatic suffix -*gu* is added, does the reflexive/reciprocal reading become central. In other words, there is no true reflexive in this language. Therefore Condition A, which is concerned with reflexive/reciprocal, cannot be applied. And Guugu Yimidhirr is not alone in this regard, there are many other Australian languages of this type. Austronesian languages like Fijian do not have true reflexive either. A third group of languages which lack reflexives are the pidgins and creoles of all origins. For example, Carden and Stewart (1986; 13f.) report that in the Northern dialect of Haitian creole, there are sentences like (96),

　　(96) Emile dwe　　ede　　　li

---

　　① ABS is the abbreviation of "absolutive", a case in ergative languages, equivalent to the object of a transitive verb and the subject of an intransitive verb in languages like English, such as *the glass* in *John broke the glass* and *The glass broke*. And ANTIP is the abbreviation of "antipassive", which, Levinson explains on page 387, is "the equivalent in an ergative language to the passive in a nominative/accusative language". But on the next page, he reveals that there is also a passive in Guugu Yimidhirr. And when the subject is a pronoun, it will have a different case ending from that used in the antipassive.

Emile should help him (from Levinson 1991: 136) in which the name and the pronoun can be co-referential. And to make the reflexive reading obligatory, one would add a particle *tèt* (head) or *kò* (body) to the pronoun, such as *tèt-a-li* or *kò-a-li*.

Therefore, Levinson proposes that perhaps we should make a distinction between languages with reflexives and those without. For the first type of languages, Condition A will be the basic one, and the other two conditions are derived from it on the basis of pragmatic principles—the Q-, I- and M-principles. For the second type of languages, however, Condition A will not be applicable, and Condition B would have to become the central one. That is, pronouns are usually non-co-referential with their antecedents in the same clause. In Levinson's terminology, "clausemate NPs are preferentially interpreted as distinct in reference" (1991: 127). And he argues this principle can be pragmatically motivated. "[I]t would seem to be a matter of inductive fact that agents normally act upon entities other than themselves; the prototypical action—what is described by the prototypical transitive clause—is one agent acting upon some entity distinct from itself. If that is how the world stereotypically is, then an interpretation of an arbitrary transitive sentence as having referentially distinct arguments is given to us by the I-principle, which encourages and warrants an interpretation to the stereotype" (ibid.).[1]

Though there are no true reflexives in the second type of languages, there are reflexive-like forms, such as *bama-gu* in Guugu

---

[1] This idea was first advanced by A. Farmer & R. Harnish (1987), known as the Disjoint Reference Presumption(DRP): The arguments of a predicate are intended to be disjoint, unless marked otherwise (p. 557).

Yimidhirr and *tèt-a-li* in the Northern dialect of Haitian creole. So there is still the question of how to derive Condition A-like pattern for these languages. To do this, Levinson proposes to view the reflexive-like forms as marked in the sense that they are longer and morphologically more complex than ordinary pronouns. Indeed, even in English, *himself* is more complex than *him* in form. Therefore their interpretation may be generated through the M-principle. That is, the use of a marked form means the opposite of the stereotypic interpretation. And this is exactly what happens in languages like Guugu Yimidhirr and the Northern dialect of Haitian creole. For example,

(97) bama-gu   gudhirra guuda-dhi
  people (ABS)-EMPH[①] two-ABS hit-ANTIP
  The two people hit each other/themselves
              (Levinson 1991: 132)

(98) Emile dwe   ede tèt-a-li
  Emile should help himself (ibid.: 136)

As for the lexical expressions like *the boy* whose interpretation is regulated by Condition C in Chomsky's theory, Levinson says, the account is familiar. That is, when a pronoun is not a clausemate with another NP as *he* in (99), there will be nothing to prevent the I-implicated tendency to co-reference (Levinson 1991:129). And if in such a position a lexical expression is used instead, as in (100), we get the complementary interpretation, i.e. disjoint reference.

(99) John said he went.[②]

---

 ① Abbreviation of "emphatic".
 ② For convenience of exposition, Levinson uses example from English rather than languages like Guugu Yimidhirr.

(100) John said the boy went.

The revised account of anaphoric pattern in the second type of languages, in which Condition B is taken as the basic one, has come to be known as the "B-first" analysis, and the earlier account based on Condition A, "A-first" analysis.

Now Levinson does not stop here. He observes that Carden and Stewart also suggest the possible development of reflexives in creoles as follows:

(i) STAGE 1: no encoded reflexives; plain pronouns used reflexively.

(ii) STAGE 2: gradual emergence of morphological reflexives (based for example on body-part metaphors) with a clause-mate, subject-antecedent condition, co-existing with but encroaching upon the use of ordinary pronouns as reflexives.

(iii) STAGE 3: the loss of the reflexive use of the ordinary pronouns. (ibid.: 137)

Stimulated by this suggestion, Levinson has examined the history of English and noticed that *self* in English was not originally a reflexive element either. According to Visser, "in the earliest Old English texts *self* could be added to the personal pronouns in the nominative whenever this was thought necessary for the sake of emphasis" (Visser 1963 Vol. 1: 420). By the time of *Beowulf* a reflexive object could only be expressed by the normal accusative pronouns, as in *ic me cloensie* (I washed me). By the time of King Alfred the two forms of a pronoun plus *self* and a simple pronoun were both used. This situation continued through the Middle English period. But "there is a distinct change in the relative frequency of the two forms: the simple pronouns, which in the beginning are numerically predominant, are gradually, and to an ever increasing extent, encroached upon by the compound pronouns (= pronouns + *self*), with the result that by the second half of the fifteenth century they are more or less in the minority in most writings" (ibid. : 432) (from Levinson1991: 138 – 9).

Therefore, he hypothesizes that A-first languages like English in fact were B-first languages in the earliest period. In otherwords, the distinction of A-first languages and B-first languages not only represents two synchronic types but also diachronic development stages. And Levinson argues if we take this diachronic perspective, then we can better account for the fact that reflexives have not only an anaphoric interpretation but also logophoric one. That is, since reflexives grow out of an emphatic use, there may very well be other contrasts than reference intended, and logophoric, the point of view contrast, may just be one of them (Levinson 1991:144).

What is more, there may be languages in the process of transition from the B-first type to the A-first, which have anaphoric patterns midway between these two. In his view, Chinese is just such a language. 自己 is not really a true reflexive yet. And this is the ultimate reason why it carries no specification of the domain in which it must be bound.①

---

　　① For example, apart from sentences like (i) in which 自己 is locally bound, there are also sentences like (ii), (iii), and (iv):
　　　(i) 小张暗暗埋怨自己。
　　　(ii) 我越想越觉得自己做得不对。
　　　(iii) 小张说小李知道自己下午没空。
　　　(iv)(a) 小张认为小李太狂妄,总是看不起自己。
　　　　 (b) 小张认为小李太自卑,总是看不起自己。
In (ii) there is no antecedent in the local domain, and 自己 is coreferential with the matrix subject. In (iii), 自己 is bound by an antecedent even higher than in (ii). And the two sentences in (iv) are identical in terms of syntactic structure, but 自己 is bound differently.

Consequently, Levinson proposes a synthesis of A-first and B-first accounts, known as "A-first plus B-first" analysis.

4.3.3 Some alternative approaches

In this section we introduce three alternatives within the pragmatics camp to Levinson's account of anaphoric patterns, proposed by Y. Huang, M. Ariel, and R. Kempson and others respectively.

Y. Huang (1991, 1994) is more concerned with the technicalities in Levinson's account. He tries to show, with Chinese examples in particular, that the latter's A-first, B-first, and A-first plus B-first analyses are all inadequate. For example, the problems of the A-first plus B-first analysis are "given that < reflexive, pronoun > forms a Horn-scale, the interpretation of a pronoun (now in terms of the Q-principle) seems to be parasitic on the interpretation of the pertinent reflexive. However, how long-distance reflexives themselves (especially in such examples as (101)) are interpreted in this analysis is not clear. If this is the case, then pronouns would be left undetermined in this account, since there would be no 'conceptual anchorage', to use Levinson's own metaphor, for pronouns to be interpreted. A second problem seems to be that unless < lexical NP, pronoun > is regarded as forming a Horn-scale, lexical NPs (especially in such examples as (102) would remain uninterpreted, since there is no longer an M-principle in this system. ① But to posit < lexical NP, pronoun > as forming

---

① This is a misunderstanding. Levinson did say there are two pragmatic principles (the I-principle and the Q-principle) at work, when he first brought the B-first analysis into the consideration of A-first languages (1991:143), but he did not say they are the only two principles. When he went on to suggest a diachronic perspective, he explicitly used the M-principle (ibid.: 134). What is more, as we have mentioned, in the B-first analysis the M-principle is indispensable for the interpretation of reflexives, even the clausemate ones.

a Horn-scale would perhaps violate both the 'entailment' and the 'equal lexicalisation' constraints on Horn-scales"(1994:128).

(101) 小明说自己在北京长大。①

(102) 小明说这个人在北京长大。

In his view, there is no need to have recourse to either Condition A or B of Chomsky's. All we need is a distinction of referential dependence between reflexives on the one hand, and other anaphoric expressions on the other. "The interpretation of reflexives, pronouns, zero anaphors and lexical NPs can then be largely determined by the systematic interaction of the M- and I-principles (with that order of priority), constrained by a world-knowledge-based DRP"(ibid.).② To illustrate, we present in some detail his arguments about the evaporation of the M-implicated contrast in reference.

He argues that the most important property of implicature is cancellability, "they tend to disappear in the face of inconsistency with (i) background assumptions (or world knowledge), (ii) meaning$_{NN}$, (iii) semantic entailments and (iv) priority pragmatic inference"(1991: 324).③ He uses the following as examples for (i), (ii), (iii) and (iv) respectively:

(103) (a) 医生$_1$ 说病人$_2$ 知道 Ø$_1$ 明天给他$_2$ 动手术。④

(b) 医生$_1$ 说病人$_2$ 知道他$_1$ 明天给他$_2$ 动手术。(ibid.)

(104) (a) 小明$_1$ 一进屋, Ø$_1$ 就把门关上了。

(b) 小明$_1$ 一进屋, 他$_1$ 就把门关上了。(cf. pp. 322, 325)

---

① Huang's examples were originally in Pinyin.

② DRP is the abbreviation of Disjoint Reference Presumption, cf. the note on page 144.

③ In his 1994 book (p. 137), Huang adds another factor "context", but there is no change in the following discussion.

④ The subscripts have been simplified.

(105) (a) 小明₁ 说 Ø₁ 下个月结婚。

(b) 小明₁ 说他₁ 下个月结婚。

(c) 小明₁ 说自己₁ 下个月结婚。

(d) 小明₁ 说小明₂ 下个月结婚。

(e) 小明₁ 说这个人₂ 下个月结婚。(pp. 319–20)

(106) (a) 小华₁, 小明₂ 一进屋, Ø₁ 就把门关上了。

(b) 小华₁, 小明₂ 一进屋, 他₁ 就把门关上了。(p. 325)

First, the M-contrast is constrained by the requirement of consistency with background assumptions. In (103b) the M-implicature that 医生 and 他 are disjoint in reference clearly runs counter to our background assumption that it is stereotypically surgeons who do operations, therefore it evaporates. Secondly, Huang claims "the M-contrast in reference must be consistent with what the speaker might clearly intend (that is, mean$_{NN}$) given the assumed state of mutual knowledge.... suppose that the hearer knows that the speaker intends to use (104b) to mean (104a) (for whatever reason), he is expecting the speaker to do so, and the speaker knows that the hearer knows all that. Then, the speaker uses (104b) instead of (104a). In that case, what the speaker clearly means$_{NN}$ is that 他 and 小明 are coreferential with each other. This is enough to cancel the M-implicature that the use of 他 in (104b) might otherwise generate"(p. 325).① (105b) will be discussed below, but (105c) illustrates that "the M-contrast in

---

① I find this argument unconvincing. The notion meaning$_{NN}$, as we mentioned in section 4.1.1, refers to the meaning intended by the speaker. Clearly a speaker is not free to use any word to mean whatever he intends to. If a man is able to mean$_{NN}$ something, he must have satisfied some conditions, syntactic, semantic, pragmatic, etc. In a sense, pragmatics is the study of the pragmatic conditions on possible meaning$_{NN}$, such as Grice's maxims, the neo-Gricean principles. So we cannot use meaning$_{NN}$ as an independent factor to support a particular interpretation. We must try to reveal the mechanism behind the meaning$_{NN}$. In my view, the difference between (104a) and (104b) lies in the tempo of delivery if it is oral. (104a) is more

reference tends to disappear when it is inconsistent with semantic constraints. ... The M-implicated local non-coreferential interpretation is outlawed by the semantics of referential dependence"(ibid.). That is, though in terms of form, 自己 in (105c) and Ø in (105a) are in contrast, in terms of meaning they are not. They are both coreferential with 小明. "Fourthly, the M-contrast in reference tends to vanish in the face of inconsistency with what is most salient/relevant. This can be seen by the fact that when there is a topic, the M-implicated referential opposition associated with the use of a pronoun where a zero anaphor could occur appears to evaporate. The use of both the zero anaphor and the pronoun is then subject to the I-implicated co-referentiality with the topic", and (106) is a case in point (ibid.).

At the end of the discussion, Huang adds "Finally the M-contrast in reference tends to evaporate when it is at variance with what is implicated by the close semantico-conceptual relationship between two clauses"(p.326). And (105b) is seen as a case in which there is a relation of indirect discourse complement. He quotes from Foley & Van Valin (1984: 269) a hierarchy of interclausal semantic relations as follows:

> *Strongest*—Causative > Modality (e.g. 'try to')① > Psych-action (e.g. 'want to') > Jussive (e.g. 'order to') > Direct perception complements (e.g. 'see S') > Indirect discourse complements (e.g. 'say that S') > Temporal adverbial clauses

---

natural in fast speech while (104b) is more natural in slower, more deliberate speech. Some evidence supporting this view is that when (104a) is written down, there is usually no comma in the middle. For example, 他只要一有空就学习(吕叔湘(主编)1984);老乡们一听见枪声就都来了(陆俭明等 1982). In other words, the contrast between Ø and 他 in this case is not referential, but stylistic. Incidentally, this shows that anaphoric expressions may differ from each other in varied ways, not just referentially or logophorically.

① Examples in the brackets are added according to Levinson (1998[1987a]:587-90).

(e.g. 'Before S, S') > Conditionals (e.g. 'If S, S') > Simultaneous actions (e.g. 'While S, S') > Sequential actions (overlapping) > Sequential actions (non-overlapping) > Action-Action (unspecified linkage)—*Weakest*

Since the indirect discourse complement relation ranks relatively higher up, Huang concludes "Such a tight interclausal semantic linkage, as Levinson (1987a) has pointed out, tends to give rise to a 'same agent/patient as the last clause' effect, hence the suspension of the M-implicature" (ibid.).

But he notes "This might raise a question: namely, why is the M-induced contrast between the lexical NP, on the one hand, and the pronoun and the zero anaphor, on the other, in (105) [i.e. between (105a) and (105b) on the one hand, and (105d) or (105e) on the other] not cancelled by the I-implicature due to the same close semantico-conceptual relationship between the two clauses? Here, I do not have a well-grounded answer. Nevertheless, my speculation is that the M-contrast between a lexical NP and, say, a pronoun is too sharp (as compared with the M-contrast between a pronoun and a zero anaphor) to be ruled out by the pertinent I-implicature"(ibid. n17).

M. Ariel (1994, 1996) thinks that Levinson's analysis of anaphora is too simplistic. Referring expressions do not occur in perfectly complementary environments. In discourses, lexical NPs may be used co-referentially. On the other hand, zero anaphors may also refer to extra-linguistic entities.① There are well-known pro-drop languages, for example. "[A]nd even English can be shown to (marginally) have zeros referring to extra-linguistic entities" as in (107).

---

① Some people distinguish between two types of reference: exophoric and endophoric. Words which refer to extralinguistic entities are exophoric and those referring intra-linguistically

(107) Ø have to leave now. (1996: 17)

Therefore, she proposes to view different referring expressions as forming a continuum rather than a dichotomy of +/-coreference. She claims "that referential systems of natural languages do not specifically code the coreference/disjoint dichotomy.... the primary function of the various referring expressions... is to mark different degrees of accessibility[①] in memory" (1996: 15). In this sense, referring expressions may be called accessibility markers.

Ariel has been examining the use of referring expressions in novels and newspaper articles since the mid-80s. On the basis of her investigation, she suggests there is a scale of accessibility marking as follows:

The Accessibility Marking Scale

zero <[②] reflexives < agreement markers < criticized pronouns < unstressed pronouns < stressed pronouns < stressed pronouns + gesture < proximal demonstrative (+ NP) < distal demon-

---

are endophoric. The problem is that words have token-reflexivity, e. g. "Spell *rhinoceros* for me", as we noted in Chapter Two. So sometimes ambiguity may arise, M. A. K. Halliday (1994: 312 [1985: 291]) is a case in point. In his example "Peter, Peter, pumpkin eater,/ Had a wife and couldn't keep her./ He put her in a pumpkin shell/And there he kept her very well", he says "*he* and *her* are anaphoric, 'point' respectively to Peter and to his wife." On the one hand, he says "*he* and *her* are anaphoric", a sub-type of endophoric, that is, they refer to other words; on the other hand, he did not italicize *Peter* and *his wife*, nor enclose them in quotation marks, suggesting that *he* and *her* refer to the two people rather than the words. Realizing the existence of this problem, J. Lyons (1977: 660) suggests to adopt an alternative formulation, to say that "an anaphoric pronoun refers to what its antecedent refers to". That is, both the pronoun and its antecedent are exophoric, referring to extra-linguistic entities. Now Ariel opts for a different solution, to say that what is referred to, whether exophoric or endophoric, is actually a mental entity, mental representation, or memory entity. In this sense, her extra-linguistic entity is not the entity itself, but its reflex in human mind.

① Ariel talks about the accessibility of an antecedent, referent or mental entity, which are interchangeable in her theory.

② Ariel seems to be using the arrowhead in the wrong direction, since forms to the left signals relatively higher accessibility than those to the right. That is, it should more logically be >.

strative (+ NP) < proximal demonstrative (+ NP) + modifier < distal demonstrative (+ NP) + modifier < first name < last name < short definite description[①]< long definite description < full name < full name + modifier. (1994: 30)

Ariel calls the analysis of referring expressions in this way Accessibility theory, which she says is "actually a more sophisticated version of Levinson's" (1994:25), or "Levinson's minimality scale[②] of potentially anaphoric expressions is actually a rudimentary Accessibility marking scale" (1996: 31).

In her view, the degree of accessibility signalled by a marker is determined by three factors: informativity, rigidity and attenuation. "The degree of informativity incorporated into the linguistic marker is crucial for its role as an Accessibility marker, for the more lexical information the marker provides the better it is suited for the retrieval of less accessible material" (1991: 449).[③] For example, "the Israeli

---

① Expressions consisting of one or two content words are short, while those of three and more are long. (Ariel 1996: 18)

② By this she means the semantic and formal hierarchy of "Lexical NP > Pronoun > Zero", which we quoted in last sub-section. Ariel (1994: 23) also calls it markedness scale, which was mistakenly arranged as "zero > pronoun > lexical NP".

③ Ariel has not elaborated on this notion any further. Judging from her argument against Levinson's I-principle, she seems to endorse a definition of informativity in inverse proportion to predictability (1994: 20 n15). Something more predictable is less informative than something less predictable. A problem here is that the notion informativity applies to accessibility markers but predictability is about the antecedents related to the markers. In her paper of 1996 (p. 29), she says "Informativity [is] measured by counting the number of content words", which is obviously not a rigorous definition. She is not aware of any differences between her informativity and Levinson's informativeness, believing the former is equal to (1994: 21), or akin to (1966: 21) the latter. In the following passage, she mistakenly equated zero with Levinson's most informative form: "Since coreference is more informative than disjointness according to Levinson, the speaker should prefer zero to pronoun and pronoun to lexical NP, wherever possible, in order to express coreference. If, on the other hand, the speaker did not choose the most informative form, the addressee is to deduce that coreference was not intended by the speaker" (1996: 14).

linguist" supplies more detailed information than "the linguist", so it signals that its antecedent, if any, is less accessible than that of "the linguist". Similarly, "this book", more informative than "this", signals an antecedent less accessible than "this" does. In general, "x + modifier" is more informative than "x", and signals lower accessibility of its antecedent than the latter. And zero anaphor, emptiest in terms of semantic content, is only used when the antecedent is most accessible.

By rigidity is meant "how uniquely referring an expression is" (1991: 450). This criterion is useful when no apparent difference between two NPs in terms of lexical content is discernible. A case in point is the distinction between "Mira Ariel" and "the Israeli linguist". They are not differentiated in the information they carry, but the proper name refers more unambiguously to an entity than the definite description. This property enables the proper name to mark lower accessibility of an antecedent than a definite description does. Ariel holds that last names and first names also differ in rigidity. There is a larger variety of last names than first names, at least in the West.

For the contrast between stressed and unstressed pronouns, Ariel invokes the criterion of attenuation, which is close to phonological size (ibid.). The stressed pronoun is less attenuated and signals a less accessible antecedent while the unstressed, being more attenuated, signals a more accessible antecedent. The contrast between expressions like "the United States of America" and "the USA" is also seen as an instance of attenuation.

Ariel (1994: 32) notes, however, that the attenuation criterion sometimes may lead to wrong predictions. For example, definite descriptions like "the table" are more attenuated than full demonstratives like "that table", since "the" is a weakened form of "that". So theoretically "the table" should be used to retrieve an antecedent of highter accessibility than "that table". But her data show that definite descriptions are used with antecedents in the same sentence 2.8% of the time and those in the last sentence 14.1%, while full demonstratives are used in these situations 4.8% and 59.5% respectively. The majority of definite descriptions are used when the antecedent is further away, 45.8% in the same paragraph and 37.3% across the paragraph, for which full demonstratives only account for 20.2% and 15.5% respectively (ibid. ;18).

The third alternative is relevance-theoretic in nature. Authors who have offered analysis in this orientation include R. Kempson (1984, 1988), R. Carston (1988, 1996, 1998), D. Wilson & D. Sperber (1998). They maintain that relevance principle can better account for anaphoric interpretation, among others, than either Horn's principles, or Levinson's.

R. Kempson (1984) represents one of the earliest attempts in this direction. What is central to her analysis of anaphora is a concept of accessibility. "If a speaker uses a pronoun or a definite NP, then he is indicating to the hearer that a representation of an NP type is immediately accessible to him in the sense specified—either from the scenario of the utterance itself, or from concepts expressed by what precedes the anaphor" (p. 4). "But the guarantee of immediate accessibility simply is an intrinsic part of the principle of relevance" (p.5). "The principle of relevance is the guarantee that the speaker believes that the form which he uttered makes immediately accessible to the hearer a context set and a proposition from which he can derive contextual implications"(p. 4).

The other writings of relevance theorists do not concern so much with the details of analysis as with the underlying principles. Carston (1998), for example, tries to show that the distinction between Q-principle and I/R-principle[①] is simply mistaken. The so-called I/R-implicature could be generated by the Q-principle, and Q-implicature by the I/R-principle. Consider,

(108) John was reading a book.

implicates: John was reading a non-dictionary.

(109) Some people like eating raw liver.

implicates: Not everyone likes eating raw liver. (p. 194)

According to Atlas & Levinson (1981: 41), (108) is a case involving the informational enrichment from non-specific to specific, and the specific information is the stereotypical one. That is, the I-principle is at work here. On the other hand, (109) involves the quantitative scale < all, some >, hence, an instance of the Q-implicature. Now Carston contends that the desired interpretations could also be derived in the opposite way. There could be a scale < dictionary, book >, so that the negative implicature could be the result of the speaker's having chosen the lower item from the scale. "And the implicature of (109) could be viewed as providing an informational enrichment of the proposition literally expressed, one whose content is obvious/stereotypical (raw liver is generally assumed to be unappetising) in the way that is typical of I/R-implicatures" (ibid.).[②]

---

① "I/R-principle" means the I-prin-ciple of Levinson's and the R-principle of Horn's. In her view, they are simply the same thing with different names.

② The trouble is that Carston's argument is not applicable to all the cases. There are two other examples in Atlas & Levinson (1981: 41) as follows:

    (1) a. The secretary smiled.

        b. The female secretary smiled.

    (2) a. John had a drink.

To support her view, Carston invokes Richardson & Richardson's (1990) argument that the Q-implicature from <and, or> and conditional perfection from I/R-principles could just as easily be given as cases of the opposite sort of implicature. She quotes from Horn(1984) the opposing schemes of Q- and R-principles as follows:

 Q-based implicature: R-based implicature

 S entails W   S entails W

 "W"implicates "not S"   "W"implicates "S"

(p. 195)

and exemplifies them with (110).

 (110) a. [P and Q] entails [P or Q]

    "[P or Q]" Q-implicates "[not [P and Q]]"

   b. [P iff Q] entails [if P, Q]

    "[if P, Q]" R-implicates "[P iff Q]" (ibid.)

In her view, the alleged clash of principles results from a confusion between what is implicated and what is conveyed. If we observe a three-way distinction between what is said, what is implicated and what is conveyed, we get the following for (110):

 (111) a. what is said: P or Q

    what is implicated: not [P and Q]

    what is conveyed: P or Q but not both

       or: just one of P, Q

   b. what is said: if P, Q

---

  b. John had an alcoholic drink.

Could we have Horn scales like <male secretary, secretary>, <non-alcoholic drink, drink>? On the other hand, could she derive the "not all" interpretation of (3) on the basis of stereotype?

  (3) Some of them went to the film.

what is implicated: if not P, not Q

what is conveyed: P iff Q   (ibid.)

That is, "in both cases, what is conveyed entails what is said and what is implicated is logically independent of what is said (not in an entailment relationship with it). ... **All** the above examples, whether Q-based or R/I-based, involve informational enrichment of what is said; as R&R (1990: 507) put it: 'What Horn, Atlas and Levinson have lost sight of is that it is quite generally the case that what is conveyed properly includes and therefore entails what is said'"(ibid.)[①]

Now Richardson & Richardson take a step further, maintaining that "the exclusive understanding of 'P or Q', which entails the inclusive understanding could be seen as a case of R-implicature and, given a bit of playing about with logical equivalences, the conditional could be claimed to generate a Q-implicature (that is, the negation of a stronger proposition) [as in (112)]" (ibid.).

(112) a. [P or-excl Q] entails [P or-incl Q]

"[P or-incl Q]" R-implicates [P or-excl Q]

b. [not [if(not P), not Q]] entails [if P, Q]

"[if P, Q]" Q-implicates [if(not P), (not Q)]

(by double negation)

But this argument is obviously faulty. First, the fact that "and" entails "or" does not mean that "P or-excl Q" entails "P or-incl Q", since "P or-excl Q" means "P or Q, but not both", while "P or-incl Q" means "P or Q, or both". For example, (113) does not entail (114), as when (113) is true, (114) is not true.

(113) He is a politician or a movie star, but not both.

[①] As we shall point out below, there is a misunderstanding of entailment here.

(114) He is a politician or a movie star, or both.

Secondly, there are severe restrictions on Horn scales. Levinson (1987b: 407) explicitly excludes the possibility of <iff, if> forming a Horn scale, as we noted in section 4.3.1.

Chapter 5: Presupposition

Before 70s, pragmatics was practised without being preached. Early pragmaticians like Grice, and Austin (whose theory we shall introduce in next chapter), did not use the term pragmatics at all.

We said in the Introduction that "pragmatics" was coined by Morris in 1937. But no linguist adopted this term until the 70s, when they discovered that there are not only semantic presuppositions, but also pragmatic presuppositions. In this sense, presupposition acted as the thin end of a wedge, which opened the way for pragmatics to come into linguistics. However, like many other important notions in pragmatics, as indeed in almost any branch of learning, presupposition has its roots in philosophy. Any discussion of it cannot but mention its philosophical tradition.

5.1 The philosophical tradition

The first philosopher who brought it to the notice of the scholarly world is Gottlob Frege, who published an article "On Sense and Reference"① in 1892. In it he first discussed expressions like "the Evening Star" and "the Morning Star", arguing that they have not only reference, but also sense. That is why (1) is tautological, telling us nothing new, whereas (2) is informative, representing an important dis-

---

① The German title is "Über Sinn und Bedeutung", also translated as "On Sense and Nominatum".

covery in astronomy.

(1) The Evening Star is the Evening Star.

(2) The Evening Star is the Morning Star.

Then he went on to examine the sense and reference of sentences. When considering the sentence "He who discovered the elliptical shape of the planetary orbits, died in misery", he said that the relative clause "who discovered the elliptical shape of the planetary orbits" has a reference, and that is Johann Kepler. From sentence (3) we can infer sentence (4).

(3) Kepler died in misery.

(4) There was a man called Kepler.

This kind of inference is not part of the logical meaning of the sentence. Sentence (3) does not tell us directly that (4) is the case. But (4) is the precondition for the use of (3). Without the existence of Kepler, one cannot talk about his dying in misery, or anything at all. Therefore Frege concluded "If anything is asserted there is always an obvious presupposition that the simple or compound proper names used have a reference" (1952 [1892]: 69). He also noted that the same presupposition obtains in the corresponding negative sentence. Sentence (5) also presupposes (4).

(5) Kepler didn't die in misery.

Apart from proper names, which give rise to presupposition, Frege noticed that temporal clauses also contain presuppositions. For example, "After the separation of Schleswig-Holstein from Denmark, Prussia and Austria quarrelled" presupposes that Schleswig-Holstein was once separated from Denmark (ibid.: 71).

The British philosopher Bertrand Russell, however, did not agree with Frege's distinction between sense and reference, which he translated as "meaning" and "denotation". In his article "On Denoting" of 1905, he argued that there are many problems in this distinction, which are "all the result of a wrong analysis of propositions whose verbal expressions contain denoting phrases" (1994 [1905]: 416). So he proposed to analyse such propositions in a different way, for example, the (a) propositions below are analysed as the ones in (b).

(6) a. I met a man.

b. I met x, and x is human.

(7) a. All men are mortal.

b. If x is human, x is mortal.

(8) a. Scott was the author of *Waverley*.

b. It is not always false of x that x wrote *Waverley*, that it is always true of y that if y wrote *Waverley* y is identical with x, and that Scott is identical with x.

In this way, the denoting phrases are broken up, analysed away, or eliminated. They are no longer there in the resultant propositions. The original proposition is now seen as a conjunction of the new propositions.

In the series of lectures delivered at London in 1918, entitled "The Philosophy of Logical Atomism", he said that sentence (9) can be analysed as (10) (1986[1918]: 219).

(9) The present King of France is bald.

(10) There is a c such that c is now King of France and c is bald.[①]

[①] This is a very loose expression. Strictly speaking, it should be "There is a c such that c reigns over France now and c is bald". Otherwise the denoting phrase *King of France* is still there.

In other words, it is analysed as a conjunction of the three propositions in (11):

(11) (a) There is a King of France.

(b) There is no one else who is King of France.

(c) The King of France is bald.

In both the 1905 article and the 1918 one, Russell held the view that (9) is false, while (12) is ambiguous. It can mean either (13) or (14). In the first sense, (12) is true, and in the second, it is false.

(12) The present King of France is not bald.

(13) It is false that there is an entity which is now King of France and is bald.

(14) There is an entity which is now King of France and is not bald.

This line of argument did not meet any criticism until about half a century later when Peter Strawson wrote his "On Referring" in 1950. Strawson not only accused Russell of confusing a sentence with the use of it, but also rose against the latter's view on the truth value of a statement like (15).

(15) The King of France is wise.[①]

He argued that in response to such a statement, nobody would say "That's untrue". If pressed for an opinion of its truth value, the hearer would be inclined to say with some hesitation that he does not think it is true, or it is false. The question of whether the statement is true or false simply does not arise, because there is no such person as the King of France. The statement has no truth value. (1971[1950]: 12)

---

① For the convenience of discussing the distinction between a sentence and its use, Strawson changed the adjective from "bald" to "wise".

When analysing "The King of France is bald", Russell said part of its meaning is that there is a King of France. Strawson did not agree with that either. He admitted that if a man seriously uttered the sentence, his uttering it would in some sense be evidence that he believed that there was a King of France. But it is not the same kind of evidence as that in a man's reaching for his raincoat for his believing that it is raining. Nor would it be the same evidence as that in the man's saying "It's raining" for his believing that it is raining. "To say 'The king of France is wise' is, in some sense, to *imply* that there is a king of France. But this is a very special and odd sense of 'imply'. 'Imply' in this sense is certainly not equivalent to entail (or 'logically implies')" (ibid.).

In the book *Introduction to Logical Theory* published in 1952, Strawson explicitly used the term "presupposition", defined in opposition to entailment. He said a statement like (16) is logically absurd, but this kind of logical absurdity is different from straightforward self-contradiction as found in (17).

(16) All John's children are asleep; but John has no children.

(17) All the men at work on the scaffolding have gone home; but some of them are still at work.

In self-contradiction, an S is conjoined with the denial of S', which is the necessary condition of the truth, simply, of S. In other words, S entails S'. In the case of (16), however, the S is conjoined with the denial of S', which is a necessary condition of THE TRUTH OR FALSITY of S. So we need a new term for the relation between S and S' here, and the one he suggested is "presupposition", or S presupposes S' (p. 175).

5.2 A semantic analysis

Since it was formally integrated into the standard theory of transformational generative grammar in 1965, the study of meaning has caught the interest of many linguists. Presupposition as a type of extra meaning has naturally been studied extensively as well. In this section, we shall introduce three early analyses of presupposition offered by linguists.

5.2.1 Presupposition vs. focus

This is the analysis proposed by Noam Chomsky in his "Deep Structure, Surface Structure and Semantic Interpretation", first published in 1970.[①] In it he discussed, among others, sentences like (18) and (19).

(18) Is it JOHN who writes poetry?

(19) No, it is BILL who writes poetry.

In (18), under the normal intonation the word *John* receives the main stress, and a possible response might be (19). Chomsky proposed to call the information carried by words like *John*, *Bill* focus, and that by the embedded clause "someone writes poetry" presupposition. (18) and (19) differ in focus, but not in presupposition. That is, "the focus is the phrase containing the intonation centre, and the presupposition is determined by the replacement of the focus by the variable" (1975 [1970]: 91). Then he went on to demonstrate that information of this kind is determined by the surface structure.

With sentences like (18) and (19) it is possible to say that the focus and presupposition are determined by the deep structure, as we can

---

① In a footnote, Chomsky mentioned that this part of the paper was drawn from lectures given in Tokyo, in the summer of 1966, and prior to that at MIT and UCLA.

postulate a deep structure of them as follows:[1]

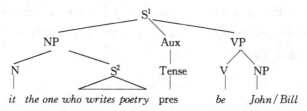

So we can say the focus is the predicate of the dominant proposition of the deep structure and the presupposition the embedded sentence.

But the focused phrase will not necessarily correspond to a phrase in the deep structure, for example, the possible responses to (20) include (21) to (26).

(20) Was he warned to look out for an ex-convict with a red shirt?

(21) No, he was warned to look out for an ex-convict with a red TIE.

(22) No, he was warned to look out for an ex-convict with a CARNATION.

(23) No, he was warned to look out for an ex-convict wearing DUNGAREES.

(24) No, he was warned to look out for an AUTOMOBILE salesman.

(25) No, he was warned to EXPECT a visit from the FBI.

(26) No, he was SIMPLY told to be more cautious.

In other words, the focus can be (a) shirt, (b) a red shirt, (c) with a red shirt, (d) an ex-convict with a red shirt, (e) to look out for an ex-

---

[1] Cf. A. Akmajian and F. Heny 1975: 281.

convict with a red shirt, (f) warned to look out for an ex-convict with a red shirt. But only one of them, i.e. (d), can be the predicate of the dominant proposition of the deep structure, which is something like the following:

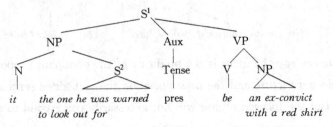

The others cannot. We cannot say "It was SHIRT that he was warned to look out for an ex-convict with a red" or any other.

Sentences like (27) and (28) are said to have derived from the same deep structure in the standard theory, the difference between them is attributed to the operation of an optional transformation known as "dative movement". ①

(27) Did John give the book to BILL?

(28) Did John give Bill the BOOK?

But clearly they differ in terms of focus and presupposition, which being *Bill* and *John gave the book to somebody* in (27), and *book* and *John gave Bill something* in (28).

If we go on to consider sentences with contrastive intonation as in (29), then it becomes more obvious that focus and presupposition are determined by the surface structure.

(29) Did John give the BOOK to Bill?

---

① This rule is something like V - NP$_1$ - {to/for} - NP$_2$ ⇒ V - NP$_2$ - NP$_1$.

This use of presupposition, i.e. in contrast to focus, is somewhat idiosyncratic, but the idea that presupposition is a feature of the surface structure has become the consensus ever since.

5.2.2 As a type of lexical information

Charles Fillmore, well known for "The Case for Case" in 1968, is more interested in explaining grammatical facts from the semantic point of view. In 1969, he published two articles: "Types of Lexical Information" and "Verbs of Judging: An Exercise in Semantic Description", setting out to specify the content of lexicon, part of the base component of transformational grammar.

In the first he explicitly argued that "the presuppositions or 'happiness conditions'① for the use of [an] item, the conditions which must be satisfied in order for [an] item to be used 'aptly'" must also be included in the lexicon (1971 [1969a]: 370). For example, the sentence "Please open the door" can be used as a command only if the hearer is in a position to know what door has been mentioned and only if the door is not at the time of speaking open. The presupposition about the existence and specificity of the door has to do with the use of the definite article and has been much discussed in the philosophical literature on referring, but the presupposition about the closed state of the door, a property of the verb *open*, deserves some discussion, too.

As for the distinction between basic meaning and presupposition, Fillmore suggests "we can separate the basic meaning of a predicate from its presuppositions by describing the former as being relevant to determining whether as an assertion it is true or false, the latter as being relevant to determining whether the sentence is capable of being an

---

① Also known as felicity conditions, discussed in detail in next chapter on speech acts.

assertion in the first place" (ibid. : 381). By way of exemplification, if he were to say (30) about somebody who is an orphan, nobody would say that he was speaking falsely, only that he was speaking inappropriately.

(30) That Harry is still living with his mother proves that he is a bad marriage risk.

The truth of the first *that*-clause is not asserted like the second, but presupposed. This can be shown by replacing *prove* with *doesn't prove*, the presuppositional aspects of (30), concerning the truth of the first *that*-clause, are unaffected by the change.

He also claims that with some verbs the presuppositional content of one is the basic meaning of the other. If somebody says (31), he presupposes that Harry regarded the editorial-writing activity as "bad" and asserts that Harry claimed that Mary was the one who did it;[①] but if he says (32), then he presupposes that Harry regarded Mary as the writer of the editorial and asserts that Harry claimed the editorial-writing behaviour or its result as being "bad".

(31) Harry accused Mary of writing the editorial.

(32) Harry criticized Mary for writing the editorial.

In the second article "Verbs of Judging", he made a detailed analysis of the meanings and presuppositions of verbs like *accuse*, *criticize*, *apologize*, *forgive*, and proposed to represent them in the lexicon as follows:[②]

ACCUSE [Judge, Defendant, Situation (of)] (Performative)

[①] See the note on page 175 for a comment.

[②] There are also sample lexical entries of *blame*, *accuse*, and *criticize* at the end of ⟨pes of Lexical Information", but of a less clear format.

    Meaning: SAY [Judge, "X", Addressee]
        X = RESPONSIBLE [Situation, Defendant]
    Presupposition: BAD [Situation]
CRITICIZE [Judge, Defendant, Situation (for)]
    Meaning: SAY [Judge, "X", Addressee]
        X = BAD [Situation]
    Presupposition: RESPONSIBLE [Defendant, Situation]
    Presupposition: ACTUAL [Situation]
APOLOGIZE [Defendant, Affected (to), Situation (for)] (performative)
    Meaning: SAY [Defendant, "X", Addressee]
        X = REQUEST [Defendant, "FORGIVE [Victim, Defendant, Situation]"]
    Presupposition: BAD [Situation]
    Presupposition: RESPONSIBLE [Defendant, Situation]
    Presupposition: ACTUAL [Situation]
FORGIVE [Affected, Defendant, Situation (for)] (Performative)
    Meaning: DECIDE [Affected, "X"]
        X = ? [Affected will not hold Situation against Defendant]
    Presupposition: BAD [Situation]
    Presupposition: RESPONSIBLE [Defendant, Situation]
    Presupposition: ACTUAL [Situation]

5.2.3 Factive and non-factive

Paul Kiparsky and Carol Kiparsky proposed to make this distinction in their article "Fact" published in 1970. They found that words like *significant* and *likely* are of two types, though they seem to be identically constructed as in (33).

(33) a. It is significant that he has been found guilty.

b. It is likely that he has been found guilty.

There are systematic differences between them as shown in the following sentences:

(34) a. The fact that the dog barked during the night is significant.

b. * The fact that the dog barked during the night is likely.

(35) a. His being found guilty is tragic.

b. * His being found guilty is sure.

(36) a. Their suddenly insisting on very detailed reports makes sense.

b. * Their suddenly insisting on very detailed reports turns out.

(37) a. * He is relevant to accomplish even more.

b. He is likely to accomplish even more.

They call the (a) type factive, which also include such predicates as *odd*, *exciting*, *matter*, *count*, *suffice*, *amuse*, *bother*; and the (b) type non-factive, including *possible*, *true*, *false*, *appear*, *happen*, *chance*, etc.

With verbs taking object clauses, these syntactic criteria effect a similar division into factive and non-factive:

Factive

regret, ignore, grasp, comprehend, take into consideration, take into account, bear in mind, make clear, mind, forget (about), deplore, resent, care (about)

Non-factive

believe, suppose, assert, allege, assume, claim, charge, maintain, conclude, conjecture, intimate, deem, fancy, figure

For example,

(38) a. I regret having agreed to the proposal.

b. * I believe having agreed to the proposal.

(39) a. Everyone ignored Joan's being completely drunk.

b. * Everyone supposed Joan's being completely drunk.

(40) a. I don't mind your saying so.

b. * I maintain your saying so.

These syntactic differences are correlated with a semantic difference: whether the embedded clause is presupposed. There is such a difference even in constructions where both are possible.

(41) a. It is odd that it is raining.

b. It is likely that it is raining.

(42) a. I regret that it is raining.

b. I suppose that it is raining.

The first in each pair carries with it the presupposition that "it is raining." The speaker presupposes that the embedded clause expresses a true proposition, and makes some assertion about that proposition. But the second does not, what is presupposed in the first is asserted as a possibility here. This, they propose, is the basic difference between the two types of predicates. In other words, factivity depends on presupposition, not assertion.

5.2.4 Presupposition-triggers

As a result of the research by linguists like the four mentioned above, the scope of presupposition has been greatly broadened. More words and constructions which give rise to presupposition, known as presupposition-triggers, have been found. In his *Pragmatics* (pp.

181-4), Levinson on the basis of Karttunen (n.d.) lists 13 types of them, which he regards as the set of core phenomena (p. 185), reproduced here with simplification and some other modifications.①

1. *Definite descriptions* (see Strawson 1950, 1952):
   John saw / didn't see *the man with two heads*.
   >> There exists a man with two heads.
2. *Factive predicates* (see Kiparsky & Kiparsky 1970):
   Martha *regrets* / doesn't *regret* drinking John's home brew.
   >> Martha drank John's home brew.
3. *Implicative verbs* (see Karttunen 1971):
   John *managed* / didn't *manage* to open the door.
   >> John tried to open the door.
   (some other implicative verbs: X *forgot to* V >> X ought to have Ved; X *happened to* V >> X didn't plan or intend to V; X *avoided Ving* >> X was expected to, or usually did, or ought to V)
4. *Change of state verbs* (see Sellars 1954; Karttunen 1973):
   John *stopped* / didn't *stop* beating his wife.
   >> John had been beating his wife.
   (some other change of state verbs: *begin*; *continue*; *start*; *carry on*; *cease*; *take* (*as* in X took Y *from* Z >> Y was at/in/with Z); *leave*; *enter*; *come*; *go*; *arrive*)
5. *Iteratives*:
   The flying saucer came / didn't come *again*.

---

① As is done in Levinson's list, the examples provide positive and negative versions separated by / ; the presupposition-triggers, except constructions like cleft sentence, are italicized; and >> stands for "presuppose".

>> The flying saucer came before.
(some other iteratives: *anymore*, *return*, *another time*, *back*, *restore*, *repeat*, *for the nth time*)
6. *Verbs of judging* (see Fillmore 1969b):
Agatha *accused* / didn't *accuse* Ian of plagiarism.
>> (Agatha thinks) plagiarism is bad.[①]
7. *Temporal clauses* (see Frege 1892):
While Chomsky was revolutionizing linguistics, the rest of social science was / wasn't asleep.
>> Chomsky was revolutionizing linguistics.
8. *Cleft sentences* (see Chomsky 1970; Atlas & Levinson 1981):
It was / wasn't Henry that kissed Rosie.
>> Someone kissed Rosie.
(Pseudo-clefts like *What John lost was his wallet* are also included here)
9. *Implicit clefts with stressed constituents* (see Chomsky ibid.; Wilson & Sperber 1979):
Linguistics was / wasn't invented by CHOMSKY.
>> Someone invented linguistics.
10. *Comparisons and contrasts* (see G. Lakoff 1971):
Marianne called Adolph a male chauvinist, and then HE insulted HER.
>> For Marianne to call Adolph a male chauvinist would be

---

① Levinson (1983: 182) comments "This kind of implication is, arguably, not really presuppositional at all; for, unlike other presuppositions, the implications are not attributed to the speaker, so much as to the subject of the verb of judging (see Wilson 1975)."

to insult him.①

(More typically comparisons and contrasts are marked by particles like *too*, *back*, *in return*, and comparative constructions.)

11. *Non-restrictive relative clauses*
The Proto-Harrappans, who flourished 2800 – 2650 B.C., were / were not great temple builders.
\>> The Proto-Harrappans flourished 2800 – 2650 B.C.

12. *Counterfactual conditionals*:
If Hannibal had only had twelve more elephants, the Romance languages would / would not this day exist.
\>> Hannibal didn't have twelve more elephants.

13. *Questions* (see Katz 1972; Lyons 1977):②
   (a) Is there a professor of linguistics at MIT?
   \>> Either there is a professor of linguistics at MIT or there isn't.
   (b) Is Newcastle in England or is it in Australia?
   \>> Newcastle is in England or Newcastle is in Australia.
   (c) Who is the professor of linguistics at MIT?

---

① This is the type of presupposition which relies on people's beliefs and is sometimes called pragmatic presupposition. A more typical example is: John called Mary a Republican and then SHE insulted HIM.

② Levinson (1983: 184) notes questions generally share the presuppositions of their assertive counterparts, and here he is concerned with the interrogative forms themselves. Yes/no questions generally have vacuous presuppositions, being the disjunction of their possible answers as in (a). Alternative questions presuppose the disjunction of their answers, but in this case non-vacuously as in (b). WH-questions introduce the presuppositions obtained by replacing the WH-word by the appropriate existentially quantified variable as in (c).

>> Someone is the professor of linguistics at MIT.

5.3 Problems in the semantic approach

Early linguists' attempts at presupposition were almost all semantic in nature. They view presupposition as a property of the particular linguistic item, verbs like *regret*, *accuse*, *stop* or constructions like cleft sentence, temporal clause. Therefore they have tried to treat presupposition in the same way as basic meaning, as information provided in the lexicon, which is especially evident in the case of Fillmore. However, presupposition differs from basic meaning in a fundamental way: it is variable with the context, both situational and linguistic. In this section, we shall follow Levinson (1983) and discuss them under the headings of defeasibility and the projection problem.

5.3.1 Defeasiblity

In chapter 3, we mentioned that conversational implicatures have some distinct properties, and defeasibility, or cancellability, is one of them. Now this seems to be a property of presupposition as well. In some contexts, a presupposition is defeasible. For example, (43) will usually have the presupposition in (44).

(43) At least John won't have to regret that he did a Ph.D.

(44) John did a Ph.D.

But if (43) is uttered when John has just failed to get into a doctoral course, then it will not have that presupposition. The situational context, the background knowledge, is in direct contradiction to the presupposition. In other words, it is cancelled, defeated, by the context, the background knowledge.

Now let's have a look at a slightly different pair of sentences: (45) and (46), while the former presupposes (47), the latter does not.

(45) Sue cried before she finished her thesis.

(46) Sue died before she finished her thesis.

(47) Sue finished her thesis.

This can be seen as a case of cancellation by a linguistic context, as the word *cried* in (45) has been changed to *died* in (46). But more generally it has to do with the background assumption about the world. That is, we assume Sue is an ordinary person. If, on the other hand, we assume her to be a spirit or somebody with magic power, then perhaps the presupposition will remain intact in (46). That is why Levinson (ibid.: 188) calls it a "belief context" to be subsumed under the situational. Another example of this type Levinson (ibid.: 187f) cites, originally due to Karttunen (1973), is (48), in which whether (49) is presupposed depends on how one classifies Simone de Beauvoir, a feminist or not. In contrast, (50) is more likely to presuppose (49), as the U.S. President will not generally be held as a feminist.

(48) If the Vice-Chancellor invites Simone de Beauvoir to dinner, he'll regret having invited a feminist to his table.

(49) The Vice-Chancellor has invited a feminist to his table.

(50) If the Vice-Chancellor invites the U.S. President to dinner, he'll regret having invited a feminist to his table.

A presupposition may also be cancelled by a linguistic context as in (51)[1] and (52).

(51) You say that someone in this room will betray you. Well maybe so. But it won't be Luke who will betray you, it won't be Paul, it won't be Matthew, and it certainly won't be John. Therefore no one in this room is actually

---

[1] The original version is due to E. L. Keenan (1971: 52).

going to betray you.

(52) A: Well we've simply got to find out if Serge is a KGB infiltrator.
B: Who if anyone would know?
C: The only person who would know for sure is Alexis; I've talked to him and he isn't aware that Serge is on the KGB payroll. So I think Serge can be trusted.

With predicates like *aware*, *know*, the use of the first person subject will also cancel the presupposition usually carried by other subjects. For example, (53) presupposes (55), but (54) does not.

(53) John doesn't know that Bill came.
(54) I don't know that Bill came.
(55) Bill came.

The cancellation of presupposition in (54) may be called intra-sentential cancellation, as against that in (51) and (52), which are inter-sentential. But the intra-sentential cancellation is really the topic of the next section, the projection problem.

5.3.2 The projection problem

The term "projection" comes from transformational grammar, in which it refers to the assignment of semantic interpretation of a sentence on the basis of the semantic interpretation of its constituents. In the present context, it refers to the interpretation of a complex sentence[①] on the basis of its constituent clauses. It is discovered that the presupposition of a constituent clause may not be inherited by the complex sentence as a whole.

First, it may be overtly denied by a constituent clause as in (56)

---

① As is noted in Chapter 3, the term "complex" covers "compound".

and (57).

(56) John didn't manage to pass his exams, in fact he didn't even try.

(57) John doesn't regret doing a useless Ph. D. in linguistics because in fact he never did do one.

It is because of this special feature of presupposition that we can say (58), which seems to support Russell's view that (12), reproduced here as (59), is ambiguous.

(58) The present King of France isn't bald, because there is no such person.

(59) The present King of France isn't bald.

R. Kempson (1977: 152) found an authentic example from Strawson's article "On Referring", the last sentence of which reads:

(60) Neither Aristotelian nor Russellian rules give the exact logic of any expression of ordinary language; for ordinary language has no exact logic.

This ambiguity explanation, however, is not acceptable to those taking the pragmatic approach, so a solution on some other principle is yet to be supplied.

Secondly, it may be suspended by a constituent clause. Karttunen (1973) suggested that the presuppositions carried by some complement clauses may be blocked by some verbs of propositional attitude like *want*, *believe*, *imagine*, *dream*, and verbs of saying like *announce*, *claim*, *say*, *tell*. For example,

(61) Loony old Harry believes he's the King of France.

(62) Nixon announced his regret that he did not know what his subordinates were up to.

(63) Nato claims that the nuclear deterrent is vital.

"However", Levinson (1983: 195) contends "it is far from clear that this is generally true." He supplied such counterexamples as:

(64) The mechanic didn't tell me that my car would never run properly again.

(65) Churchill said that he would never regret being tough with Stalin.

Even in (66), a modified (61), there would not be the so-called suspension.

(66) Loony old Mary believes she's the Queen of England.

More convincing examples of suspension are perhaps induced by *if*-clauses, as shown in the following:

(67) John didn't cheat again, if indeed he ever did.

(68) Harry clearly doesn't regret being a CIA agent, if he actually ever was one.

The *if*-clause in these examples throws doubt on the presupposition, or calls it into question. In (69) below, the presupposition is directly made conditional, therefore it evaporates. ① The disjunction in (70) has a similar function as the conditional in (69).

(69) If John does linguistics, he will regret doing it.

(70) Either John has no wife, or his wife is away.

---

① When discussing the difference between *even though* and *even if*, Quirk et al (1985: 1099) have said something related to the question we are considering here. In reference to (1) and (2), they remark "Whereas the *even though* clause in (1) presupposes 'you dislike ancient monuments', the *even if* clause in (2) leaves open whether that is so or not. The presupposition of (1) can [also] be cancelled by adding modal *may* or a hedging adverbial such as *perhaps*."

(1) Even though you dislike ancient monuments, Warwick Castle is worth a visit.

(2) Even if you dislike ancient monuments, Warwick Castle is worth a visit.

5.4 The pragmatic approach

Problems in the semantic approach forced linguists to find some alternative solutions. The one that seems most promising is the pragmatic approach. In this section, we shall introduce three such proposals.

5.4.1 Holes, plugs and filters

These notions were first proposed by L. Karttunen in his "Presuppositions of Compound Sentences" of 1973, and developed in two papers written together with S. Peters: "Conventional Implicature in Montague Grammar" in 1975 and "Conventional Implicature" in 1979.

In comparison to entailment, presupposition may survive in some linguistic contexts, the best known of which is negation. For example, (71) has both a presupposition as in (72) and an entailment as in (73), whereas (74) only has the presupposition in (72), but not the entailment in (73).

(71) The chief constable arrested three men.
(72) There is a chief constable.
(73) The chief constable arrested two men.
(74) The chief constable didn't arrest three men.

The other contexts, in which presupposition will survive while entailment will not, include modal operators such as *possible*, *perhaps*, *may*, conditionals and disjunctions. Thus, presupposition (72) will also survive in (75). And the presupposition of (76), i.e. (77), will survive in (79) and (80), but the entailment of (76), i.e. (78), will not.

(75) It's possible that the chief constable arrested three men.
(76) The two thieves were caught again last night.

(77) The two thieves had been caught before.

(78) One of the two thieves was caught last night.

(79) Either the two thieves were caught again last night, or P. C. Katch will be losing his job.

(80) If the two thieves were caught again last night, P. C. Katch will get an honourable mention.

These contexts, which allow presuppositions to go through, but not entailments, are termed holes by Karttunen.

In contrast to holes, Karttunen at that time thought verbs of propositional attitude like *want*, *believe*, *imagine*, *dream* and verbs of saying like *announce*, *claim*, *say*, *tell* are plugs to block presuppositions to go through. But as has been pointed out earlier that this is a bit dubious.

Now as a matter of fact, the holes are not always functional either. However, Karttunen contends there are filtering conditions as follows: [①]

1. In a sentence of the form *if p then q*, (and also, perhaps, in a sentence of the form *p & q*) the presupposition of the parts, *r*, will be inherited by the whole UNLESS *q* presupposes *r* and *p* entails *r*;

2. In a sentence of the form *p or q*, the presupposition of the parts, *r*, will be inherited by the whole UNLESS *q* presupposes *r* and ~ *p* entails *r*.

And the conditional, disjunction, and conjunction, which let some presuppositions through but not others, are known as filters.

In this way the cancellation of presupposition in sentences like

---

[①] From Levinson (1983: 197), with a minor modification.

(69) and (70), reproduced here as (81) and (82), Karttunen claims, can be explained systematically.

(81) If John does linguistics, he will regret doing it.

(82) Either John has no wife, or his wife is away.

That is, the presupposition of q in (81), i.e. "John does linguistics", is entailed by p; and that of q in (82), i.e. "John has a wife", is entailed by $\sim p$.

In their later works, Karttunen and Peters reallocated what is generally known as presupposition to other pragmatic inference. In "Conventional Implicature", for example, they argued that the subjunctive conditional construction (or counterfactual conditional) is not really a presupposition-trigger. They considered sentences (83), (84) and (85).

(83) If it were raining outside, the drumming on the roof would drown out our voices.

(84) If Mary were allergic to penicillin, she would have exactly the symptoms she is showing.

(85) If Shakespeare were the author of *Macbeth*, there would be proof in the Globe Theater's records for the year 1605.

In their view, only (83) presupposes that the antecedent is false. The antecedent of (84), on the other hand, is true. This is offered as a possible reason why Mary has the symptoms she is showing, so it indicates at least that the speaker does not know that the antecedent is false.

As for (85), its antecedent could be true or false depending on its context. In the context where the Globe Theater's records for the year 1605 have just been searched and found to lack any evidence of Shakespeare's authorship, the antecedent is false. But in the context where one is speculating about how the authorship of *Macbeth* could be established, the antecedent could be true. And if one goes on to say "Let's go through them once more to make sure we didn't overlook that proof", then the falsity assumed in the first context also evaporates.

Therefore the authors propose to treat the supposed counterfactual presupposition as a case of particularized conversational implicature, which varies with the context, and can be explained on the basis of the Gricean maxims. For example, when the consequent clause is obviously false, as is the case in (83), the hearer will, on the basis of the maxim of Quality, work out that the antecedent is false.

They also argue that particles like *too*, *either*, *also*, *even*, *only*, factive verbs like *forget*, *realize*, *take into account*, implicative verbs like *manage*, *fail*, cleft and pseudo-cleft constructions are not presupposition-triggers either. The so-called presuppositions are only instances of conventional implicatures. They discussed in detail the word *even*, which we mentioned in section 3.2.3.

After they have successfully reallocated, to their mind at least, presupposition to implicature, they set out to account for conventional implicature in the framework of Montague grammar, in which meanings are represented by logical expressions. The logical expressions, and hence the phrases whose meaning they represent, are systematically related to nonlinguistic objects, such as individuals, truth values, sets, properties, propositions, and the like. In order to account for implicature, Karttunen and Peters extended Montague's system. They suggest there are two types of meaning, so there should be two types of expression as well. They renamed the logical expression in Montague's original system extension expression and called the new expression implicature expression. Each phrase is associated with these two types of expression in the lexicon. Then there is a third expression to govern the projection of implicature, to determine whether the complex sentence will inherit the implicature of its constituents, known as heritage expression. In this way, the notions of holes, plugs and filters are incorporated into the new system.

For example, the heritage expression that captures the filtering condition for conditionals, according to Levinson (ibid.: 208), will be something like:

> The conventional implicatures of *if p then q* (and also perhaps of *p and q*) are the conventional implicatures of *p* together with the expression "if *p* then the conventional implicatures of *q*".

The different presuppositions[①] carried by sentences (86) and (87) can thus be explained as: (86) has the implicatures (88) and (89); whereas (87) has (88) and (90), the second of which is tautological and vacuous.

(86) If John has children, he will regret doing linguistics.
(87) If John does linguistics, he will regret doing it.
(88) John exists.
(89) If John has children, he does linguistics.
(90) If John does linguistics, he does linguistics.

Plugs and holes will also have their respective heritage expressions that block or allow the implicature expressions to ascend to become the conventional implicatures, or presuppositions, of the whole.

But there are also problems with this theory. As is shown in the heritage expression for conditionals, the heritage expression for con-

---

[①] In Levinson's (1983: 217) view, Karttunen and Peters' argument that the so-called presuppositions are in fact implicatures was little more than a terminological switch.

junctions is identical to it. In that case, it will incorrectly predict that (91) and (92) presuppose (93).

(91) It is possible that John has children and it is possible that his children are away.

(92) Perhaps John has children but perhaps John's children are away.

(93) John has children.

A way out is to allow (91) and (92) to be interpreted as non-modal first. However, if the first clause is negative as in (94), the revised version will produce contradiction.

(94) Perhaps John has no children but perhaps John's children are away.

Then perhaps we would have to interpret the *but* in (94) as *or*, to say that there are two alternative speculations here. "So", Levinson (ibid.: 210) concludes "it is the use of an utterance in discourse for specific conversational purposes, rather than the logical properties of the particular connective, that seems to determine the appropriate filtering condition."

5.4.2 Potential and actual presuppositions

This distinction was proposed by G. Gazdar in his *Pragmatics: Implicature, Presupposition and Logical Form* and "A Solution to the Projection Problem", both published in 1979.

His theory has two main characteristics. First he makes a distinction between the potential and the actual, both of implicature and presupposition. And he calls the potential implicature im-plicature, the potential presupposition pre-supposition. In his view, sentences have their potential implicatures and presuppositions all the time, but only those "which are satisfiable in the context of utterance actually emerge as the implicatures and presuppositions of the utterance" (1979b: 68). That is, the context, both the situational and linguistic, is a cancelling mechanism, which determines which potentials will become actuals. And it is defined, in Levinson's (1983: 212) words, as "a set of propositions that are mutually known by participants, or which would at least be accepted to be non-controversial." What is more, the context augments as the conversation goes on. The propositions expressed by the utterance, both explicitly and implicitly, i.e. those entailed, implicated and presupposed by the utterance, will be added to the context, if they are consistent with propositions already in the context. In other words, with reference to implicatures and presuppositions, only those actual implicatures and presuppositions will become part of the new context. Those potential implicatures and presuppositions which are not satisfiable in the existing context, not consistent with it, will be cancelled. To ensure the correct generation of implicatures and presuppositions, this augmentation of context proceeds in a particular order: entailments > implicatures (clausal > scalar) > presuppositions.[①] And this is the second important feature of the theory.

Now let's have a look at the way this theory works in practice. (95) is the example we considered earlier as (43).

(95) At least John won't have to regret that he did a Ph.D.

Since *regret* is a factive verb, the embedded clause is pre-supposed. But whether this potential presupposition will get through depends on the context. Suppose it is uttered when John finally got a job after obtaining a Ph.D., then the pre-supposition will become actual. But if it is uttered when John failed to get into a doctoral course, then the

---

[①] Cf. Gazdar (1979a: 135) and Levinson (1983: 213).

context will block it. The cancellation of pre-supposition (97) of (96), and (99) of (98) may be explained in the same way.

(96) Kissinger ceased to be Secretary of States before the third world war started.

(97) The third world war started.

(98) The student said that he hadn't realized that Wales was a republic.

(99) Wales is a republic.

The pre-suppositions in these examples are cancelled by the situational context, the knowledge of the world. Now we shall turn to cases in which the pre-suppositions are cancelled by entailments, which may be regarded as linguistic context in another sense.

(100) John doesn't know that Bill came.

(101) I don't know that Bill came.

(102) Bill came.

(100) to (102) are (53) to (55) reproduced, in which (101), unlike (100), does not have the presupposition in (102), which is inconsistent with the entailment of (101), namely, "as far as I know it is not the case that Bill came". As entailment is ordered before presupposition, by the time we come to process presupposition, the entailment "Bill didn't come" has already been built into the context. So the presupposition "Bill came" will be blocked.

(103) John didn't manage to pass his exams, in fact he didn't even try.

(104) John doesn't regret doing a useless Ph. D. in linguistics because in fact he never did do one.

(103) and (104), (56) and (57) reproduced, are also cases of presuppositions being directly denied by entailments.

Armed with this mechanism of cancellation, we can better account for sentences like "The present King of France isn't bald, because there's no such person". That is, the potential presupposition carried by the definite description is cancelled by the entailment.

The clausal implicature will also have this function to stop those potential presuppositions which are inconsistent with it from becoming actual. The sentence about Simone de Beauvoir, reproduced here as (105), is a case in point.

(105) If the Vice-Chancellor invites Simone de Beauvoir to dinner, he'll regret having invited a feminist to his table.

Other examples of this type are:

(106) It's possible that John is sorry that he was rude.

(107) If there is a King of France, the King of France doesn't any longer live in Versailles.

For examples of pre-supposition blocked by scalar implicature we may reconsider (51), reproduced here as (108).

(108) You say that someone in this room will betray you. Well maybe so. But it won't be Luke who will betray you, it won't be Paul, it won't be Matthew, and it certainly won't be John. Therefore no one in this room is actually going to betray you.

That is, the use of *maybe* at the beginning, which means the same as *possibly*, implicates that "it is not necessarily so", since *possibly* and *necessarily* are on the same scale, and the former is a weak term while the latter strong. In this way the pre-supposition that "it is necessarily the case that someone in this room will betray you" is cancelled.

5.4.3 A principled account

The examples above suggest that Gazard's theory works quite

well. However, Levinson is not satisfied with it on one account, namely, Gazard has to supply the potential presupposition one by one. He argues it is more preferable to predict the presuppositions from the semantic content of presupposition-triggers, e.g. *regret*, *aware*, by means of general pragmatic principles (1983: 216). The item-by-item treatment suggests that presuppositions are attached to presupposition-triggers merely by arbitrary conventions, but the linguistic items that give rise to presuppositions seem to be universal across language boundaries. The translation equivalents in languages of quite different families seem to have similar presuppositions. Hence Levinson has proposed a principled account, which first appeared in an article "It-clefts, Informativeness and Logical Form: Radical Pragmatics" of 1981, written in collaboration with J. D. Atlas, and was repeated in his *Pragmatics* of 1983.

Their basic idea is that the presupposition carried by a linguistic item is determined by its semantic content. As long as a word has the required semantic content, it will generate a particular presupposition, though the relation between the semantic content and the form is arbitrary. And there are pragmatic principles governing the realization of presuppositions, i.e. whether a particular presupposition will be realized depends on the use. Therefore their task is two-fold: to specify the semantic content, or what they call the logical form, of words and sentences; and to establish pragmatic principles which are generally applicable.

For example, Levinson (1983: 221) says the logical form for (109) would be something like (110).

(109) It was John that Mary kissed.

(110) $\lambda x \ (x = \text{John}) \ (\gamma x \ \text{kiss} \ (\text{Mary}, \ x))$

The logical device lambda-extraction is used to construct complex properties, such as, "x equals John", "x has the property of being kissed by Mary". And the gamma-operator, also known as group-operator, constructs collective terms, i.e. terms which refer to a group of individuals. So this logical form means the term x has a complex of properties, which include "x equals John" and "x as a group has the property of being kissed by Mary". Adding these two together we get "A group kissed by Mary has the property of being identical to John". This logical form indicates that the logical subject of (109) is "a group kissed by Mary", which is responsible for the inference in (111).

(111) Mary kissed somebody.

Levinson claims that the logical subject of a sentence identifies its topic, or what it is about. And there should be a general pragmatic principle, "if a sentence is about t, then the existence or actuality of t can be assumed to be non-controversial or given, unless there are specific indications or assumptions to the contrary" (ibid.).

Now one may notice what this pragmatic principle postulates is what is more usually known as presupposition. But Levinson calls it entailment on the ground that it satisfies the condition for entailment, i.e. whenever (109) is true, (111) is also true; and if (111) is not true, (109) will not be true either. This is in fact a very general phenomenon. The notorious example about the King of France, reproduced here as (112), may be said to entail (113), pace Strawson (1950, 1952).

(112) The present King of France is bald.

(113) There is a King of France now.

Unlike their negative counterparts, these sentences are not subject to overt denial, which may be seen as evidence supporting this treatment.

For example, (114) and (115), in contrast to (116) and (117), are not acceptable.

(114) * It was John that Mary kissed, but in fact she didn't kiss anyone.

(115) * The present King of France is bald, but there is no King of France now.

(116) John didn't manage to pass his exams, in fact he didn't even try.

(117) John doesn't regret doing a useless Ph. D. in linguistics because in fact he never did do one.

For the negative sentences, Levinson has a different analysis. The logical form of (118), he suggests, is (119), reading "It is not the case that a group that Mary kissed has the property of being identical to John".

(118) It wasn't John that Mary kissed.

(119) $\sim (\lambda x \ (x = \text{John}) \ (\gamma x \ \text{kiss}(\text{Mary}, x)))$ (ibid.: 222)

In other words, the negation is external, or of wide-scope, i. e. the whole sentence is negated. But, Levinson argues, this kind of negation is not informative. It merely states that something is not the case, without indicating how it fails to be true, e. g. whether it is because Mary didn't kiss anybody at all, or she kissed somebody else. So Levinson proposes another pragmatic principle which allows us to read into an utterance more information than it actually contains. This principle is dubbed the principle of informativeness. As is mentioned in the section on neo-Gricean principles, this principle has been developed into a full-blown theory later. It instructs the speaker to "say as little as necessary", but requires the hearer to "amplify the informational content of the speaker's utterance, by finding the most SPECIFIC interpretation, up to what [he] judge[s] to be the speaker's m-intended point". And specifically the hearer should "(a) assume that stereotypical relations obtain between referents or events, ... (b) assume the existence or actuality of what a sentence is 'about' if that is consistent with what is taken for granted.①..." (Levinson 1987b: 402).

Concerning (118), Levinson suggests, if nothing indicates to the contrary, its logical form should be enriched as (120), reading "A group that Mary kissed has the property of not being identical to John".

(120) $\lambda x(x \neq \text{John})(\gamma x \text{ kiss}(\text{Mary}, x))$ (1983: 222)

That is, it becomes an internal, or narrow scope, negation, only the predicate is negated. The logical subject, as in the positive, is still "a group kissed by Mary". Hence the inference in (111) is still there.② But this enriched interpretation, the internal negation interpretation, is an implicature, which is obtained on the assumption that the speaker is observing the Gricean cooperative principle and its maxims, including the I-principle. And the inference in (111) is also an implicature. What is more, as it is an implicature which obtains when nothing indicates to the contrary, i. e. the default interpretation, or preferred reading, it belongs to the generalized type.

To summarize, in this approach the logical form of the negative particle *not* is external, or of wide-scope. In actual use it will be inter-

---

① This (b) is the previous principle we considered. In other words, in this new form these two principles are no longer separated.

② If one wants to use negation in the external sense, one has to use a marked form, by adding "in fact she didn't kiss anyone", just as "The King of France isn't bald, there is no such person", or "It won't be Luke who will betray you, it won't be Paul, it won't be Matthew, and..."

preted as internal, or of narrow scope, if nothing indicates to the contrary. This treatment is like that for *or* before. The logical meaning of *or* is inclusive, the exclusive interpretation is due to a generalized implicature: the use of *or* implicates the stronger term *and* does not hold.

In this way, Levinson reallocated the presupposition of positive sentences to entailment and that of their negative counterparts to conversational implicature. A problem arises is whether presuppositions share the basic features of conversational implicature. For example, it is generally held that presuppositions are tied to certain aspects of the surface structure, to particular words and constructions, e.g. *regret, manage, stop*, cleft sentence, temporal clause. In other words, they are detachable. If one changes the surface form, uses a synonym or near-paraphrase, the presupposition will disappear. Now Levinson argues this problem is more apparent than real. In fact, presuppositions are, like conversational implicatures, also non-detachable (ibid.: 223). For example, (121 a-g) all presuppose (122).

(121) a. John regrets that he ate all the pudding.
b. John is sorry that he ate all the pudding.
c. John repents of having eaten all the pudding.
d. John is unhappy that he ate all the pudding.
e. John feels contrite about eating all the pudding.
f. John feels penitent about eating all the pudding.
g. John feels remorse about eating all the pudding.

(122) John ate all the pudding.

If Levinson were right, that is, presupposition could be reallocated to entailment and conversational implicature, then in this chapter we begin with the discovery of presupposition, but end with the disappearance of it. However, I do not think he is. It is awkward, to me at least, to treat the positive of a sentence and its negative counterpart as having two types of inference, and this very peculiarity may be used as evidence for treating presupposition as a special type of inference, different from both entailment and conversational implicature.

A more serious problem is that Levinson attributes the entailment "Mary kissed somebody" to the principle that the existence or actuality of what the subject refers to should be non-controversial, on the condition that there are no indications to the contrary. This implies if there are contrary indications, there would be no such entailment, i.e. the entailment is cancellable. If so, then there is no difference between entailment and conversational implicature any more, since one can say *some* means (i.e. entails) *not all*, if nothing indicates to the contrary. What is more, as pointed out earlier, Levinson later (1987) incorporated this principle into his principle of informativeness, which makes the generation of entailment dependent on pragmatic principles as well. This again blurs the distinction between entailment and conversational implicature.

Chapter 6: Speech Acts

Speech act theory is the first major theory in pragmatics, initially proposed in the 50s and widely discussed in the 60s and 70s. There is an enormous literature on it from both the philosophical and linguistic point of view. In this chapter, however, we shall first confine our attention to the ideas of John Langshaw Austin and John R. Searle, and only touch on the suggestions raised by linguists in the latter part.

J. L. Austin, the originator of speech act theory, was one of the ordinary language philosophers[1] at Oxford, and a leading one at that. As a result of the work of scholars like G. Frege, B. Russell, G. Moore and L. Wittgenstein, there was a linguistic turn in western philosophy at the beginning of this century. Philosophers then formed the opinion that many philosophical problems were in fact problems of language, and could be solved if we did a proper analysis of language. Consequently this movement of philosophy came to be known as analytic philosophy, or linguistic philosophy, of which ordinary language philosophy was a major development. Another major school of analytic philosophy was called logical positivism, or logical empiricism, represented by people like Moritz Schlick, Rudolf Carnap, Alfred Tarski and Alfred Ayer. At the risk of oversimplification, these two schools differ in that logical positivism thinks that everyday language is defi-

---

[1] Other notable philosophers of this school include H. Paul Grice and P. Strawson.

cient and needs to be improved, or replaced by an ideal, logical, or artificial language, while ordinary language philosophy maintains otherwise.

Another difference between them concerns the theory of meaning. Logical positivists argue that unless a sentence can be verified, i.e. tested for its truth or falsity, it is meaningless. And they have developed a theory of meaning on the basis of truth conditions. Ordinary language philosophers hold a different view. P. Strawson (1950), for instance, insists on making a distinction between a sentence and the use of a sentence. To his mind, a sentence in the abstract cannot be assigned any truth value. It is only when a sentence is used in actual situations, will it be possible to say whether it is true or not.

The theory we are concerned with in this chapter grows out of Austin's conscious effort to combat the traditional bias, which culminates in logical positivism, to the study of sentences capable of being true or false. His first shot at the theory is that there are two types of sentence: those that are used to do things and those that are used to describe things. The former is dubbed performative, which cannot be said to be true or false, and the latter constative.

6.1 The performative-constative dichotomy

In this section, we are going to present an overall view of this dichotomy: how it came into being, Austin's efforts to characterize performatives, and its collapse.

6.1.1 Early development

Austin began to form ideas about this distinction in the late 30s, when he was working on the question of "promising". He discovered that to say "I promise" is not just to say something, not just to make an autobiographical assertion about oneself like "I play cricket", but to do it, i.e. to make a promise. Then he started to think about the general phenomenon of utterances which look autobiographical, as if the speaker were saying of himself that he does something, whereas in fact he is—essentially, primarily—*doing* it.①

In his article "Other Minds" published in 1946, Austin compared "I know" to "I promise". He argued that the dictum "If I know, I can't be wrong" only makes sense in the following way: "You are prohibited from saying 'I know it is so, but I may be wrong', just as you are prohibited from saying 'I promise I will, but I may fail'. If you are aware you may be mistaken, you ought not to say you know, just as, if you are aware you may break your word, you have no business to promise" (Austin 1970: 98). "When I say 'I know', I *give others my word*: I *give others my authority for saying* that 'S is P'" (ibid.: 99). In other words, the sentence "If I promise, I can't fail" means I am committed to performance; you are entitled to expect, rely on, and indeed demand that. And the sentence "If I know that S is P, I can't be wrong" means I am specifically committed to the proposition that S is P, and that you are entitled to rely on that and indeed to say, on my authority, that you know it too.② Austin called expressions like "I promise", "I know" ritual phrases, and said "Utterance of obvious ritual phrases, in the appropriate circumstances, is not *describing* the action we are doing, but *doing* it" (ibid.: 103).

---

① Cf. G. J. Warnock (1989: 105-6).

② We must hasten to add that although Austin's general observation about ritual phrases here is illuminating, his grouping of "I know" together with "I promise" seems regrettably wrong. When someone says "I promise", he is performing the action of promising. But when someone says "I know", he is obviously not, in saying it, performing the action of knowing. Austin may have felt something queer about it when he was writing *How to Do Things with Words*. That is why the verb "know", though included in the category of expositives, has a question mark beside it like some other verbs (see p. 216).

In 1952, Austin began to give a series of lectures entitled "Words and Deeds" in Oxford. In 1955, when he went to the United States to deliver the William James lectures, he revised the lecture notes and renamed it "How to Do Things with Words". The book of the same title compiled by J. O. Urmson in 1962 was based on these notes. It consists of 12 lectures, in the first 7 of which Austin discussed the performative-constative dichotomy.

He first isolated sentences like (1), (2) and (3),

(1) I name this ship the *Queen Elizabeth*.

(2) I give and bequeath my watch to my brother.

(3) I bet you sixpence it will rain tomorrow.

arguing that they form a special class in that

A. they do not "describe" or "report" or constate anything at all, are not "true or false"; and

B. the uttering of the sentence is, or is a part of, the doing of an action, which again would not *normally* be described as, or as "just", saying something. (Austin 1975 [1962]: 5)[1]

For example, (1) said by the Queen of England at a ship-launching ceremony is not a description of what she was doing at the time of speaking. To utter this sentence is to perform the very action of naming the ship. It is different from (4) said by a chemistry teacher in a demonstration of an experiment, which describes the teacher's action at the time of speaking.

(4) I pour some liquid into the tube.

The utterance of this sentence is not the performance of the action of pouring some liquid. The teacher cannot pour any liquid into a tube by

---

[1] Quotations of Austin from this book will henceforth be given only page numbers.

simply uttering these words. He must accompany his words with the actual pouring of some liquid into the tube. Otherwise one can accuse him of making a false statement. But one cannot say the Queen made a false statement, even though she did not accompany her words with the action of actually writing *Queen Elizabeth* on the ship. Sentences like (1) are named by Austin performatives, and those like (4) constatives.

6.1.2 Felicity conditions

Although performatives cannot be true or false, there are still ways in which they will go wrong, be unhappy, or infelicitous. In other words, there are conditions to be met to produce an appropriate performative. And the felicity conditions Austin suggested in these lectures are as follows:

(A. 1) There must exist an accepted conventional procedure having a certain conventional effect, that procedure to include the uttering of certain words by certain persons in certain circumstances, and further,

(A. 2) the particular persons and circumstances in a given case must be appropriate for the invocation of the particular procedure invoked.

(B. 1) The procedure must be executed by all participants both correctly and

(B. 2) completely.

(Γ.[①]1) Where, as often, the procedure is designed for use by

---

[①] Austin (pp. 15-6) explains that the use of a Greek letter instead of the Roman ones is meant to bring out a distinction between them. When any of the first four rules is violated, the intended act is void, not achieved, or without effect, known as misfire. Whereas in the

persons having certain thoughts or feelings, or for the inauguration of certain consequential conduct on the part of any participant, then a person participating in and so invoking the procedure must in fact have those thoughts or feelings, and the participants must intend so to conduct themselves, and further

(Γ. 2) must actually so conduct themselves subsequently.

(pp. 14−5)

When illustrating condition A1, Levinson (1983: 229f.) says in Muslin cultures, a man may achieve a divorce by saying to his wife "I hereby divorce you" three times in succession.① The utterance of these words constitutes the performance of divorce. As a British citizen, however, he cannot divorce his wife in this way. There is no such a conventional procedure in British society. To explain condition A2, we may continue with the case of the Muslin divorce. That is, according to the Muslin tradition only the man has the right to divorce his wife in this way, and he has to address it to his wife, otherwise it will still be infelicitous. As for the conditions of the second class, the Muslin man must use the correct sentence. If he does not, then it will not have the expected effect. And he must say it three times in succession. Once or twice is not enough to bring it off. Thirdly, the speaker must mean what he says. When promising, for example, he must be prepared to fulfill it. And he must do so subsequently.

---

latter two cases, a violation will result in an abuse of the procedure.

① In feudal China, there was a similar convention, though by the written medium in this case. That is, a man could divorce his wife by writing a letter of divorce. And as a matter of fact, the Muslin tradition is also changing. In Egypt, for example, a law was passed in the early 80s, stipulating that divorce is no longer exclusively a man's right. And it must be approved by the legal authorities.

In the discussion of these conditions, however, Austin gradually realized that they are not really useful for separating performatives from constatives. For example, it is true that with some performatives, there will be a conventional procedure and the procedure must be executed correctly and completely. So at the wedding ceremony in Britain, when the priest asks the bridegroom, "Wilt thou have this woman to thy wedded wife... and, forsaking all other, keep thee only unto her, so long as ye both shall live?" he could only answer "Yes, I will". He cannot use other expressions, even if they are synonymous. But it is also true that with some performatives, there may not be such a strict restriction. At a ship-launching ceremony, the namer may either use "name" or "christen". To make a promise, one can either say "I promise" or "I give my word". On the other hand, the so-called constatives may also be infelicitous in these ways. "The present King of France is bald" is infelicitous in the same way as "I bequeath you my Sansovino" said by someone who does not have a Sansovino. They both presuppose the existence of something. And the person who makes a statement must also have the requisite thoughts, feelings and intentions. To make a promise one must have the intention to carry it out. Similarly, to state that something is the case, one must believe it. One cannot say "The cat is on the mat, but I don't believe it".[1]

6.1.3　Collapse of the dichotomy

Having failed to separate performatives from constatives by means of felicity conditions, Austin tried to explore whether there are some grammatical criteria for distinguishing them. He noticed that the

---

[1]　This phenomenon has already been noticed by G. E. Moore, known as Moore's paradox.

classic examples of performatives have some common features, namely, they take the first person singular subject, simple present tense, indicative mood, and active voice. So (5), (6), (7) and (8) are not performatives.

(5) She names this ship the *Queen Elizabeth*.

(6) I'm naming this ship the *Queen Elizabeth*.

(7) Name this ship the *Queen Elizabeth*.

(8) This ship is named the *Queen Elizabeth*.

However, he immediately refuted it on the ground that they are neither sufficient nor necessary conditions on a performative. On the one hand, constatives may also have this form as is shown in (4). On the other, performatives may take other forms as well. The subject may be first person plural, second person or third person, and the voice may be passive.

(9) We promise to clean the room afterwards.

(10) You are hereby authorized to pay for the purchase.

(11) Passengers are warned to cross the track by the bridge only.

(12) Notice is hereby given that trespassers will be prosecuted.

In informal situations, other moods than the indicative may be used. Instead of "I order you to turn right", one may say simply "Turn right".[①] Other tenses may also be used, in place of "I find you guilty" the jury may say "You did it".

[①] On the evidence of utterances of this type, Austin (pp. 32f., 69ff.) makes a distinction between explicit performatives and implicit (also known as primary, primitive) performatives. Implicit performatives, which do not employ performative verbs like *order*, *promise*, will be ambiguous in their force. As far as the mere utterance is concerned, the utterer of "Turn right" may also be advising or entreating. Similarly, "I'll buy the tickets" may be a promise or an offer.

And vocabulary is not a reliable criterion either. To issue an order, one does not have to use the word *order*, as we noted just now. The performative verbs may also be used in constative ways, which is illustrated by examples (5) – (8).

As a result, at the end of the 7th chapter and the beginning of the 8th, Austin declares that "it seemed that we were going to find it not always easy to distinguish performative utterances from constative", and "It is time then to make a fresh start on the problem." That is, he is not going to maintain this distinction any more. Levinson (1983: 231) accuses Austin of "playing cunning" here. He says "Readers of *How to Do Things with Words* should be warned that there is an internal evolution to the argument, so that what is proposed at the beginning is rejected by the end." But this accusation is in fact not justifiable. It is true that by this time, i.e. 1955 or earlier, Austin no longer believed in this distinction. But the way he presented his ideas in *How to Do Things with Words* has to do with its being a text of lectures rather than any intention to mislead. As Warnock (1989: 106) comments "in lecturing Austin was not merely expounding, he was teaching; and to be shown alternative byways and blind alleys, how what at first sight seems hopefully luminous can turn out to be deceptive, how persistent thought about a problem can twist and turn, is more philosophically educative than to plod expositorily along an absolutely straight road."

When he was not lecturing, he would state clearly what his position was on this question from the very beginning. In 1958 he attended an Anglo-French conference and presented a paper entitled "Performative-Constative". At the end of the first paragraph, he asked "Ought we to accept this Performative-Constative antithesis?" (Austin 1971:

13) In other words, he was going to challenge this distinction, to show that this is not a valid distinction and should be abandoned. In fact, even in *How to Do Things with Words*, he disclosed his real intention whenever possible. For example, there is a footnote to the heading of the first section of the first chapter, reading "Everything said in these sections is provisional, and subject to revision in the light of later sections" (p. 4).

Anyway, for Austin the question now is not why we should make this distinction, but why this distinction is inadequate. Now one may wonder since he himself was the one to propose it in the first place why not simply withdraw the proposal. This way of thinking misses the point. The dichotomy between performative and constative was not discussed for its own sake, it serves another purpose, it paves the way for a new theory—the theory of illocutionary acts.

6.2 The theory of illocutionary acts

In chapter 8 of *How to Do Things with Words*, Austin made a fresh start on the problem and considered it from the ground up again, i.e. in what sense to say something is to do something. In this section, we first introduce Austin's answer, then discuss some other proposals concerning it.

6.2.1 Three kinds of speech act

The first sense in which to say something can be understood as doing something Austin proposes, is the ordinary sense of the movement of vocal organs to produce a stretch of meaningful sounds. In his words, it is "the utterance of certain noises, the utterance of certain words in a certain construction, and the utterance of them with a certain 'meaning' in the favourite philosophical sense of that word, i.e. with a certain sense and with a certain reference" (p. 94). That is, in this sense, when somebody says "Morning!", we can ask a question like "What did he do?" instead of "What did he say?" And the answer could be that he produced a sound, word or sentence—"Morning!" The act performed in this sense is dubbed a locutionary act.

By itself the first sense is an uninteresting, or trivial, observation, but it leads us to something interesting and important. That is, "in performing a locutionary act we shall also be performing such an act as: asking or answering a question, giving some information or an assurance or a warning, announcing a verdict or an intention, pronouncing sentence, making an appointment or an appeal or a criticism, making an identification or giving a description, and the numerous like" (pp. 98 – 9). For example, to the question "What did he do?" when the person concerned said "Morning!", we could perfectly well answer "He offered a greeting."

In other words, when we speak, we not only produce some units of language with certain meaning, but also make clear our purpose in producing them, the way we intend them to be understood, or they also have certain forces as Austin prefers to say. In the example of "Morning!" we can say it has the force of a greeting, or it ought to have been taken as a greeting.[1] This is the second sense in which to say something is to do something, and the act performed is known as the illocutionary[2] act.

---

[1] Austin acknowledges that "force" can be regarded as part of "meaning", when the latter is used in a broad sense. So we can say "He meant it as a greeting". "But I want to distinguish *force* and meaning in the sense in which meaning is equivalent to sense and reference, just as it has become essential to distinguish sense and reference" (p. 100), he emphasizes.

[2] The prefix "il" means "in, within", not "not", so the translation of it as 言外行为 is misleading.

The third sense in which to say something can mean to do something concerns the consequential effects of a locution upon the hearer. By telling somebody something the speaker may change the opinion of the hearer on something, or mislead him, or surprise him, or induce him to do something, or what not. Whether or not these effects are intended, they can be considered as part of the act that the speaker has performed. This act is called perlocutionary, as it is performed through, by means of, a locutionary act.

To explain these new notions further, Austin used "Shoot her" as an example. The speaker's production of these two words in this order and with determinate sense and reference, such as "open fire at Miss Smith", is a locutionary act which may be described by the hearer as "He said to me 'Shoot her'". The illocutionary act performed in saying it may be described as "He urged/advised/ordered me to shoot her", as in different contexts, it may have these different illocutionary forces. When you are fighting with a woman, who is going to kill you with the weapon in her hand, then your friend in saying "Shoot her" is offering you a piece of advice. If you are a soldier and the woman is an escaping criminal who is on the verge of success, then this utterance from the mouth of an officer is an order. The perlocutionary act, as is explained, concerns the effect of a locution. Somebody's saying of "Shoot her" may lead you to the actual shooting of the woman referred to, and this act may be described as "He persuaded me to shoot her". If, on the other hand, you did not shoot the woman willingly, then you can be said to have been forced to shoot her. The utterance may also have the effect of frightening the woman concerned, or produce in you an irritation towards the speaker. These are perlocutionary acts performed by the speaker of "Shoot her", too, though they may not be what he had intended originally. This brings up another difference between illocutionary and perlocutionary acts, i.e. one is related to intention and the other not.

In this general theory then, every utterance is a speech act, consisting of three sub-acts: locutionary, illocutionary and perlocutionary.① Utterances are no longer performative or constative. The original performatives are just a special type in which the illocutionary force is made explicit by the performative verb. Thus, "I promise to return it tomorrow" is a promise, and "I warn you that the bull will charge" is a warning. In this sense, "state" is also a performative verb in "I state this is only a personal opinion". Among the three acts: locutionary, illocutionary and perlocutionary, the second is the most important. The theory of speech acts can in fact be said to be the theory of illocutionary acts.

6.2.2 Some counter-arguments

Since the proposal of the three acts, there have been many arguments against them, especially the distinction between locutionary act and illocutionary act. The most fierce of them is the one voiced by J. Cohen (1964), who denies that meaning and force, and consequently the locutionary act and illocutionary act, are distinguishable. For example, he argues, in "Is it raining?" or "I ask whether it is raining", the meaning of the locutionary act is the same as the illocutionary force, i.e. asking whether it is raining.

---

① Leech (1983: 199) characterizes the three acts as: a locutionary act performing the act *of* saying something, an illocutionary act performing an act *in* saying something, and a perlocutionary act performing an act *by* saying something. On page 201, he compares them to the description of an event in a football match as: The centre-forward has kicked the ball; moreover, he has scored a goal; and furthermore, he has won the match!

On one occasion, Austin lists some devices other than the performative verb which also help make explicit the illocutionary force. Among the examples are

"Shut it, do" resembles "I order you to shut it".

"Shut it—I should" resembles "I advise you to shut it".

"Shut it, if you like" resembles "I permit you to shut it".

"Very well then, shut it" resembles "I consent to your shutting it".

"Shut it if you dare" resembles "I dare you to shut it". (p. 73)

Cohen contends "Austin seems to hold that all such devices clarify illocutionary force, not meaning. But on this view there can be no difference of meaning at all between such utterances as 'It must have rained, because the streets are wet' and 'It must have rained, therefore the streets are wet.' Yet most ordinary speakers of English, let alone linguists and interpreters, would be very surprised indeed to hear that such a pair of utterances have the same meaning" (Cohen 1971 [1964]: 585). It is obvious that Cohen is using "meaning" in a broader sense than Austin.

Searle, on the other hand, has tried to solve the problem from the other direction, i.e. to use some other types of act to replace the locutionary act. The locutionary act, in Austin's terms, is the utterance of certain noises, certain words in a certain order and with a certain meaning. These three utterances are given three names respectively: phonetic act, phatic act and rhetic act (Austin 1975 [1962]: 95). Now Searle argues that the rhetic act is in fact the same as the illocutionary act. For example, Austin says "He said 'Get out'" reports a phatic act, whereas "He told me to get out" reports a rhetic act; "He said 'Is it in Oxford or Cambridge?'" reports a phatic act, whereas

"He asked whether it was in Oxford or Cambridge" reports a rhetic act. In other words, "the verb phrases in the reports of *rhetic* acts invariably contain *illocutionary* verbs. They are indeed very general illocutionary verbs, but they are illocutionary nonetheless" (Searle 1971 [1968]: 266). As a possible way out, Searle suggests that in characterizing the locutionary-illocutionary distinction "Austin may have had in mind the distinction between the content or, as some philosophers call it, the proposition, in an illocutionary act and the force or illocutionary type of the act" (ibid.: 272).

This idea first appears in an earlier paper of 1965, entitled "What Is a Speech Act?" There Searle has considered the following sentences:

Will John leave the room?
John will leave the room.
John, leave the room!
Would that John left the room.①
If John will leave the room, I will leave also.

"The first would, characteristically, be a question, the second an assertion about the future, that is, a prediction, the third a request or order, the fourth an expression of a wish, and the fifth a hypothetical expression of intention. Yet in the performance of each the speaker would characteristically perform some subsidiary acts which are common to all five illocutionary acts. In the utterance of each the speaker *refers* to a particular person John and *predicates* the act of leaving the room of that person. In no case is that all he does, but in every case it is a part of what he does. I shall say, therefore, that in each of these cases, although the illocutionary acts are different, at least some of the

---

① This is an archaic form for expressing a wish.

non-illocutionary acts of reference and predication are the same". And he proposes to call this common content proposition①(1971 [1965]: 618).

So instead of Austin's locutionary act (made up of phonetic, phatic and rhetic acts) and illocutionary act, we have now the following four types of acts:

Phonetic acts

Phatic acts

Propositional acts

Illocutionary acts (Searle 1971 [1968]: 275)

In his *Speech Acts*, Searle repeats himself except that phonetic and phatic acts have been conflated into one type: utterance act. In other words, the new types of acts are:

(a) Uttering words (morphemes, sentences) = performing *utterance acts*.

(b) Referring and predicating = performing *propositional acts*.

(c) Stating, questioning, commanding, promising, etc. = performing *illocutionary acts*. (1969: 24)

He goes on to explain "I am not saying, of course, that these are separate things that speakers do, as it happens, simultaneously, as one might smoke, read and scratch one's head simultaneously, but rather that in performing an illocutionary act one characteristically performs propositional acts and utterance acts. Nor should it be thought from this that utterance acts and propositional acts stand to illocutionary acts

---

① Searle notes he makes a distinction between proposition and assertion. The proposition that John will leave the room is expressed in all the five sentences, but only in the second is that proposition asserted (1971[1965]: 619).

in the way buying a ticket and getting on a train stand to taking a railroad trip. They are not means to ends; rather, utterance acts stand to propositional and illocutionary acts in the way in which, e.g., making an 'X' on a ballot paper stands to voting" (ibid.). This new typology of acts has an advantage over that of Austin's in that it makes clear that sentences may differ in not only locutionary meaning and illocutionary force, but also utterance. Sentences like "I promise to return it tomorrow", "I give my word to return it tomorrow", and "I'll return it tomorrow", referring to the same person, object and time, and predicating the same action, are different utterances, though they perform the same propositional act, and even the same illocutionary act.

6.3 Classes of illocutionary acts

The last topic Austin's 1962 book is concerned with is the classification of illocutionary acts, which is seen as a very important part of the study of the things one can do with words. In what follows, we introduce Austin's original classification and Searle's revision in succession, and discuss the problems in them meanwhile.

6.3.1 Austin's classification

In the last, the 12th, chapter of *How to Do Things with Words*, Austin attempted a preliminary classification of illocutionary acts. But the idea that illocutionary acts are of different classes does not come up all of a sudden. Austin has been letting it out from the very beginning. In a footnote on page 5, he declares the choice of examples like "I name this ship the *Queen Elizabeth*" is not "without design: they are all 'explicit' performatives, and of that prepotent class later called 'exercitives'". And in his efforts to separate the performative from the constative, he had noticed time and again that some classes of utterances pose more difficulties than others, and anticipated the classification presented in the last chapter from very early on. For example, in the 4th chapter, he mentions verdictives like "I find the accused guilty" may satisfy all the felicity conditions, but still be unhappy in the sense that the verdict may be unjustified or incorrect. On page 85, he notes that expositives like "I argue that there is no backside to the moon" generally have the straightforward form of a statement, but according to the tests he envisages there, the verbs are of the performative type.

Verdictives, exercitives and expositives are three of the five classes Austin distinguishes, the other two being commissives and behabitives. As explicit performative verbs make clear the illocutionary forces of utterances, they are used as a basis for the classification.[1]

(i) Verdictives

Verdictives are concerned with the delivery of a verdict, a finding, a judgement, or an assessment, upon evidence or reasons. For example, when the jury acquit somebody of some crime, they give a verdict, a judgement on the basis of the evidence they hear. Examples are:

> acquit, convict, find (as a matter of fact), hold (as a matter of law), interpret as, understand, read it as, rule, calculate, reckon, estimate, locate, place, date, measure, put it at, make it,

---

[1] It is for this reason that Searle (1979 [1975a]: 9 – 11) accuses Austin of confusing illocutionary verbs with illocutionary acts. But Leech (1983: 176 – 7) maintains that Searle himself was also thinking in terms of illocutionary verbs in his revision. In Leech's view, the realities to which the categories of speech-act verbs apply are often scalar or indeterminate, so "it is pointless to attempt a rigid taxonomy of illocutionary acts". And Wittgenstein's answer to the question "how many kinds of sentences are there?" that "there are countless kinds" is probably as sensible as any other reply to the question "How many speech acts are there?" (p. 225). In other words, the most we can do is to classify the meanings of speech-act verbs. And he presents a detailed classification of English speech-act verbs in his book (pp. 198 – 228).

take it, grade, rank, rate, assess, value, describe, characterize, diagnose, analyse

(ii) Exercitives

Exercitives are concerned with the exercising of powers, rights or influence. "It is a decision that something is to be so, as distinct from a judgement that it is so; it is advocacy that it should be so, as opposed to an estimate that it is so; it is an award as opposed to an assessment; it is a sentence as opposed to a verdict" (p. 155). Examples are:

appoint, degrade, demote, dismiss, excommunicate, name, order, command, direct, sentence, fine, grant, levy, vote for, nominate, choose, claim, give, bequeath, pardon, resign, warn, advise, plead, pray, entreat, beg, urge, press, recommend, proclaim, announce, quash, countermand, annul, repeal, enact, reprieve, veto, dedicate, declare closed, declare open

(iii) Commissives

"The whole point of a commissive is to commit the speaker to a certain course of action" (p. 157). When someone promises, he undertakes the obligation to perform the action promised. Examples are:

promise, covenant, contract, undertake, bind myself, give my word, am determined to, intend, declare my intention, mean to, plan, purpose, propose to, shall, contemplate, envisage, engage, swear, guarantee, pledge myself, bet, vow, agree, consent, dedicate myself to, declare for, side with, adopt, champion, embrace, espouse, oppose, favour

(iv) Behabitives

Behabitives have to do with attitudes and social behaviour, e.g., reaction to other people's behaviour and fortunes. Examples are:

1. For apologies we have "apologize".

2. For thanks we have "thank".
3. For sympathy we have "deplore", "commiserate", "compliment", "condole", "congratulate", "felicitate", "sympathize".
4. For attitudes we have "resent", "don't mind", "pay tribute", "criticize", "grumble about", "complain of", "applaud", "overlook", "commend", "deprecate", and the non-exercitive uses of "blame", "approve", and "favour".
5. For greetings we have "welcome", "bid you farewell".
6. For wishes we have "bless", "curse", "toast", "drink to", and "wish" (in its strict performative use).
7. For challenges we have "dare", "defy", "protest", "challenge".

(v) Expositives

"Expositives are used in acts of exposition involving the expounding of views, the conducting of arguments, and the clarifying of usages and of references" (p. 161). Examples are:

1. affirm, deny, state, describe, class, identify
2. remark, mention, ? interpose
3. inform, apprise, tell, answer, rejoin
3a. ask
4. testify, report, swear, conjecture, ? doubt, ? know, ? believe
5. accept, concede, withdraw, agree, demur to, object to, adhere to, recognize, repudiate
5a. correct, revise
6. postulate, deduce, argue, neglect, ? emphasize
7. begin by, turn to, conclude by
7a. interpret, distinguish, analyse, define

7b. illustrate, explain, formulate

7c. mean, refer, call, understand, regard as

There are some problems with this classification. One of them is that the classes are not clear-cut. There are overlapping cases, as Austin himself concedes. But the most serious is that there is no consistent principle behind it. Austin claims that these classes are based on their illocutionary force and he uses the explicit performative verb in the first person singular present indicative active form as a test. This is, however, not even true of the sample verbs listed. Among the commissives, there is the verb "shall", which he explicitly labels as a primary, i. e. implicit, performative verb. What is more, he groups "intending" and "promising" together on the ground that both can be expressed by the locutions "shall probably", "shall do my best to", "shall very likely" (p. 158).

6.3.2 Searle's revision

At the time of writing *Speech Acts*, Searle thought the question whether there are some basic illocutionary acts to which the others are reducible was difficult to answer. "Part of the difficulty in answering such questions is that the principles of distinction which lead us to say in the first place that such and such is a different kind of illocutionary act from such and such act are quite various" (Searle 1969: 69). Two years later, i.e. in 1971, he seemed to have changed his mind. That year, he delivered a lecture to the Summer Linguistics Institute in Buffalo, NY, entitled "A Taxonomy of Illocutionary Acts", which appeared in print in 1975. In it he first discussed 12 dimensions in which illocutionary acts may differ from one another. And the four important ones are the illocutionary point, the direction of fit between words and the world, the psychological state expressed and the propositional content.

By illocutionary point is meant the point or purpose of an illocution. For example, "[t]he point or purpose of an order can be specified by saying that it is an attempt to get the hearer to do something. The point or purpose of a description is that it is a representation (true or false, accurate or inaccurate) of how something is. The point or purpose of a promise is that it is an undertaking of an obligation by the speaker to do something" (Searle 1979 [1975a]: 2). Illocutions may also differ in their directions of fit between words and the world. Some have as part of their illocutionary point to get the words to match the world, e.g. assertions; others to get the world to match the words, e.g. promises and requests. In the performance of an illocutionary act with a propositional content, the speaker usually also expresses some attitude, some psychological state, to that propositional content. "A man who states, explains, asserts or claims that *p expresses the belief that p*; a man who promises, vows, threatens or pledges to do *A expresses an intention to do A*; a man who orders, commands, requests *H* to do *A expresses a desire (want, wish) that H do A*; a man who apologizes for doing *A expresses regret at having done A*; etc." (ibid.: 4) The propositional content, as is explained in section 6.2.2, is concerned with the reference and predication of a locution. When using it as a criterion to separate different illocutionary acts, Searle emphasizes the differences that are determined by illocutionary force indicating devices (IFID for short).[①] "The differences, for example,

---

[①] Illocutionary force indicating devices include word order, stress, intonation contour, punctuation, the mood of the verb, and the most important, the explicit performative verb if there is one.

between a report and a prediction involve the fact that a prediction must be about the future whereas a report can be about the past or present" (ibid.: 6).

In his *Speech Acts*, Searle suggests that felicity conditions[①] should not only be seen negatively as ways in which an utterance can go wrong, but also positively as rules, the observance of which constitutes or creates the speech act. For example, apart from general conditions like "Normal input and output conditions obtain", there are the following conditions for promising:

1. Propositional content conditions:
    (a) S expresses the proposition that p in the utterance of T.[②]
    (b) In expressing that p, S predicates a future act A of S.
2. Preparatory conditions:
    (a) H would prefer S's doing A to his not doing A, and S believes H would prefer his doing A to his not doing A.
    (b) It is not obvious to both S and H that S will do A in the normal course of events.
3. Sincerity condition:
    S intends to do A.
4. Essential condition:
    S intends that the utterance of T will place him under an obligation to do A. (Searle 1969: 57 - 60)

---

① Searle's felicity conditions are different from those proposed by Austin. His felicity conditions on promises will be listed below and those on requests and questions will be mentioned in Section 6.5.

② S is the abbreviation of *speaker*, H *hearer*, A *act*, p *proposition*, and T stands for sentence.

Now Searle relates the dimensions in which illocutionary acts differ from each other with his felicity conditions. The illocutionary point corresponds to the essential condition, the psychological state expressed to the sincerity condition, and the propositional content to the propositional content condition. He uses these three together with the direction of fit between words and the world as the main criteria for the classification of illocutionary acts into the five categories of assertives, directives, commissives, expressives and declarations.

(i) Assertive

The point or purpose of this class is to commit the speaker to something being the case, to the truth of the expressed proposition. The direction of fit is words to the world. The psychological state expressed is Belief (that). So this class is symbolized as

$$\vdash \downarrow B\ (p)^{①}$$

The simplest test of an assertive is: can you literally characterize it as true or false. In this sense this class equals what Austin originally called constatives.

(ii) Directives

The illocutionary point of a directive is to get the hearer to do something. The direction of fit is the world to words. The psychological state expressed, or the sincerity condition, is Want (or Wish or Desire). And the propositional content is that the hearer H does some future action A. In Searle's view, questions are a sub-class of direc-

---

① $\vdash$ is the sign used by some philosophers for assertion. $\downarrow$ means the direction of fit is words to the world, i.e. the upside stands for words and the bottom the world. B is the abbreviation of *belief*, and *p proposition*. Similarly, W is the abbreviation of *want*, C *commissive*, I *intention*, E *expressive*, D *declaration* and Da *assertive declaration* in the other symbols.

tives, since they are attempts by S to get H to answer, i.e. to perform a speech act. To use the exclamation mark for the illocutionary point of this class, the symbol for the directive is:

$$! \uparrow W \ (H \text{ does } A)$$

(iii) Commissives

The illocutionary point in this class is to commit the speaker to some future course of action. The direction of fit is the world to words. The sincerity condition is Intention. And the propositional content is that the speaker S does some future action. So it can be symbolized as

$$C \uparrow I \ (S \text{ does } A)$$

(iv) Expressive

The illocutionary point is simply to express the psychological state specified in the sincerity condition about a state of affairs specified in the propositional content. But there is no direction of fit between words and the world. In performing an expressive, the speaker is neither trying to get the world to match the words nor the other way round, rather the truth of the expressed proposition is presupposed. When someone apologizes for having stepped on your toe, it is not his purpose to report a past event that he has stepped on your toe nor to try to bring about a future state of affairs, i.e. to get your toe stepped on, but to express his attitude about an existing fact that your toe has been stepped on by him. The utterance cannot get off the ground unless there already is a fit between words and the world.

The psychological state expressed in this class is a variable, depending on the illocutionary point. The propositional content ascribes some property (not necessarily an action) to either S or H, e.g. S's stepping on H's toe, H's winning a race, or H's good looks.

Therefore it is symbolized as
$$E \varnothing (P^{①}) (S/H + \text{property})$$

(v) Declarations

The illocutionary point is to bring about some alteration in the status or condition of the referred to object. The successful performance of a declaration guarantees that the propositional content corresponds to the world. If somebody successfully performs the act of appointing you chairman, then you are chairman; if somebody successfully performs the act of declaring a state of war, then war is on. So the direction of fit is both words to the world and the world to words: $\updownarrow$. The saying of something causes something to become reality. The performance of a declaration brings about a fit between words and the world by its very successful performance. In this sense, this class corresponds to the typical performatives. There is no sincerity condition in the sense that no personal attitude is involved in declarations. The speaker is acting as a spokesman of an institution. He is not expressing any psychological state of his own. The propositional content is also a variable, depending on the illocutionary point. Its symbol is:

$$D \updownarrow \varnothing (p)$$

But some members of this class overlap with members of the assertive class. When the judge declares "You are guilty", he has not only brought about some change in the status of the person referred to, but also asserts that it is true that you have committed a crime, and he believes in this verdict. So there is a difference of the illocutionary

---

① P, different from the small p in the fourth position, is a variable ranging over the different possible psychological states expressed in the performance of the illocutionary acts in this class.

point, the direction of fit, and the psychological state in this sub-class, which may be called "assertive declarations" and symbolized as

$$Da \downarrow \updownarrow B(p)$$

Searle claims that the successful classification of illocutionary acts shows that "there are a rather limited number of basic things we do with language: we tell people how things are, we try to get them to do things, we commit ourselves to doing things, we express our feelings and attitudes and we bring about changes through our utterances" (1979 [1975a]:29).

Levinson (1983: 240) says Searle's classification is a disappointment in that it lacks a principled basis, and it is not even built in any systematic way on felicity conditions. I think this is a groundless criticism. There IS a principled basis, i.e. the dimensions in which illocutionary acts differ from each other, and they are closely related to the felicity conditions. In my view, one of the failings of Searle's system concerns the criterion of the direction of fit, which has nothing to do with the felicity conditions, yet occupies a central position in the classification. Searle wishes that he could build the taxonomy entirely around this distinction (Searle 1979 [1975a]: 4), and even tries to group directives and commissives together on the ground that they have the same direction of fit between words and the world (ibid.: 14). But a more serious failing is that the number of classes, i.e. five, is too small. For example, to ask a question should not be regarded as a sub-class of directives. It is not convenient to say somebody who has asked a question has made a directive. The fact that Searle has a sub-class of assertive declaration also points to the need for more specific classes.

6.4 A semanticist view

After the proposal of Austin's theory of speech acts, there arose numerous attempts to incorporate it into a theory of grammar, especially generative semantics. Among them the most representative is "On Declarative Sentences" written by John Ross in 1970. In the terminology of G. Leech (1983), we call the view expressed by these linguists a semanticist view. And we begin with, in some detail, a presentation of J. Ross's proposal, known as the performative hypothesis. Then following G. Gazdar (1979), we examine one by one the sub-claims of the strongest possible performative hypothesis.

6.4.1 The performative hypothesis

Ross observes that we can say (13), but not (14), which suggests reflexives like *himself* must have antecedents. But (15) is odd in that there seems to be no antecedent for *myself* either, yet it is acceptable. In note 19 (Ross 1970: 263), he mentions (16) is in a similar situation as (15).

    (13) Tom believed that the paper had been written by Ann and himself.

    (14) * The paper had been written by Ann and himself.

    (15) This paper was written by Ann and myself.

    (16) Was this paper written by Ann and yourself?

His solution to this puzzle is that the antecedent of *myself* and *yourself* appear in the deep structure of (15) and (16), which in a simplified form is something like the following

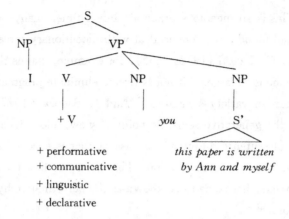

He has adduced six other arguments, such as the fact that (17) and (19) are acceptable, while (18) is not, to support the claim that "a higher subject *I* must be postulated to exist in all deep structures for declarative sentences" (ibid. : 238).

(17) I told Albert that physicists like himself were a godsend.
(18) * Physicists like himself don't often make mistakes.
(19) Physicists like myself were never too happy with the parity principle.

Then he collects three arguments for the claim that the verb in the deep structure has the features [+ communicative, + linguistic, + declarative] and another three for the claim that the deep structure for all declaratives contains an indirect object *you*. And the final argument for his performative analysis is based on sentences like (20), in which the *for*-clause does not provide a reason for Jenny's absence, but a reason for the speaker to assert that she is absent. So this sentence most probably derives from a deep structure in which it is an object clause of some verb of saying.

(20) Jenny isn't here, for I don't see her.

This is an ingenious proposal. For a time, many people thought they had found a way out to deal with illocutionary force in semantics proper. G. Lakoff (1972a: 655), for example, claims that "What we have done is to largely, if not entirely, eliminate pragmatics, reducing it to garden variety semantics." And J. Sadock (1977: 67) argues "from the generative semantic point of view, illocutionary force is an aspect of sentence meaning", an aspect that is encoded as an abstract verb in semantic representation. This theory of illocutionary force, or speech acts, has come to be known as the performative hypothesis, PH for short. [1]

6.4.2 A detailed examination

In order to examine its tenability, Gazdar (1979: 18) summarizes the sub-claims the strongest possible PH requires as follows:

For ∃ sentences S, in all natural languages, the deep structure of S
(a) has a clause containing a PERFORMATIVE verb. [2]
(b) the subject of this clause is *I* and the indirect object is *you*. [3]
(c) this clause is the HIGHEST clause in the deep structure. [4]
(d) this clause is DELETABLE when the verb is marked to allow this, [5] and the deletion transformation is MEANING-PRESERVING (early generative semantics assumption).
(e) the verb in the clause is the ONLY verb in the sentence which

---

[1] Ross himself calls it performative analysis.
[2] "Every deep structure contains one and only one performative sentence as its highest clause" (Ross 1970: 261).
[3] Ross 1970: passim.
[4] Note [2] above.
[5] Ross 1970: 249.

is performative.①

(f) the verb represents the ILLOCUTIONARY FORCE of the sentence.②,③

(g) illocutionary force is SEMANTIC.④

(h) ∃ is the UNIVERSAL quantifier.⑤

Gazdar (ibid.) notes this summary "does not represent a position which any particular proponent of the PH has ever attempted to defend as a whole. G. Lakoff, for example, has never maintained (b), and (d) makes little sense in grammars that allow transderivational⑥ constraints." And he has indicated the source at the end of each sub-claim, which I have copied as notes except for some typographic corrections.

Now let's have a closer look at these sub-claims.

(a) The verb is performative.

The attentive reader will have noticed that this is the one feature which Ross did not touch on in his arguments for his performative analysis. When summarizing his 14 arguments, Ross said "Paradoxically, the one facet for which I have the least support is the claim that

---

① Note ② on the previous page.

② "Illocutionary force... is to be represented in logical form by the presence of a performative verb" (G. Lakoff 1972: 561).

③ The illocutionary force of an uttered sentence is that aspect of its meaning which is represented by the performative clause in the semantic structure of the sentence" (Sadock 1977: 67).

④ "There will be a uniform deep structural configuration on which to base the semantic notion *speech act*" (Ross 1970: 248). And Note ③ above.

⑤ Note ② on the previous page.

⑥ "Transderivational rules characterize what happens in one derivation on the basis of what is the case in one or more other, related derivations" (Gordon and Lakoff 1975 [1971]: 104).

the verb of the deleted higher clause has the feature [+performative] and is in fact a performative in (7)[1]. Aside from the rather weak argument which is mentioned in Section 3.4 below, I have no syntactic justification for this claim" (Ross 1970: 248). The weak argument is presented when he was discussing the rule to delete the performative part in the deep structure. One of the questions concerned with this rule is whether it can apply to its own output and produce infinite ambiguity. That is, can the deep structure of a sentence like (15) above be embedded again in the object of a higher performative verb of saying? Ross's answer is "no". The reason is "there is an independently necessary constraint that prohibits any verb from having a performative interpretation when it is embedded as the complement of another verb. Thus while (21a), said in isolation, constitutes an admission, and (21b) a promise,

(21) a. I admit that I'll be late.
b. I (hereby) promise that I'll be late.

when (21b) appears as the object of *admit*, as in (22)

(22) I admit that I (* hereby) promise that I'll be late.

---

[1] (7) is the deep structure of "Prices slumped" as follows:

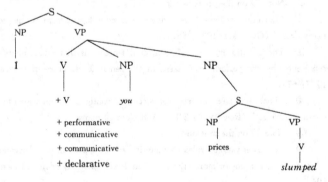

the result is an admission of having made frequent promises, but it is not a promise. This fact is also reflected in the inability of the adverb *hereby* to precede *promise* in (22).① Thus, since performative verbs cannot be used performatively in complements, rule (92)② will not produce infinitely ambiguous surface structures. This point provides some nonsemantic evidence for including the feature [+ performative] in (7) and in (92)" (ibid.: 251f.). In other words, (a) relies on the plausibility of (e) and (f), if neither of them can be maintained then there is no point in attempting to defend (a).

(b) The subject is *I* and the indirect object is *you*.

The trouble with this claim, as Leech (1981 [1974]: 325) points out, is that there are "impersonal styles of discourse in which first and second person pronouns are taboo (for example, in legal documents, regulations, bureaucratic instructions). Here the performative analysis forces us to allow first-person and second-person pronouns in the underlying structure of a sentence, but not to allow them in its surface structure." But it would be difficult to supply such a deep structure for (23) and (24), and at the same time maintain (e) and (f).

(23) The company hereby undertakes to replace any can of Doggo-Meat that fails to please, with no questions asked.

(24) The court finds the accused not guilty.

Even in informal discourses there are utterances which are difficult to derive from deep structures with *I* as the subject and *you* as the indirect object.

(25) Johnny is to come in now.

---

① This in my view is the main reason why Ross did not recognize conclusively that the verb is performative. He noted on page 270 that it is odd to say: * I hereby tell/ say to you that prices will skyrocket.

② The Performative Deletion rule.

(26) What am I to do?

(c) The clause is the highest in the deep structure.

This condition is necessary in that Ross insists on it that performative verbs cannot be used performatively in complements. However, there are sentences like (27), in which the highest verb *regret* is not performative, while the performative *inform* is in a lower clause. And there are no known transformations available to derive (27) from a deep structure with *inform* in the highest clause.

(27) I regret to inform you of the death of your goldfish.

Sadock (1974: 64) proposes a "fairly wild transformation" whose details are "fairly obscure" as follows:

(*I* INFORM *you* (S AND (*I regret* S)))
$\Downarrow$

(*I regret* (*I inform you* S)) (from Gazdar 1979: 22)
Yet Sadock (ibid.) acknowledges "the necessity for such an enormously powerful and unique transformation is a serious drawback to the proposal [i.e. the PH] under consideration". In other words, sentences like (27) constitutes irremediable counterexamples to claim (c).

(d) The deletion transformation is meaning-preserving.

This claim is perhaps the least tenable. The principle that transformation, including deletion transformation, preserves meaning was only maintained, as Gazdar notes, in the early days of generative semantics. In cases like (28) and (29), one can barely maintain that they mean the same.

(28) I order you to go.

(29) Go!

With sentences like (30) and (31), however, it is no longer possible to do so.

(30) I state to you the earth is flat.

(31) The earth is flat.

They differ in truth conditions. The sentence in (30) is true as long as the speaker has uttered it, the truth of the complement "the earth is flat" is irrelevant. In (31), on the other hand, this is exactly what the truth hinges on.

Gazdar (1979: 25) argues that even if we ignore the truth conditions, they have quite different conditions of use. "Speakers do not generally fail to delete highest performatives—if they were to, and produced utterances like (32) instead of (33), then they would either not be understood at all, or else they would be taken to be implying something more than that carried by the performative complements."

(32) I request that you listen to me. I declare that your violin playing is excruciating. I request you to tell me why you don't do it elsewhere.

(33) Listen to me. Your violin playing is excruciating. Why don't you do it elsewhere?

(e) There is only one performative verb.

As mentioned earlier, Ross maintains that a performative verb used in complements is no longer performative. His example, to repeat, is

(34) I admit that I (* hereby) promise that I'll be late.

However Fraser (1971: 4) found examples like (35), which is both an announcement and a promise.

(35) I announce that I hereby promise to be timely.

(from Gazdar 1979: 26)

Sadock (1974: 134 - 7) has considered sentences like (36) and (37), which are wholly or partly interrogative, but on some occasion of use will count as reminders.

(36) Isn't Danish beautiful.[①]

(37) Danish is beautiful, isn't it. (from Gazdar ibid.)

And he suggests that their possible deep structures would be something like the following:

((*I* REMIND *you* S) AND (*I* REQUEST *you* (*you* CONFIRM S)))

(ibid.)

In other words, there are two performative verbs.

(f) The verb represents the illocutionary force.

A problem with this claim is that one has to postulate a deep structure with the same verb for all the sentences that have the same illocutionary force. For example, the following sentences can all have the illocutionary force of a request, but one would be hard put to it to suggest a deep structure with the verb request for most of them.

(38) Close the door.

(39) I request you to close the door.

(40) I must ask you to close the door.

(41) I'm asking you to close the door.

(42) I want you to close the door.

(43) You must close the door.

(44) Why don't you close the door.

(45) Will you close the door.

(46) How about closing the door.

[①] There is a practice in linguistics literature to use the full stop to show that the sentence does not have the interrogative force. J. Thomas (1995: 93) has even found an example in real life (in the changing rooms at the swimming pool at the University of Warwick) to use a full stop at the end of an interrogative with a request force—"Would users please refrain from spitting."

(47) Close the door, will you.

(48) You may close the door.

(49) Can you close the door. (from Gazdar 1979: 27)

G. Green (1975) has considered four approaches to solving this problem.[①] The first was suggested by Sadock (1970), who dubbed sentences like (50)—(54), interrogative in form but imperative in force, whimperatives.

(50) Will you close the door please?

(51) Can you lend me a dime please?

(52) Won't you have a seat please?

(53) Could you move over please?

(54) Do you want to set the table now?

And his suggestion is that they should be analyzed as a conjunction of a question and a request as follows, the first conjunct accounting for the form and the second the force.

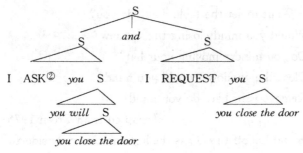

(from Green 1975: 108)

In this approach, however, the conjunction reduction and perfor-

---

① As the second is not very different from the first, we shall leave it out here.

② The words *ask*, *request*, and *will* are **Q**, *Imp* and **MODAL** respectively in Green's original, the present adaptation has been made in accordance with Gazdar (1979: 28).

mative deletion would have to be obligatory, otherwise the sentence would be ill-formed as in (55).

(55) * I ask you if you can close the door, and I order you to do it.

As an alternative, Green suggests we might turn to something a little closer to the surface for a source of whimperatives. That is, to derive (50) from something like (56), which in turn is derived from (57).

(56) Close the door, will you?

(57) Close the door!

This proposal appears to be simpler and more plausible. But not all the sentences with a request force may be derived in this way. (54), for example, does not have a corresponding (58). And with sentences like (59) and (60), the corresponding forms (61) and (62) are morphologically dissimilar, to say the least.[①]

(58) * Want to set the table now, do you?

(59) Would you mind closing the window?

(60) Do you mind removing your hat?

(61) Close the window, would you mind?

(62) Remove your hat, do you mind?

(adapted from Green 1975: 118)

Gordon and Lakoff (1971) is the last one Green considered. They claim that the underlying or logical structure of a whimperative is not an imperative, but an interrogative. For example, the underlying form of (51) is something like (63).

(63) I request that you tell me whether you can lend me a

[①] Green (1975: 118) herself finds them a bit dubious.

dime.①

They (Gordon and Lakoff 1975 [1971]: 86f.) suggest there are conversational postulates such as,

ASK $(a, b,$ CAN $(b, Q))^{*②} \rightarrow$ REQUEST (a, b, Q)

where Q is of the form FUT (DO (b, R)) ["b will do act R"]

That is, if A asks B a defective question whether B has the ability to do something, then A is effectively requesting B to do it.

Green (1975: 131) argues this approach to postulate the same deep structure for different illocutionary forces, such as question and request, apart from its other inadequacies, "seriously undermines many of the rather convincing arguments given in support of abstract performative verbs". In other words, it directly contradicts claim (f).

(g) Illocutionary force is semantic.

This is the central claim of the PH. That is, the illocutionary force of a sentence could be captured by the semantic representation of it. For example, the underlying verb of a sentence will have the features of [+ performative, + communication, + linguistic, + declarative].③ The problem is that illocutionary force has not only to do with

---

① Cf. Green 1975: 118.

② Gordon and Lakoff (1975 [1971]: 87) hold that a sentence like (51) is ambiguous. It can be a real question, i.e. a request for information about the hearer's ability to lend the speaker a dime; or a request for action, a real request that the hearer lend the speaker a dime. And only when the hearer assumes that the speaker does not intend it to be a question, will it become a real request. And the asterisk shows the condition that as a question it is defective.

③ As noted earlier, these features were meant for the verb of a declarative by Ross. But at the end of his paper, Ross expresses the hope that his performative analysis would be broadened to encompass all sentence types. As a matter of fact, the imperative had always been thought of as derivative from a declarative with *order*. And there had been suggestions that the interrogative be treated as a type of request for information, such as Katz and Postal 1964, Langacker 1969, to name just two. Therefore it would not be too farfetched to suppose that these features are applicable to the underlying verb of any sentence.

truth conditions but also felicity conditions. One of the conditions (64) must satisfy in order to be felicitous is that the door is not open at the time of speaking.

(64) Open the door.

So the PH proponent will have to specify it as a feature of *open* in the lexicon, as Fillmore would like to see.[1] But no one has ever demonstrated how this could be actually done.

The honourable exception is G. Lakoff in that he did come up with a suggestion to account for felicity conditions by pure semantic means. In his view, truth conditions can be interpreted in two different senses. In the technical sense used by logicians, "*true* has been made into the relative term *true in a model* (*given a point of reference*)" (G. Lakoff 1975: 260). And it is in this sense that we say (30) is true as long as it is a fact that the speaker has made that statement. In the everyday sense, on the other hand, performatives like (65), including (30), do not have truth value, as Austin argued. One cannot say whether they are true or false.

(65) I bet you sixpence that it will rain tomorrow.

Therefore Lakoff chooses to talk about "satisfaction conditions" instead. "[I]n a natural logic, satisfaction conditions would be given for each atomic predicate, including all of the performative predicates; the satisfaction conditions are at once both truth conditions and felicity conditions" (ibid.: 268). "What we need to do is to extend the assignment of truth values for nonperformative sentences to the assignment of felicity values for performative sentences. Just as we have valuations like $V_w[P] = 1$ for 'P is true in world w', where P is non-

---

[1] Cf. section 5.2.2.

performative, we will let $V_w[P] = 1$ stand for 'P is felicitous in world w', where P is performative" (G. Lakoff 1972b: 570). In other words, "truth conditions" in the technical, i.e. broad, sense, are called "satisfaction conditions" by Lakoff. Felicity conditions are just satisfaction conditions for performative sentences, and truth conditions in the everyday, i.e. narrow, sense are satisfaction conditions for nonperformatives.

Specifically, he has proposed meaning postulates like the following,

$$\text{Request}(x, y, P) \supset \text{attempt}(x, \text{cause}(y, P))$$

(G. Lakoff 1975: 268)

which he claims could account for the entailment relationship in (66) and (67).

(66) Henry requested of Jill that she take her clothes off.

(67) Henry attempted to get Jill to take her clothes off.

But Gazdar (1979: 31) argues that if (66) entails (67), then (68) should make Henry sound completely irrational and (69) should be contradictory.

(68) Henry requested of Jill that she take her clothes off because it was the only way he knew of preventing her from doing so.

(69) Henry requested of Jill that she take her clothes off but he was only attempting to shock her.

As one of the felicity conditions on orders is that the speaker has authority over the addressee, Lakoff (1975: 269) also says (70), (71) and (72) entail (73).

(70) Sam ordered Harry to get out of the bar.

(71) Sam didn't order Harry to get out of the bar.

(72) Sam may order Harry to get out the bar.

(73) Sam has authority over Harry.

Again, Gazdar (1979: 31f.) has found that illogical as we can say (74), (75) and (76).

(74) Sam ordered Harry to get out of the bar but Harry reminded him that he didn't have the authority.

(75) Sam didn't order Harry to get out of the bar because he didn't have the authority to do so.

(76) Sam may order Harry to get out of the bar even though he doesn't have the authority to do so.

(h) All sentences have a higher performative clause.

This amounts to the claim that all sentences are performative in the deep structure. But if verbs like *say*, *tell* cannot be shown conclusively to be performative as we demonstrated earlier, it is hardly legitimate to call the clause performative. What is more, G. Lakoff (1975: 284 – 5) notes there are sentences which do not contain deictic elements like (77), (78) and (79).

(77) Two plus two equals four.

(78) Force equals mass times acceleration.

(79) Whales are mammals.

And they can be considered in the abstract, away from the situation of use, in other words, not uttered in the performance of a speech act—typically an assertion. In such a case, they would not have a performative clause in the logical structure.

To sum up, Gazdar (1979: 35) argues "the strongest hypothesis possible in the light of the discussion above" is

Some sentences contain, in their surface structure representations, one or more performative verbs.

In other words, the PH is not tenable.

6.5 Indirect speech acts

When discussing felicity conditions, Searle (1969: 58f.) realizes that the word *promise* may be used with other illocutionary forces than promising. For example, the utterance of (80) has an illocutionary force of a warning or a threat.

(80) If you don't hand in your paper on time I promise you I will give you a failing grade in the course.

And when somebody accuses you of stealing money, your reply (81) is an emphatic denial.

(81) No, I didn't, I promise you I didn't.

On the other hand, seldom does one actually need to use the explicit *I promise* to make a promise. One may say *I'll do it for you*, as long as in saying it he is undertaking an obligation to perform a future action for you, i.e. the essential condition for a promise is satisfied. Similarly, one may say *I wish you wouldn't do that* to express a request rather than a wish, if the point of saying it is to get you to do something, or rather to stop doing something as in this case, i.e. the essential condition for a request is satisfied.

"This feature of speech—", Searle points out, "that an utterance in a context can indicate the satisfaction of an essential condition without the use of the explicit illocutionary force-indicating device for that essential condition—is the origin of many polite turns of phrase. Thus, for example, the sentence 'Could you do this for me?' in spite of the meaning of the lexical items and the interrogative illocutionary force-indicating devices is not characteristically uttered as a subjunctive question concerning your abilities; it is characteristically uttered as a request" (ibid.: 68).

This kind of speech acts, or illocutionary acts, "in which one illocutionary act is performed indirectly by way of performing another" (1975b: 60), Searle calls indirect speech acts.① In a sense, last section is mainly a discussion of the semantic account of indirect speech acts. Now in this section we shall come to Searle's views on them, which are expressed in two articles: "Indirect Speech Acts" and "Speech Acts and Recent Linguistics", both published in 1975.

6.5.1 A pragmatic analysis

Searle is in direct opposition to the generative semanticists we discussed above. He argues that sentences like (82) do not have an imperative force as part of their logical meaning, since it is possible without inconsistency to connect it with the denial of any imperative intent as in (83).

(82) I'd like you to do this for me, Bill.

(83) I'd like you to do this for me, Bill, but I am not asking you to do it or requesting that you do it or ordering you to do it or telling you to do it. (1975b: 67)

Then how can (82) be used as a request? Searle attributes this possibility to the existence of the felicity conditions for illocutionary acts.② After the discussion of felicity conditions on promises in his *Speech Acts*, Searle (1969: 64ff.) extends the analysis to other types

---

① As a matter of fact, all speech acts, except for very few explicit performatives, are indirect to some degree. Therefore J. Thomas (1995: 94) thinks "Searle's introduction of the new term seems an unnecessary refinement".

② Searle (1975b: 60f.) says the theory of speech acts as presented in his 1969 book, more specifically the felicity conditions, is not a complete answer to this question. So he has developed it by including the general principles of conversation suggested by Grice, and mutually shared background information of the speaker and the hearer, together with an ability on the part of the hearer to make inferences.

of illocutionary act, and suggests that the felicity conditions on requests and questions, among others, are as follows:

	Request	Question
Propositional content	Future act A of H.	Any proposition or propositional function.
Preparatory	1. H is able to do A. S believes H is able to do A. 2. It is not obvious to both S and H that H will do A in the normal course of events of his own accord.	1. S does not know "the answer", i.e., does not know if the proposition is true, or, in the case of the propositional function, does not know the information needed to complete the proposition truly (but see comment below). 2. It is not obvious to both S and H that H will provide the information at that time without being asked.
Sincerity	S wants H to do A.	S wants this information.
Essential	Counts as an attempt to get H to do A.	Counts as an attempt to elicit this information from H.
Comment:	*Order* and *command* have the additional preparatory rule that S must be in a position of authority over H. *Command* probably does not have the "pragmatic" condition requiring non-obviousness. Furthermore in both, the authority relationship infects the essential condition because the utterance counts as an attempt to get H to do A *in virtue of the authority of S over H*.	There are two kinds of questions, (a) real questions, (b) exam questions. In real questions S wants to know (find out) the answer; in exam question, S wants to know if H knows.

241

As we noted in our discussion of Sealer's classification of illocutionary acts, he regards felicity conditions not just negatively as ways in which an utterance may go wrong, but also positively as rules the observance of which constitutes the relevant speech act. In his "Indirect Speech Acts", Searle (1975b: 72) reiterates this view and suggests that as a consequence of these rules, together with certain other information, namely, the factual background information and the general principles of conversation, there are the following generalizations for requests, or more generally, directives:

GENERALIZATION 1: *S can make an indirect request (or other directive) by either asking whether or stating that a preparatory condition concerning H's ability to do A obtains.*

GENERALIZATION 2: *S can make an indirect directive by either asking whether or stating that the propositional content condition obtains.*

GENERALIZATION 3: *S can make an indirect directive by stating that the sincerity condition obtains, but not by asking whether it obtains.*

GENERALIZATION 4: *S can make an indirect directive by either stating that or asking whether there are good or overriding reasons for doing A, except where the reason is that H wants or wishes, etc., to do A, in which case he can only ask whether H wants, wishes, etc., to do A.*

To exemplify his approach, Searle has considered in detail the use of (84) at the dinner table by X as a request of Y to pass the salt instead of just asking a question about his ability to do so.

(84) Can you pass the salt?

A bare-bones reconstruction by Searle (ibid.: 73f.) of the steps necessary for Y to derive the request force from the utterance is as follows:

STEP 1: *X has asked me a question as to whether I have the ability to pass the salt (fact about the conversation).*

STEP 2: *I assume that he is cooperating in the conversation and that therefore his utterance has some aim or point (principle of conversational cooperation).*

STEP 3: *The conversational setting is not such as to indicate a theoretical interest in my salt-passing ability (factual background information).*

STEP 4: *Furthermore, he probably already knows that the answer to the question is yes (factual background information). (This step facilitates the move to Step 5, but is not essential.)*

STEP 5: *Therefore, his utterance is probably not just a question. It probably has some ulterior illocutionary point (inference from Steps 1, 2, 3, and 4). What can it be?*

STEP 6: *A preparatory condition for any directive illocutionary act is the ability of H to perform the act predicated in the propositional content condition (theory of speech acts).*

STEP 7: *Therefore, X has asked me a question the affirmative answer to which would entail that the preparatory condition for requesting me to pass the salt is satisfied (inference from Steps 1 and 6).*

STEP 8: *We are now at dinner and people normally use salt at dinner; they pass it back and forth, try to get others to pass it back and forth, etc. (background information).*

STEP 9: *He has therefore alluded to the satisfaction of a preparatory condition for a request whose obedience conditions it is quite likely he wants me to bring about (inference from Steps 7 and*

8).

STEP 10: *Therefore, in the absence of any other plausible illocutionary point, he is probably requesting me to pass him the salt* (*inference from Steps* 5 *and* 9).

"According to this analysis," he goes on, "the reason I can ask you to pass the salt by saying *Can you pass the salt?* but not by saying *Salt is made of sodium chloride* or *Salt is mined in the Tatra mountains* is that your ability to pass the salt is a preparatory condition for requesting you to pass the salt in a way that the other sentences are not related to requesting you to pass the salt" (ibid.: 74).

In appearance Searle's solution is very similar to that of Gordon and Lakoff's (1971), but Searle (1979 [1975c]: 174f.) argues that there are drastic differences between them. His solution is based on a general theory of speech acts, a theory of conversation of the Gricean type, and knowledge about speakers' and hearers' powers of inference and rationality. But Gordon and Lakoff's solution in terms of conversational postulates is entirely ad hoc and unmotivated. In fact, theirs is not a solution at all. They simply turned the problem to be solved into the solution to itself. For example, one of the questions is why we can use a question concerning the hearer's ability to do something as a request of the hearer to do it. Gordon and Lakoff did not answer this question, but simply said that this is a conversational postulate, i.e. a rule.

There is a further problem with Gordon and Lakoff's argument that only when the hearer discovers that questions like (84) are defective, will he take them as requests. Searle (ibid.: 177) uses (85) as a counter-argument.

(85) Can you eat the square root of Mount Everest?

6.5.2 Idiomatic, but not idioms

Searle (1975b: 68 – 70, 75f.) also refutes the attempt to explain indirect speech acts as idioms. He makes a distinction between idiom and being idiomatic. In his view, sentences like (84) are not idioms like *kicked the bucket* in (86).

(86) Jones kicked the bucket.

When these sentences are used as requests, they still have their literal meaning, so that literal responses are also appropriate. In response to (84), one can say (87). The question in (88) can also be responded to in a literal way as in (89).

(87) Yes, I can. (Here it is.) / No, sorry, I can't, it's down there at the end of the table.

(88) Why don't you be quiet?

(89) Well, there are several reasons for not being quiet. First, ...

Idioms, however, cannot be understood literally. In response to (90) one would not very likely say (91).

(90) Do you remember Old Pete? He kicked the bucket.

(91) Really? Did he hurt his leg?

Another reason for claiming that indirect speech acts are not idioms is that a word for word translation of these sentences into other languages will generally produce sentences with similar illocutionary act potential, but idioms will not.

Nevertheless, Searle admits that not all the sentences synonymous with these can be used as requests. For example, (92) cannot be used as a request, at least not very easily. Even within the pair in (93), there is a difference in indirect illocutionary act potential.

(92) Is it the case that you at present have the ability to reach the

salt?

(93) a. Can you do A?

b. Are you able to do A?

The way out provided by Searle is to say indirect speech acts are idiomatic, or conventional, ways of making requests. But this has to do with conventions of usage rather than conventions of meaning. That is, to request is not part of the literal meaning of sentences like (93a). The request force comes from the way we use language, the way conversations generally go. Consequently Searle proposes to add another manner maxim to Grice's inventory, namely,

Speak idiomatically unless there is some special reason not to.

Levinson (1983: 273 fn. 21) points out, as Gazdar (1981) argues, when Searle claims that sentences like (93a) have literal question meanings, he overlooks a problem. That is, these sentences as questions are infelicitous. They do not meet the felicity conditions on questions, e.g. the sincerity condition of question is "S wants this information", the essential condition is "it counts as an attempt to elicit this information from H".① Even though in response to *Can you pass the salt?* one can say *Yes, I can*, we can also leave this part out, and this is the more usual. And sentences like (94) are also infelicitous in that the speaker has performed the act of reminding without the permission being granted.

(94) May I remind you that jackets and ties are required if you wish to use the bar on the 107th floor, sir?

This shows either the position that indirect speech acts have literal meanings is not tenable, or the felicity conditions as envisaged by Searle are wrong. Even if we make the concession to grant that Searle's analysis of indirect requests is correct, he still has to explain

conversations like the following:
(95) A: That's the telephone.
B: I'm in the bath.
A: O.K.②

---

① Cf. the table on page 241.
② Searle intends his analysis to be of general application. At the beginning of "Indirect Speech Acts" (p. 61ff.), he did consider a case of general nature:
(1) Student X: Let's go to the movies tonight.
(2) Student Y: I have to study for an exam.
And he suggests X might take ten steps to derive the illocutionary force of Y's response. But these steps are not as closely related to speech act theory as the ten steps we quoted earlier. And Searle will be hard put to it to derive the request force of answering the phone from "That's the telephone".

Chapter 7: Conversation Analysis

Conversation analysis is an integral part of the study of language in use, though in their exemplification of theories, pragmaticians seem to use single sentences only.① The simple fact that Grice named his first paper on implicature "Logic and Conversation" and the most important type of implicature "conversational implicature" is a strong indication of the place of conversation in his theory.

And this is the ultimate reason why Levinson has a chapter on this topic in his 1983 book.② Nevertheless, it is in the work of some sociologists, or ethnomethodologists, notably, Harvey Sacks, Emanuel Schegloff and Gail Jefferson that we find the most illuminating results concerning the structure of conversation. In this chapter, therefore,

---

① J. Thomas (1995: 199f., 209) says the criticism that pragmatics restricts itself to single, isolated utterances is only true of Austin, Grice, Searle and introductory textbook writers. And there are "obvious practical reasons why writers of all the currently available introductory texts have compromised on the quantity of data used for purposes of illustration. In the first place, they are trying to introduce a very large number of concepts as quickly and as clearly as possible for readers who are new to the discipline—it is not possible to find just one text capable of illustrating adequately a wide range of theoretical issues. Secondly, the text chosen must be readily accessible to readers from a variety of backgrounds." In my view, these two reasons are applicable to the early writers as well.

② 廖秋忠 (1992: 195) compares it to the last chapter of *The Sound Pattern of English* by Noam Chomsky and Morris Halle in the sense that the previous chapters are formal and speculative while this one is descriptive and empirical.

we shall first introduce their findings, then go on to review the approaches to conversation by neo-Gricean and speech act theorists.

7.1 Turn-taking

One of the most important discoveries made by Sacks and his associates is that people take turns at talking: in a given conversation there is only one person talking at a time, only when he stops will another begin to talk. In H. Sacks's words, "at least and no more than one party talks at a time".①

Since it is a conversation, a verbal activity, naturally there will be at least one person speaking. If a person does not speak when it is his turn to, his silence may be interpreted in a number of ways, the exact nature of which will be discussed in next section.

That there should be no more than one person talking at a time seems also to be self-explanatory. If there are more than one person talking at the same time, one will not be able to hear the speaker, or in fact, speakers, clearly. But Levinson (1983)② questions this explanation in a footnote on page 301: "It is also worth pointing out that the motivation for turn-taking is not as obvious as it may seem: as Miller has noted (1963: 418) turn-taking 'is not a necessary consequence of any auditory or physiological inability to speak and hear simultaneously; one voice is poor masking for another' (cited in Goodwin, 1977: 5). The possibility of simultaneous translation bears wit-

---

① H. Sacks (MS), from M. Coulthard (1985 [1977]: 59). This remark does not mean that there are no overlaps or silences whatsoever in conversation, but that if there are more or less than one party talking, participants will set out to remedy the situation immediately, and the overlap or silence will be short-lived.

② The citations of Levinson in this chapter are all from this book, unless otherwise indicated.

ness to this (see Goldman-Eisler, 1980)." Apart from observations like it is polite not to speak at the same time as someone else, is there any intrinsic motivation for the organization of conversation in terms of turns? This is the question we shall try to explore in what follows.

7.1.1 Rules for turn-taking

In order to maintain the situation that at least and no more than one party talks at a time, it is essential for the participants to know when is the time for one of them to start talking, and who this one is.

In other words, first, the next speaker should know when the current speaker has finished, and therefore he can begin to speak. Is that possible? Let us have a look at some examples.

(1) *Penny*: An'the fact is I-is-I jus' thought it was so kind of stupid[①]
// I didn' even say anything // when I came ho:me.
Janet: Y- Eh-
(0.3)
Janet: Well Estelle jus' called 'n...
(from Sacks et al 1998 [1974]: 217)

(2) *Ken*: I saw 'em last night // at uhm school.
Jim: They're a riot (ibid.)

(3) *Louise*: I think it's really funny // to watch.
Roger: Ohhh God! (ibid.)

(4) *Tourist*: Has the park cha:nged much,
Parky: Oh::ye:s,
(1.0)
Old man: th' *Funfair* changed it 'n//ahful lot//didn' it.
Parky: Th- That-

[①] For transcription conventions, see the appendix at the end of this chapter.

Parky: *That changed* it, (ibid.)

In appearance, the answer seems to be negative to our question. The fact that there are overlaps, there are cases in which the next speaker tries to come in before the current speaker stops, suggests that next speakers are not able to know where the current speaker will stop. But if we look at them more closely, we shall discover that these overlaps do not occur randomly. They do not just happen anywhere. In (1), Janet tried to start talking twice before her actual turn, once after "...stupid" and once after "...anything". And what is significant of them is that they are both at the end of a sentence, where Penny could have stopped. In (2) and (3), the next speaker's utterance overlaps with the last adverbial of the previous speaker's. As these are optional adverbials, the next speakers may still be said to have started at the end of a sentence. Parky's first attempt at talking after the old man's turn in (4) is a little different. It starts after an "and", which is a conjunction, suggesting that something more is coming.

However, considering the briefness of "n" and the fact that it occurs after a sentence, it will not be too far-fetched to regard it also as a case of overlap at sentence boundaries. ① These examples show that listeners look carefully for sentence boundaries, and try to start at these places rather than in the middle of a sentence, especially a simplex one. And they may be so successful in doing this that the next speaker's utterance follows the previous one's without any gap.

(5) *J*: Those shoes look nice when you keep on putting stuff on 'em.

---

① Words like "and", "but" and "however", Sacks notes, are often used by speakers to turn a potentially complete sentence into an incomplete one. Cf. Coulthard 1985 [1977]: 64.

```
C:    Yeah I 'ave to get another can cuz cuz it ran out. I mean
      it's a//lmost(h) ou(h)t =
J:              Oh:::ah he .hh heh =
C:    = yeah well it cleans 'em and keeps // 'em clean.
J:                                          Yeah right =
C:    = I should get a brush too you should getta brush 'n
      // you should-fix you hiking boo//ts
J:    Yeah suh::                            my hiking boots
C:    which you were gonna do this weekend.
J:    Pooh, did I have time this wk-well::
C:    Ahh c'mon =
J:    = wh'n we get-(uh:: kay), I haven't even sat down to
      do any-y'know like .hh today I'm gonna sit down 'n
      read while you're doing yur coat, (0.7) do yur-hood
```
(from Sacks et al 1998 [1974]: 210)

Therefore Sacks suggests that next speakers are not concerned with actually completed utterances. They do not wait to hear if the current speaker has actually stopped. All they are concerned with are points of possible completion.[①] In their paper " A Simplest Systematics for the Organization of Turn-taking of Conversation" of 1974, Sacks, Schegloff and Jefferson call these points of possible completion "transition relevance place", TRP for short.

Secondly comes the question who shall speak next when the current speaker stops. Unless the order of speakers is predetermined, the next speaker is usually selected in two ways: through the nomination of the current speaker or self-selection.

---

① H. Sacks (MS), cf. Coulthard 1985 [1977]: 61.

According to Coulthard (1985 [1977]: 60 - 1), Sacks thinks that a current speaker can exercise three degrees of control over the next turn. First, he can select both the participant to speak next by naming him "John", and also select the type of next utterance by producing the first part of an adjacency pair①, such as a question or a greeting, which constrains the next speaker to produce an appropriate answer or returning greeting. Secondly, the current speaker may simply constrain the next utterance, without selecting the next speaker. He may simply ask a question, so that anyone who can answer it is entitled to speak next. Thirdly, he can select neither, and let the others self-select completely.

Sacks emphasizes that these options are in an ordered relationship—the first over-rides the second and the second over-rides the third. If a next speaker has been selected by the current speaker, he alone should talk next. Even when an unselected speaker usurps the turn already assigned to a selected, the right of the selected speaker is usually preserved:

 (6) A (to C): Tell us about yourself so we can find something
    bad about you.
  B: Yeah hurry up.

What is more, these selection techniques operate only utterance by utterance: there is no mechanism in conversation by which the current speaker can select the next-but-one speaker—choice of the next speaker is always the prerogative of the current speaker if he chooses to exercise it. But pre-sequences,② especially pre-announcements, can be seen as a

---

 ① This notion will be discussed in detail in section 7.2.
 ② They will be discussed in detail in section 7.4.1.

technique to select oneself as the next-but-one speaker. For example,
    (7) A: Have you heard the one about the pink Martian?
        B: No.
        A: ((Story))

Even if somebody else takes the next-but-one turn, the original speaker can still be sure of a chance in the end.
    (8) K: You wanna hear muh-eh my sister told me a story last night.
        R: I don't wanna hear it. But if you must,
        A: What's purple an' an island. Grape-Britain. That's what iz sis//ter-
        K: No. to stun me she says uh there was these three girls...((Story follows))
                (Sacks 1974: 338)

    In their 1974 paper, Sacks and his associates have summarized the rules for the organization of turn-taking as follows:

    The following seems to be a basic set of rules governing turn-construction, providing for the allocation of a next turn to one party, coordinating transfer so as to minimize gap and overlap:

1 for any turn, at the initial transition-relevance place of an initial turn-constructional unit:

  (a) If the turn-so-far is so constructed as to involve the use of a "current speaker selects next" technique, then the party so selected has the right and is obliged to take next turn to speak; no others have such rights or obligations, and transfer occurs at that place.

  (b) If the turn-so-far is so constructed as not to involve the use of a "current speaker selects next" technique, then self-selection for next speakership may, but need not, be instituted; first starter acquires rights to a turn, and transfer occurs at that place.

(c) If the turn-so-far is so constructed as not to involve the use of a "current speaker selects next" technique, then current speaker may, but need not, continue unless another self-selects.

2 If, at the initial transition-relevance place of an initial turn constructional unit, neither 1(a) nor 1(b) has operated, and, following the provision of 1(c), current speaker has continued, then the rule-set (a) to (c) reapplies at the next transition-relevance place, and recursively at each next transition-relevance place, until transfer is effected. (Sacks et al 1998 [1974]: 198)

7.1.2 The significance of the rules

We said at the beginning that the organization of conversation in terms of turns does not mean that there are no overlaps or silences at all in conversation. The significance of the rules for turn-taking is that they can better account for the occurrence of overlaps and silences when they do occur.

Sacks et al (1998 [1974]: 201) note that there are two reasons for the occurrence of overlaps. First, "Rule 1(b), in allocating a turn to that self-selector who starts first, encourages earliest possible start for each self-selector. It thereby provides for overlap by competing self-selector for a next turn, when each projects his start to be earliest possible start at some possible transition-relevance place, producing simultaneous starts." Their examples are:

(9) *Parky*:   *Oo what* they call them dogs that pull the sleighs.

```
                    (0.5)
         Parky:    S-sledge dogs.
                    (0.7)
         Old man:  Oh uh //:: uh
         Tourist:           Uh-Huskies. =
         Old man:  = // Huskies. Mm,
         Parky:             Huskies. Yeh Huskies.
                            (from Sacks et al 1998 [1974]: 201)
```

(10) *Lil*: Bertha's lost, on *our* scale, about fourteen pounds.
     Damora: Oh //:: no::.
     Jean: *Twelve* pounds I think wasn't it. =
     Daisy: = // Can you *believe* it?
     Lil: *Twelve* pounds on the Weight Watcher's scale.   (ibid.)

(11) Mike: I know who d' guy is. =
     Vic: = // He's ba::d.
     James: You know the gu:y?   (ibid.)

Another reason for the occurrence of overlaps is that the current speaker may vary the last part of his talk, by lengthening the last syllable, adding a term of address or a tag question, which will result in overlap between a current turn and a next. For example,[①]

(12)   A: Sixty two feet is pretty good si://ze.
      B: Oh:: boy.   (ibid.: 202)

(13)   A: Uh *you* been down here before // havenche.
      B: Yeh.

[①] Example 4 above may also be regarded as one of this type.

(ibid.)

(14)　　A： What's yer name again please // sir,
　　　　B：　　　　　　　　　　　　　　F. T. Galloway.

(ibid.)

　　Now silences are of different types depending on the places they occur. Sacks et al (1998 [1974]: 240 n26) classify silence into three types: intra-turn silence (not at a transition-relevance place) is a pause; silence after a transition-relevance place is a gap; and an extended gap is a lapse. And they add that a gap may be transformed into a pause, if the person who was speaking before it continues with another turn.① On pages 209 to 211, however, their account is somewhat different, where a pause is defined as the silence after a next speaker has been selected.

　　Levinson (p. 299) uses the two terms "silence" and "pause" in a way which is opposite to Sacks and his associates. He calls the selected next speaker's silence "significant silence", "attributable silence", or "silence" simply, while the term "pause" is used as a general cover term. But this terminological difference in no way mars his analysis of this silence. That is, the fact a person does not speak when it is his turn to suggests that there is something odd, abnormal with the utterance to be provided. For example,

(15)　M： What's the time-by the clock?
　　　R： Uh
　　　M： What's the time?

---

　　① This seems to suggest that a transition-relevance place may be changed into a non-transition-relevance place, which invalidates the notion transition-relevance place to some extent.

(3.0)
M: (Now) what number's that?
R: Number two
M: No it's not
What is it?
R: It's a one and a nought

(from Levinson 1983: 327)

By asking the child a question, the mother has selected him as the next speaker, so the silence is the child's. And the mother takes it that the child is unable to answer the question, so she rephrases it to make it easier.

In (16) below, after the receiver's *Hello*, the caller issues a greeting, after which there is a pause of two tenths seconds. Though it is relatively short, it still suggests something odd on the receiver's side, and the most likely reason is that the receiver cannot identify the caller just on the basis of the greeting *Hello Charles*, so the receiver hastens to add *This is Yolk*. That this is the right analysis of this silence is proved by (17), in which after the caller's greeting, there is a silence of 1.5 seconds and then the receiver explicitly asks *Who's this*. Sometimes the silence may be taken as a negative answer. In (18) there is a silence of 0.2 seconds after A's invitation, fearing that the hearer might reject it, A immediately goes on to elaborate his invitation. That a silence may be interpreted as a rejection is more obviously shown in (19).

(16) C: ((rings))
R: Hello?
C: Hello Charles.
(0.2)

       C: This is Yolk.　　　(ibid.)
(17)　C: ((rings))
       R: Hello?
       C: Hello
         (1.5)
       R: Who's this.　　　(ibid.: 328)
(18)　A: C'mon down he:re, = it's oka:y,
         (0.2)
       A: I got lotta stuff, = I got be:er en stuff　　(ibid.)
(19)　C: So I was wondering would you be in your office on Monday (.) by any chance?
         (2.0)
       C: Probably not
       R: Hmm yes =
       C: = You would?
       R: Ya
       C: So if we came by could you give us ten minutes of your time?　　　(ibid.: 320)

Levinson (p. 321) says these examples show that the turn-taking system has the power to literally make something out of nothing: to assign significance to silence. It is fair to say that the phenomenon that we can make something out of silence has already been noticed and has always been exploited by writers, especially playwrights, which is known as pregnant silence.

7.2　Adjacency pairs

The second important discovery in this approach is that utterances are paired. "Given a question, regularly enough an answer will follow".① Similarly, a greeting from A is followed by a greeting from B; an offer is followed by either an acceptance or rejection; a warning is followed by an acknowledgment; and a complaint is followed by an apology or justification.

Schegloff and Sacks (1973) offer us a characterization of adjacency pairs as follows:

adjacency pairs are sequences of two utterances that are:
(i) adjacent
(ii) produced by different speakers
(iii) ordered as a first part and a second part
(iv) typed, so that a particular first part requires a particular second (or range of second parts)—e. g. offers require acceptance or rejections, greetings require greetings, and so on

(from Levinson 1983: 303 – 4)

7.2.1 Insertion sequences

This characterization of conversation as sequences of paired utterances is related to the turn-taking system, since a question from A is a means to select the next speaker and a constraint on the type of next utterance, i.e. the turn after a question should be issued by the questioned and the response should be an answer. However, there are problems in this characterization. First, strict adjacency is too strong a requirement. There are conversations in which a first part, such as **Q1** below, is not followed by a second part A1 immediately.

(20) B: ... I ordered some paint from you uh a couple of weeks ago some vermilion

---

① H. Sacks (1967 – 1971), from Coulthard 1985 [1977]: 69.

A: Yuh

B: And I wanted to order some more the name's Boyd

A: Yes // how many tubes would you like sir ((Q1))

B:　　　　An-

B: U:hm (.) what's the price now eh with V.A.T. do you know eh ((Q2))

A: Er I'll just work out for you =

B: = Thanks

(10.0)

A: Three pounds nineteen a tube sir ((A2))

B: Three nineteen is it = ((Q3))

A: = Yeah ((A3))

B: E::h (1.0) yes u:hm ((dental click)) ((in parenthetical tone)) e:h jus-justa think, that's what three nineteen. That's for the large tube isn't it ((Q4))

A: Well yeah it's the thirty seven c.c.s ((A4))

B: Er, hh I'll tell you what I'll just eh eh ring you back I have to work out how many I'll need. Sorry I did-wasn't sure of the price you see ((A1))

A: Okay　　　　　　　　(Levinson 1983: 305)

Sacks does not think exchanges like this detrimental to the theory of adjacency pairs. He argues that in conversation many things may be absent and go unnoticed, but the absence of a second part is noticeable and noticed. People regularly complain "You didn't answer my question" or "I said hello, and she just walked past".[1]

But Schegloff (1972) proposes to replace the strict criterion of adjacency with the notion of conditional relevance. That is,

---

[1] Cf. ibid.: 70.

the **Q** [question] utterance makes an **A** [answer] utterance conditionally relevant. The action the **Q** does ([e. g.], direction asking) makes some other action sequentially relevant ([e. g.], giving directions by answering the **Q**). Which is to say, after the **Q**, the next speaker has that action specifically chosen for him to do and can show attention to, and grasp of, the preceding utterance by doing the chosen action then and there. If he does not, that will be a notable omission. (from Coulthard 1985 [1977]: 73)

In other words, the paired structure of conversation means that a second part is relevant to its first part. Whenever there is a first part, one may always expect that there will be a second part following, though not necessarily immediately. In this sense the utterances used between Q1 and A1 in the above example are inserted into them. Therefore, Schegloff calls the embedded utterances "insertion sequences". They are used because the speaker does not understand, or because he does not want to commit himself until he knows more, or because he is simply stalling, delaying.[①] What structure an insertion sequence has, he does not specify, though he seems to assume that the insertion sequence is an adjacency pair in itself.

Jefferson (1972) finds a different sequence from that of Schegloff's and labels it "side sequence", of which (21) and (22) may serve as examples.

(21) A: Hey the first time they stopped me from sellin' cigarettes was this morning.
(1. 0)
B: From *sell*ing cigarettes?

---

① Cf. ibid.: 73.

　　　　A: From buying cigarettes.

　　　　　　　　　(from Schegloff, Jefferson and Sacks 1977: 370)
(22) Ken: 'E likes that waiter over there,
　　　Al: Wait-*er*?
　　　Ken: Waitress, sorry,
　　　Al: 'At's better, (ibid.: 377)

Jefferson initially suggests that it has a three-turn structure: a statement, a misapprehension and a clarification.[①] It differs from the insertion sequence in that the statement is not a first part, there is no indication of who should speak at the end of the sequence or of what type of utterance should follow, so the other items are in no sense inserted. On the other hand, misapprehension-clarification looks like a pair, but there is actually a compulsory third element in the sequence, an indication by the misapprehender that he now understands and the sequence is now terminated, as is realized by '*At's better* in (22), which may be called "terminator".

7.2.2　Three-turn structures

　　The last point in the above discussion leads to a second problem in the theory of adjacency pair: not all utterances seem to be paired. A telephone conversation, for example, usually begins with the receiver's *Hello*, followed by the caller's greeting if they are friends and familiar with each other's voice, then the receiver will return a greeting. It seems that there are three turns here, not just a pair as predicted. Schegloff (1972) argues that the receiver's first *Hello* is not a real greeting here. It is the answer to a summons, i.e. the ringing of the telephone. Though it appears to be the first turn at the talk, it is actually

---

[①] Cf. ibid.: 75.

the second move at the interaction, the first being the caller's action to dial the receiver's telephone number. And the summons and answer form an adjacency pair by themselves.

Levinson (p. 312) has summarized the structure of telephone opening as follows:

    C: ((rings))   ((SUMMONS))
    R: Hello   ((ANSWER)) + ((DISPLAY FOR RECON-
                      GNITION))
    C: Hi   ((GREETINGS 1ST PART))
                      ((CLAIM THAT C HAS RECOGNIZED R))
                      ((CLAIM THAT R CAN RECOGNISE C))
    R: Oh hi::   ((GREETINTS 2ND PART))
                      ((CLAIM THAT R HAS RECOGNIZED C))

In other words, the turns in such openings are multifunctional. "[A] single minimal utterance or turn can be the locus of a number of quite different overlapping constraints—it can thus perform, and can be carefully designed to perform, a number of quite different functions at once" (ibid.: 311). Face-to-face interactions like (23) and (24) also show evidence of this.

    (23) Ch: Mummy
         M: Yes dear
           (2.1)
         Ch: I want a cloth to clean (the) windows
                          (from Levinson 1983: 309 – 10)
    (24) A: John?
         B: Yeah?
         A: Pass the water wouldja?   (ibid.: 310)

The summons-answer adjacency pair differs from others in that it is always a prelude to something. It is not done for its own sake, one summons somebody in order to achieve some other purposes. So the second part, the answer, usually takes the form of a question. And the summoner will produce another utterance in response to the question, which specifies the reason for summons. Levinson (p. 310) calls an exchange of this type a three-turn sequence, a three-turn structure constructed out of two adjacency pairs.

But the analysis may be carried further. The third turn in which the reason is given is in fact not the last turn in this interaction, there will be another turn to meet the request, even if it is not realized verbally, since the summons may not be realized verbally either, as in the case of a telephone call. For example, we could add another turn, such as (25), to (24).

(25) B: Here you are.

Nevertheless there ARE three-turn structures. 李月菊（1994：27-28）reports a dialogue at a talent exchange fair as follows：

(26) A：哎，你搞什么专业的？
　　　B：我是搞计算机的。
　　　A：计算机的。
　　　B：计算机的。
　　　A：嗯::,你是哪个学校毕业的？
　　　B：大连理工大学。
　　　A：啊？
　　　B：大连工学院的。
　　　A：大连工学院啊,大连工学院,那你怎么上这儿来了？
　　　B：我是分在这儿了。
　　　A：分在这儿(.),你是哪年分的？
　　　B：九::,九一年的(.)。

A：九一年的(.)，你老家是哪儿的？
B：河北的。
A：东北的。
B：河北的,河北的。
A：河北的啊(.)，想到大连去啊？
……

Speaker A is in a habit of echoing what B has said. After the question-answer pair, there is always a third part. The third part does not carry the main information, but it is not without any significance either. One of its functions is to assure the listener that his previous information has been received. Another is to help the listener check whether the speaker has understood him properly. If not, there may be chance for timely correction, as shown by 东北的 above.

7.3 Preference organization

A phenomenon that looms large in the analysis of conversation is that some types of utterances are preferred to others in the sense that they are used more frequently. In what follows we discuss this phenomenon in relation to repair, and the alternative second parts of an adjacency pair.

7.3.1 Preference in repair

The idea that some utterances are preferred to others was first put forward by Schegloff, Jefferson and Sacks in their article "The Preference for Self-correction in the Organization of Repair in Conversation" published in 1977. In it they discussed the question of how speakers correct mistakes occurring in conversation. In order for the analysis to have a more general applicability, they introduced the term "repair", which covers not only the correction of real mistakes but also the imagined mistakes, misunderstandings, mishearings, even non-hearings as in (27), or self-editing to make the expression more exact, more precise as in (28) and (29).

(27) A: Were you uh you were in therapy with a private doctor?
B: yah
A: Have you ever tried a clinic?
B: What?
A: Have you ever tried a clinic?
B: ((sign)) No, I don't want to go to a clinic.
(Schegloff, Jefferson and Sacks 1977: 367)

(28) N: she was givin' me a:ll the people that were go:ne this yea:r I mean this quarter y'//know
J: Yeah (ibid.: 364)

(29) L: An 'en but all of the doors 'n things were taped up =
= I mean y' know they put up y' know that kinda paper'r stuff, the brown paper. (ibid.: 366)

They discover that there is a preference organization of repair in conversation, i.e. self-initiated self-repair is preferred to other-initiated self-repair, which is itself preferred to other-initiated other-repair.① Listeners do not usually initiate a repair as soon as they have detected some deficiency in speech. They wait for some time for the speaker to initiate it himself. Only when the speaker fails to do that during the waiting period, do they begin to initiate it. For example, before B initiates a repair in example (21) on page 262, there is a one second lapse. And there are even fewer cases of listener repairing. As far as possible, they will leave it to the speaker to do the repair, as is shown

---

① This is a simplified representation of their idea. In the original, they also emphasize that mid-turn self-initiated self-repair is preferred to a turn-end one.

in (22). Only when the speaker fails to respond to the initiation as it is, will they go out of their way to do it. A case in point is (30).

(30) Lori: But y'know single *beds*'r *aw*fully *thin* to *sleep* on.
    Sam: What?
    Lori: Single beds. // They're-
    Ellen: Y'mean narrow?
    Lori: They're awfully *na*rrow yeah.   (ibid.: 378)

Now Schegloff and others consider other-repair to be highly constrained, and Levinson (p. 342) calls it a rare event. However, 赵晓泉(1996) finds that it is not the case according to his data. He recorded ten discussions of a linguistic circle, and collected 260 instances of repair. A categorization of the data shows there are 126 (48%) cases of self-initiated self-repair, 47 (18%) other-initiated self-repair, 67 (26%) other-initiated other-repair, and 20 (8%) self-initiated other-repair. In other words, though self-repair makes up a majority, 66% in total, other-repair accounts for not an insignificant percent, 34%, a strong one third. What is more, if we look at the initiation only, self-initiation does not have a comfortable majority, only 56%. And among those other-initiated, 59% are other-repaired. Why is it that the discoveries of Schegloff and others are not born out here? The author suggests perhaps it has to do with the nature of the discussions he recorded. They are academic discussions, in which accuracy of information is of utmost importance. So if possible, others would try to repair the speaker. Another reason may have to do with the Chinese culture. Is it possible that we Chinese tend to repair others more often than Americans do? But whatever the reason, one thing is certain, that is, other-repair is not a rare event, at least the frequency of other-repair varies with the type of conversation, the content of conversation, or the situational context.

7.3.2 Preferred and dispreferred seconds

The idea of preference organization has been extended to other areas of conversation, especially the alternative second parts to the first part of an adjacency pair. Thus Levinson (p. 333) says the alternative second parts to the first part of an adjacency pair are not of equal status: some second parts are preferred and others dispreferred. For example,

(31) A: Why don't you come up and see me some
　　　　　//times
　　　B: I would like to

(from Levinson 1983: 333)

(32) A: Uh if you'd care to come and visit a little while this morning I'll give you a cup of *coffee*
　　　B: hehh Well that's awfully sweet of you, I don't think I can make it this morning. . hh uhm I'm running an ad in the paper and-and uh I have to stay near the phone.

(ibid.: 333-4)

He links this distinction to the notion of markedness in morphology: the preferred is the unmarked and dispreferred the marked. He says categorically that the notion of preference he is using is not a psychological one, it has nothing to do with the speaker's or hearer's individual desires, or preferences.[①] Rather it is a structural notion. The preferred second parts are structurally simpler, i.e. consisting of fewer constituents, sometimes even a single *yes* will do. The dispreferred second parts on the other hand, are structurally more complex, con-

---

① Cf. Levinson 1983: 307, 332f.

sisting of more constituents, such as, delays, insertion sequences, even explanations for the use of the dispreferred. Specifically, the dispreferred second parts have the following features:

(a) *delays*: (i) by pause before delivery, (ii) by the use of a preface (see (b)), (iii) by displacement over a number of turns via use of *repair initiators* or insertion sequences

(b) *prefaces*: (i) the use of markers or announcers of dispreferreds like *Uh* and *Well*, (ii) the production of token agreements before disagreements, (iii) the use of appreciations if relevant (for offers, invitations, suggestions, advice), (iv) the use of apologies if relevant (for requests, invitations, etc), (v) the use of qualifiers (e.g. I *don't know for sure, but*...), (vi) hesitation in various forms, including self-editing

(c) *accounts*: carefully formulated explanations for why the (dispreferred) act is being done

(d) *declination component*: of a form suited to the nature of the first part of the pair, but characteristically indirect or mitigated (pp. 334 – 5)

To illustrate, Levinson (pp. 335 – 6) provides the examples below:

(33) *Illustrating (a)(i)*
    Ch: Can I go down an see 'im
       (2. 0)
       ( )
       (1.8)
       C'mo::n
       (1.5)
       Come'n te see 'im

(1.6)
C'mo::n
M: No::

(34) *Illustrating (a)(ii), (b)(iii), (c), (d)*
B: She says you might want that dress I bought, I don't know whether you do
A: Oh thanks (well), let me see I really have lots of dresses

(35) *Illustrating (a)(iii)*
Ch: I wan my ow:n tea .hh my*self*
M: (You) want what? =
Ch: = My tea my*se:lf*
M: No:w? We are all having tea together

(36) *Illustrating (b)(i), (c)*
R: What about coming here on the way (.) or doesn't that give you enough time?
C: Well no I'm supervising here

(37) *Illustrating (b)(v), (d)*
C: Um I wondered if there's any chance of seeing you tomorrow sometime (0.5) morning or before the seminar
(1.0)
R: Ahum (.) I doubt it

(38) *Illustrating (b)(vi) (R has been complaining that C's fire in the apartment below has filled R's apartment with smoke)*
C: ...is it-it's all right now-you don't want me to put it out?
R: E::r (1.5) well on the whole I wouldn't bother because er huhuh (2.0) well I mean what-what (0.5) would it

involve putting it out
(0.5)
C: Hahaha ( ) hahah

(39) *Illustrating* (*b*)(*iv*)
A: ((to operator)) Could I have Andrew Roper's extension please?
(9.0)
B: Robin Hardwick's telephone (1.0) hello
A: Andrew?
B: No I'm awfully sorry Andrew's away all week

On page 336 Levinson goes further to correlate the content of the second parts in adjacency pairs with their format as follows:

FIRST PARTS:	Request	Offer/Invite	Assessment	Question	Blame
SECOND PARTS:					
Preferred:	acceptance	acceptance	agreement	expected answer	denial
Dispreferred:	refusal	refusal	disagreement	unexpected answer or non-answer	admission

When discussing the responses to assessments, however, he notes that there is an asymmetry in the significance of a pause after an ordinary assessment and that after a self-deprecation assessment. For example,

(40) A: God isn't it dreary!
B: ((SILENCE = DISAGREEMENT))
(41) A: I'm gettin fat hh
B: ((SILENCE = AGREEMENT)) (p.339)

That is to say, the same structural device may have different significance. Silence does not necessarily indicate dispreferred response

Levinson has attributed this asymmetry to the existence of another principle, namely, a norm enjoining the avoidance of criticism.

But the problem lies deeper. There are also problems in the correlation of expected answer with preferred and unexpected with dispreferred. First, Levinson does not specify what is expected and what is unexpected. Presumably, this is a pair of semantic notion like "acceptance/refusal, agreement/disagreement, denial/admission", which have to do with the content of the answer (e.g. positive or negative to a polar question), and the psychological state of the speaker and hearer, i.e. their expectation, whether they expect to hear a positive or negative answer. However, if we consider it in some depth, we soon discover that the distinction between expected and unexpected is hard to maintain in relation to a yes/no question. The use of a yes/no question itself suggests that there are two possible answers to it, one positive and the other negative.① Both of them are anticipated, or expected; neither one will come as a surprise. If one is absolutely sure of a positive answer, there would be no need of a polar question. One could instead ask a question which presupposes a positive answer. For example, before an interviewing counter, one could ask 你们需要多少经济法专业的？rather than 你们需要经济法专业的吗？On the other hand, if one is sure of a negative answer, then there is no need for any question at all. Since you know the answer will definitely be negative, then why bother to ask?② So for polar questions at least, the answers

---

① Both of them are presuppositions of a yes/no question, see section 5.2.4 for the details.

② We are only considering real questions here, not including rhetorical questions, or questions for other stylistic purposes.

cannot be distinguished in terms of content into expected and unexpected, but only positive and negative, which are more in line with the other content distinctions, such as, agreement and disagreement.

Second, in terms of structure, there are answers which are marked or unmarked in the sense that some are simple and others are complex. But there is no correlation between this distinction and the content distinction of positive or negative. Among the data collected by 李月菊(1994), there are negative answers given both in the marked form and unmarked form, and the positives are usually given in the marked form, i.e. with insertion sequences in between. For example,

(42) A：需要经济法的吗？
　　 B：经济法不要。
(43) A：学俄语的要吧？
　　 B：俄语的不要。
(44) A：哎,同志,你这个俄语的还招吗？
　　 B：招,25岁到30岁,大学以上。你是学专业俄语的？
　　 A：我不是,我是学国际经济学的。
　　 B：那不行,我们要专业俄语的。
　　 A：哦,这个经济的行吗？
　　 B：哪个？
　　 A：那个经济。((用手指招聘牌上写的条目))
　　 B：哪个,你说哪个经济,这里哪有经济,你给我看看。
　　 A：这个(.),就要大学的是吧？
　　 B：唉。
　　 A：这个行吗？
　　 B：这个行啊::？你是哪个学校毕业的,你给我简历看看。
　　 A：我现在还没毕业,我是应届毕业生。
　　 B：哎哟！那太急了！这样吧,明年吧,噢::

(45) A: 你们这儿缺外语方面的人吗?
    B: 你是::
    A: 学英语的。
    B: 英语(.), 哪届毕业生?
    A: 明年。
    B: 明年(.)硕士
    A: 唉,
    B: 硕士生,需要
    ……

(46) A: 你这儿还需要自动化的吗?
    B: 你指的是::,应届?
    A: 应届的。
    B: 可以啊。

(47) A: 那个烟台外语需要什么专业?
    B: 那::个::,你学的什么语种?
    A: 英语,英文的=
    B: =英文的(.),哪儿毕业的?
    A: 北大的。
    B: 啊,填个表,填个表

This may have to do with the nature of insertion sequences. As we noted in section 7.2.1, Schegloff points out that insertion sequences may be used for three reasons: (i) the hearer does not understand what the speaker has just said; (ii) the hearer does not want to commit himself until he knows more; or (iii) he is simply stalling, delaying an answer. It is only in the third case, will the answer eventually given be most likely negative. In the first two cases the answer may still be positive, if the information provided subsequently is satisfactory to the inquirer. So we cannot conclude simply from the use of insertion sequences that it is a negative answer. The mother's response in example (35), reproduced here as (48), can in fact be interpreted in two ways: a real question for clarification, or a question in disguise, with the implicature of a refusal. This is born out by (49).

(48) Ch: I wan my ow::n tea .hh my*self*
  M: (You) want what? =
  Ch: = My tea my*se:lf*
  M: No:w? We are all having tea together

(49) C: ... Do you have in stock please any L.T. one eight eight?
  R: One eight eight
  C: Yeah =
  R: = Can you hold on please
  C: Thank you
  (1.5)
  R: Yes I have got the one
  C: Yes. Could I-you hold that for H.H.Q.G please
          (Levinson 1983: 348)

This is not only true of questions. In response to requests, offers, or invitations, one may also use insertion sequences before giving an acceptance, as is shown in (50). In other words, there may not be a simple correlation between the content and format of a second part in the adjacency pair. At least the use of insertion sequences does not necessarily mean a dispreferred second part in the sense of a refusal, for example,

(50) A: May I borrow your bike tomorrow?
  B: When will you be back?
  A: About two o'clock.

B: Okay.

7.4 A neo-Gricean interpretation

Levinson (1998 [1987a]: 562) holds the view that "a conversational principle had better show up in conversation", and has tried to interpret conversational activity in terms of neo-Gricean principles, especially the I-principle. His first attempt in this direction was made in his *Pragmatics* of 1983. The discussion of preferred and dispreferred second parts in terms of markedness mentioned in last section, as he recalls later, was meant to show that by the I-principle "the unmarked form should implicate the informative, stereotypical response, while the marked form will Q/M implicate the complement of the I-principle" (1998 [1987a]: 568 – 9). But a more explicit reference to the I-principle was made in connection with pre-sequences.

7.4.1 Pre-sequences

Pre-sequences can be defined as utterances which are not the substantive part of a conversation in themselves but are used to prefigure, to lead to that part. For example, summons may be seen as a pre-sequence① for a request. According to the content that is prefigured, pre-sequences may be of different kinds: pre-invitations, pre-requests, pre-arrangements, pre-announcements, pre-offers, etc. On the basis of pre-invitations like (51) and (52),

(51) A: Whatcha doin'?

B: Nothin'

---

① The term "pre-sequence" is sometimes used with a systematic ambiguity, i.e. it may refer to a single turn such as a summons, or a sequence of turns such as summons + answer +, even, reason for summons + follow up. So Levinson introduces "pre-s" for the single turn in his 1983 book.

> A: Wanna drink? (from Levinson 1983: 346)

(52) R: Hi John
> C: How ya doin =
> = say wh*at*'r you doing?
> R: Well we're going out. Why?
> C: Oh, I was just gonna say come out and come over here an' talk this evening, but if you're going out you can't very well do that (ibid.)

Levinson proposes the following structure for pre-sequences:
> T[urn]1 (Position 1): a question checking whether some precondition obtains for the action to be performed in T3
> T2 (Position 2): an answer indicating the precondition obtains, often with a question or request to proceed to T3
> T3 (Position 3): the prefigured action, conditional on the "go ahead" in T2
> T4 (Position 4): response to the action in T3 (pp. 346 – 7)

But the order of the turns may not always coincide with that of the positions. In example (49), reanalyzed here as (53), there are two insertion sequences, consisting of T2 and T3, T4 and T5 respectively.

(53) C: ... Do you have in stock please any L. T. one eight eight? ((T1)) ((POSITION 1))
> R: One eight eight ((T2))   ((INSERTION
> C: Yeah = ((T3))   SEQUENCE 1))
> R: = Can you hold on please ((T4)) ((INSERTION
> C: Thank you ((T5))   SEQUENCE 2))
> (1.5)
> R: Yes I have got the one ((T6)) ((POSITION 2))

C: Yes. Could I-you hold that for H. H. Q. G. please ((T7)) ((POSITION 3))

Position 2 in fact is realized by T6. Therefore Levinson ends up with "position" and "turn" separated. The former refers to the structural place an utterance occupies in relation to others, while the latter refers to its place in terms of a pure sequential order. His characterization of pre-announcements, for instance, is as follows:

Position 1: pre-sequence first part, generally checking on newsworthiness of potential announcement in position 3

Position 2: pre-sequence second, generally validating newsworthiness, and first part of second pair, namely a request to tell

Position 3: second part to second pair—the announcement delivered

Position 4: news receipt (p. 350)

Indirect speech acts may also be analyzed in this way. For example,

(54) A: Hi. Do you have uh size C flashlight batteries? ((POSITION 1)) ((PRE-REQUEST))
B: Yes sir ((POSITION 2)) ((GO AHEAD))
A: I'll have four please ((POSITION 3)) ((REQUEST))
B: ((turns to get)) ((POSITION 4)) ((RESPONSE))

(from Levinson 1983: 357)

Now Levinson argues that pre-sequences can be interpreted in terms of conversational principles. One of the reasons why people use pre-announcements may be to secure a longer turn to speak, to let others know that he has a story to tell. But a more important reason may be to check whether what he is going to say is really worth saying, or newsworthy. If it is not, he would withhold the intended information. In other words, people prefer silence to speech if possible. This idea has been developed into the I-principle by Levinson as we mentioned in section 4.3.1, namely, "Say as little as necessary". In cases of bad news, the use of a pre-announcement may prompt a guess from the listener, so that the action of the speaker's telling the news could be entirely avoided, as is exemplified in (55).

 (55) D: I-I-I had something *terrible* t'tell you. So
    // uh
   R: How terrible *is* it.
   D: Uh, th-as worse it could *be*.
    (0.8)
   R: Wm-y'ean Edna?
   D: Uh yah.
   R: Whad she do, die?
   D: Mm:hm, (ibid.; 356)

Pre-requests may also prompt the hearer to provide an offer on his own initiative, so that the speaker would have no need to make a request at all. For example,

 (56) C: Do you have pecan Danish today?
   S: Yes we do. Would you like one of those?
   C: Yes please
   S: Okay ((turns to get)) (ibid.;359)
 (57) C: Hullo I was just ringing up to ask if you were going to
    Bertrand's party
   R: Yes I thought you might be
   C: Heh heh
   R: Yes would you like a lift?

       C: Oh I'd love one
       R: Right okay um I'll pick you up from there...
                                                           (ibid.)

Sometimes a request may be fulfilled by a pre-request alone, i.e. Positions 2 and 3 may simply be left out. Consider (58), (59) and (60).

    (58) S: Have you got Embassy Gold please? ((POSITION 1))
         H: Yes dear ((provides)) ((POSITION 4))
                                                (ibid.: 361)
    (59) C: Do you have Marlboros? ((POSITION 1))
         S: Yeah. Hard or soft? ((INSERTION
         C: Soft please   SEQUENCE))
         S: Okay ((POSITION 4))   (ibid.)
    (60) S: Can I have two pints of Abbot and a grapefruit and whisky? ((POSITION 1))
         H: Sure ((turns to get)) ((POSITION 4))
            ((later)) There you are ...   (ibid.: 362)

In (61), the pre-request is taken as such, and declined. But not much face has been lost, since the request was not made in the first place.

    (61) M: What're you doing wi' that big bow-puh tank. Nothing.
         (0.5)
         V: ((cough)) uh-h-h (1.0) I'm not into selling it or giving it. That's it.
         M: Okay   (ibid.)

To save face, some people explicitly resort to this means. Sacks has an example of a child asking his parent "Can you fix this needle?"

When he gets the answer "I'm busy", he protests "I just wanted to know if you can fix it". ①

That this principle is at work is also supported by the fact that in telephone conversations, people are reluctant to overtly identify themselves. The caller would simply produce a *Hello* as a clue for the recipient to recognize. Only when the recipient fails to do so, will the caller go on to give his first name, or also last name, for example,

(62) R: Hello
     C: Hello
     R: Hi   (ibid.: 343)
(63) R: Hello,
     C: Hi Susan?
     R: Ye:s,
     C: This's Judith (.) Rossman
     R: Judith!   (ibid.)

7.4.2 Minimization in conversation

In his "Minimization and Conversational Inference" of 1987, Levinson devotes a section to a detailed examination of the connection between neo-Gricean principles and conversation analysis. In what follows we shall mainly introduce his arguments for the claim that there is something analogous to the Q- and I-principles in the works of Sacks and his associates.

Levinson notes Sacks in his article "Everyone Has to Lie" of 1975 demonstrated that answers to the question "How are you?" are constrained in a number of ways. For example, "(a) an honest answer might lead away from the business in hand (and the kind appropriate

---

① Cf. Coulthard 1985 [1977]: 72.

to the interlocutor), and (b) news about troubles and successes ought to go in a well-ordered sequence, to one's nearest and dearest first" (Levinson 1998 [1987a]: 563). This shows a simple-minded application of the first maxim of Quantity "say as much as is required" is out of place. There must be some principles of minimization at work as well.

In his lectures of 1971, Sacks was even closer to Grice in having a maxim "Don't tell people what they already know". This consideration, as we mentioned in last section, may be what motivates the use of pre-announcements in the first place.

On the other hand, Sacks and his associates observe that hearers or readers may enrich the information they receive in a certain way. Sacks in his paper "On the Analyzability of Stories by Children" written in 1972 suggests that the hearer or reader of a two-sentence children's story like "The baby cried. The mommy picked it up" might infer:

(i) The baby and the mommy are co-family members.
(ii) It is stereotypical that babies cry;
It is non-reprehensible that this baby cried.
(iii) It is stereotypical that mothers comfort babies; the mother did the proper thing.
(iv) The event described in the first clause (E1) comes before the event described in the second (E2).
(v) E2 occurred *because* of E1.

(from Levinson 1998 [1987a]: 567)

Schegloff in his 1972 paper "Notes on a Conversational Practice: Formulating Place" points out that when calling a police department for help, the speaker will usually give the location in terms of a bare street name, and the hearer will assume that they are in the same city. Similarly, if A and B are both in New York, a description that "John is in the East" would implicate that John is not in New York, even though "the East" would normally be taken to include New York.

Sacks and Schegloff also notice that different principles of conversational organization may interact in an interesting way. In "Two Preferences in the Organization of Reference to Persons in Conversation and their Interaction" of 1979, they suggest that there are two principles at work in reference to third persons. One is a principle of minimization, which amounts to a preference for single reference forms. The other is a principle of recognition, a preference for forms which will enable the recipient to recognize the referent easily. These two principles may be satisfied at the same time by the use of a name such as "John" or "Mary", which is both minimal and recognitional. But they may be in conflict. For example,

(64) A: ...well I was the only one other than that the uhm tch Fords? Uh Mrs Holmes Fords?

B: (pause)

A: You know uh

// the the cellist

B: Oh yes. She's the cellist

A: Yes   (from Levinson 1998 [1987a]: 573 – 4)

Speaker A uses a minimal name first, which upon non-recognition is expanded to title plus names, and lastly to a description. This suggests that the resolution of a conflict between different principles is achieved interactionally. That is, "one can try a minimal form and see if it works, if not, escalate" (Levinson 1998 [1987a]: 599). In terms of neo-Gricean principles, this means "Try letting the I-principle win in the first instance, i.e. go for minimal forms; if that doesn't work escalate step by step towards a Q-principle solution" (ibid.).

Levinson (ibid.: 607 n12) notes "Emanuel Schegloff provides me with another kind of evidence. When a speaker has a 'word-search' problem, and cannot find a name for someone, he may use a description which allows the recipient to recognize the referent. Yet, despite the fact that recognition is now achieved, neither may be satisfied until the minimal reference form is found, indicating that recipient design (motivating the goal of referent-recognition) and minimization (motivating the search for a single minimal reference form) are independent, and independently satisfiable."

In this way Levinson hopes to have shown that the neo-Gricean principles are "in fact well grounded in the details of conversational organization" (ibid.: 562).

7.5 Searle on conversation

In 1981, Searle delivered a lecture introducing a conference on dialogue at the University of Campinas, Brazil, which was first published as "Notes on Conversation" in 1986. Because of its importance for conversation analysis, and for pragmatics in general, Herman Parret and Jef Verschueren invited eight scholars from a diversity of perspectives to write comments on Searle's article, and published them together, with the addition of Searle's reply in 1992 under the title of (*On*) *Searle on Conversation*. In this section, we shall concentrate on two of the questions discussed by Searle and his critics: the structure of conversation and turn-taking rules.

7.5.1 The structure of conversation

The central theme of Searle's article is to explore whether conversations are structured. In Searle's view, speech acts are the basic units of language use. Conversations are made up of speech acts. So his exploration starts with the question: "Could we get an account of conversation parallel to our account of speech acts? Could we, for example, get an account that gave us constitutive rules for conversations in a way that we have constitutive rules of speech acts?" (Searle et al 1992: 7).①

He argues "Just as a move in a game creates a space of possible and appropriate countermoves, so in a conversation, each speech act creates a space of possible and appropriate response speech acts. The beginnings of a theory of the conversational game might be a systematic attempt to account for how particular 'moves', particular illocutionary acts, constrain the scope of possible appropriate responses" (p.8). And he first considers the relationship between pairs of speech acts like question/answer, greeting/greeting, offer/acceptance or rejection, to which he thinks the term "adjacency pair" has been misleadingly applied.

It seems that there are tight constraints on what constitutes an ideally appropriate response in these cases. If somebody asks you a yes/no question, then your answer has to count either as an affirmation or a denial of the propositional content presented in the original question. If it is a wh-question, the inquirer has expressed a propositional function, and your appropriate response has to fill in the value of the free variable. The form of an appropriate answer is determined by the form of the question. In cases of offers, bets and invitations, the constraints are even stronger. Following a bet, the hearer must go on to accept it. And a bet not accepted is not a bet properly made.

---

① All quotations in this section are from this book, henceforth only page number will be given.

But constraints of this kind do not apply to all types of speech acts. Assertions, in particular, are not subject to these constraints. "For example," Searle argues, "if I say to you 'I think the Republicans will win the next election', and you say to me, 'I think the Brazilian government has devalued the Cruzeiro again,' at least on the surface your remark is violating a certain principle of relevance. But notice, unlike the case of offers and bets, the illocutionary point of my speech act was nonetheless achieved. I did make an assertion, and my success in achieving that illocutionary point does not depend on your making an appropriate response" (p. 10).

Then Searle examines the possibility of using "relevance" as a constraint on conversational sequence. In his view relevance is a relative notion. In relation to one conversational purpose, an utterance may be relevant, while in relation to another it may not. Suppose a man and a woman are having a conversation as follows:

(65) A: How long have you lived in California?
B: Oh, about a year and a half. (p.13)

The relevant response by A depends on his conversational purpose. If he is trying to pick up the woman in a bar, the following response might be relevant.

(66) A: I love living here myself, but I sure am getting sick of the smog in L.A. (ibid.)

On the other hand, if he is a doctor interviewing a patient, then the relevant response would be something like (67).

(67) A: And how often have you had diarrhoea during those eighteen months? (ibid.)

Another example he employs is "Suppose, ... I am having a conversation with my stock broker about whether or not to invest in IBM.

Suppose he suddenly shouts, 'Look out! The chandelier is going to fall on your head!' Now is his remark relevant? It is certainly not relevant to my purpose in investing in the stock market. But it certainly is relevant to my purpose of staying alive. So, if we think of this as one conversation, he has made an irrelevant remark. If we think of it as two conversations, the second one which he just initiated being about my safety, then he has made a relevant remark" (p. 14). In other words, relevance depends on the identity of conversation. Therefore, Searle maintains, to use relevance as a criterion of conversation is circular.

Searle sometimes denies that conversations have purposes, but his wording is not always consistent. On page 14, he says "there is no GENERAL purpose of conversations, qua conversations" (emphasis mine), while on page 20 he declares "conversations as such lack a PARTICULAR purpose or point" (emphasis mine). And he claims that the lack of a purpose is the reason why conversations do not have an inner structure in the sense that speech acts do. He lists such talk exchanges as in (68), and asks whether there is a well defined structure common to all of these. The suggestion that they all have a beginning, a middle and an end has aroused ridicule from Searle, for a glass of beer also has a beginning, middle and end.

(68)   A woman calling her dentist's office to arrange an appointment.

Two casual acquaintances meeting each other on the street and stopping to have a brief chat in which they talk about a series of subjects (e.g. the weather, the latest football results, the president's speech last night).

A philosophy seminar.

A family spending a Sunday afternoon at home watching a football game on television and discussing the progress of the game among various other matters.

A meeting of the board of directors of a small corporation.

(pp. 20−1)

Now commentators have voiced various disagreements against Searle, but in this section we shall only present those more closely related to the nature of conversation. David Holdcroft, for example, thinks that the talk exchange about the Republicans and the Brazilian government is not a conversation. And Searle's conclusion that one does "not violate a constitutive rule of a certain kind of speech act or conversation just by changing the subject" is not valid. In his view, "if by 'changing the subject' is meant introducing another topic for discussion, then perhaps this could be an extremely clumsily executed case of changing the subject" (p. 63). Suppose the first participant continues with "Oh I didn't know that their inflation was that bad", and the second with "Les Miserables is a great success", "then surely no conversational moves at all can be attributed to [the second], and what we are dealing with is not a conversation" (ibid.).

Andreas H. Jucker argues from the point of view of relevance theory as established by D. Sperber and D. Wilson that "What is relevant to the participants changes continually along with the changing set of background assumptions" (p. 83). In the case of Searle's conversation with his stock broker, the relevance of (69) lies in the fact that a new stimulus, the falling down of the chandelier, has changed the context, hence the change of the degree of relevance of the utterances made by the two participants. Searle's stock broker "can safely assume that it will be of more immediate relevance for Searle to know that he should jump out of the way than to know whether or not to invest in IBM" (p. 84).

(69) Look out! The chandelier is going to fall on your head!

Jucker also disagrees with the comparison between a conversation and a glass of beer. These two things have considerable differences. "The beginning and the end of, let us say, a fairy tale are clearly distinguishable. 'Once upon a time there was...' and 'They lived happily ever after' cannot be exchanged. The first and the last gulp of a glass of beer, on the other hand, are not distinct from a structural point of view even though they may be quite different from a beer drinker's point of view" (pp. 78 – 9).

The circularity question of relevance, Marcelo Dascal thinks, partly arises from the fact that Searle takes the position of an observer from the outside. He suggests if you are a participant in the conversation, then you will naturally know your purposes, and can make judgements about relevance without much difficulty.

7.5.2 Turn-taking "rules"

In his article, Searle discusses at length the turn-taking rules suggested by Sacks and his associates as a possible candidate for the description of the structure of conversation.

After quoting the rule-set from Sacks et al (1974), which we reproduced in section 7.1.1, Searle paraphrases it "in plain English" as follows:

> In a conversation a speaker can select who is going to be the next speaker, for example, by asking him a question. Or he can just shut up and let somebody else talk. Or he can keep on talking. Furthermore, if he decides to keep on talking, then next time

there is a break[①] in the conversation, (that's called a "transition relevance place") the same three options apply. (p.16)

But he objects to call it a rule. He argues "The notion of a rule is logically connected to the notion of following a rule, and the notion of following a rule is connected to the notion of making one's behavior conform to the content of a rule because it is a rule. For example, when I drive in England, I follow the rule: Drive on the left-hand side of the road. Now that seems to me a genuine rule. Why is it a rule? Because the content of the rule plays a causal role in the production of my behavior. If another driver is coming directly toward me the other way, I swerve to the left, i.e. I make my behavior conform to the content of the rule" (pp. 16 – 7). In his view the Sacks et al rule is like a description of his driving behavior in England as he keeps the steering wheel near the centerline and the passenger side nearer to the curb.[②] Though it describes his behavior and makes predictions accurately, it is only a consequence of following the rule to drive on the left, not the rule itself.

This is especially true of rules 1(b) and (c). To his mind, rule 1 (b) "just means that there is a break and somebody else starts talking. That 'rule' says that when there is a break in the conversation anybody can start talking, and whoever starts talking gets to keep on talking" (p. 18). And rule 1 (c) "just says that when you are talking, you can keep on talking" (ibid.). In the case of rule 1(a), that is,

---

　① According to Schegloff, in the 1986 version the word "pause" was used instead of "break".

　② In his reply, Searle further compares it to a description of his driving behavior in England as driving on the side of the road opposite his birth mark.

when a current speaker selects a next speaker by, say, asking him a question, Searle thinks, the real rule is a speech act rule about asking questions.

Schegloff in his commentary argues that there is something important missing in Searle's paraphrase of the rule-set. That is, the notion of "turn-constructional unit". Turn-constructional units are the building blocks of conversation, at the end of which whether ending the turn or continuing it, transfer of the turn or its retention becomes relevant. That is why the points at which they end are known as transition-relevance places. And "'transition-relevance place' does *not* translate into plain English as 'pause'" (p. 117). Most transition-relevance places *are* not accompanied by silences, let alone being recognized by them. On the other hand "there are silences in the talk during which others specifically *withhold* intervention, and these are when the silences occur at other than possible completions of the turn-constructional units, that is, when they are *not* at transition-relevance places" (ibid.).[①]

Concerning the interpretation of rule 1(b), Schegloff again points out the question of "pause" or "break". Then he argues that there is a condition on the application of this rule, that is, the current speaker has not selected a next speaker. So it is not simply that at a transition-relevance place "anybody can start talking". Thirdly, the self-selected speaker does *not* get to keep on talking. "That person's talk will also be composed of a turn-constructional unit which will itself fairly rapidly come to a possible completion, which will be transition-relevant, af-

---

① Searle in his reply explains that "by 'break' or 'pause' I did not mean a simple temporal gap, but rather the boundaries of an intentionally defined chunk" (p. 146).

fording another participant the opportunity for turn-transfer" (p. 121).

The same considerations apply to rule 1(c). It is not just when you are talking, you can keep on talking. "[I]t says more than that, and less" (p. 122). On the one hand, it is subject to the condition that the previous two rules have not been applied. On the other hand, you have the option to go on talking or not, only when you have come to a transition-relevance place. Otherwise you have no choice but to go on talking, even when the hearer has already understood what you are saying.

On the status of rule 1(a) as a speech act rule or turn-taking rule, Schegloff holds that when a speaker asks somebody a question, he is both asking a question and selecting a next speaker. That these two acts are distinct and only partially overlapping is shown by the fact that we may ask a question without asking SOMEBODY a question. And there are other ways of selecting a next speaker than the use of a particular term of address. For example, "Y'want some nuts, babe?" selects the daughter who has not had any yet to be the next speaker rather than the husband who has, for whom the utterance would have been "Y'want some more nuts, babe?" (p. 124).

As for the name, Schegloff is quite prepared to have a change. He does not insist on calling it "rule", "practices" is quite acceptable to him.

Appendix: **transcription conventions** (adapted from Levinson 1983: 369–70)

//	point at which the current utterance is overlapped by that transcribed below
(0.0)	pauses or gaps in what is very approximately tenths of seconds
(.)	micropause—potentially significant but very short pause, somewhere below 0.2 seconds' duration
( )	uncertain passages of transcript
(( ))	used to specify some non-verbal action
italics	syllables stressed by amplitude, pitch and duration
: :	lengthened syllables
-	glottal-stop self-editing marker
= =	"latched" utterances, with no gap
?	not a punctuation mark, but a rising intonation contour
.	used to indicate falling intonation contour
,	used to indicate maintained ("continuing") intonation contour
hh / .hh	indicates an audible out-breath / in-breath

Bibliography

Akmajian, A. & Heny, F. W. (1975). *An Introduction to the Principles of Transformational Syntax*. Cambridge, Mass.: The MIT Press.

Arens, E. (1994). *The Logic of Pragmatic Thinking: from Peirce to Habermas*. (tr. by D. Smith) New Jersey: Humanities Press.

Ariel, M. (1988a). Referring and accessibility. In *Journal of Linguistics*, **24**, 65-87.

——— (1988b). Retrieving propositions from context: why and how. In *Journal of Pragmatics*, **12**, 567-600.

——— (1991). The function of accessibility in a theory of grammar. In *Journal of Pragmatics*, **16**, 443-63.

——— (1994). Interpreting anaphoric expressions: a cognitive versus a pragmatic approach. In *Journal of Linguistics*, **30**, 3-42.

——— (1996). Referring expressions and the +/- coreference distinction. In T. Fretheim & J. K. Gundel (eds.) (1996: 13-35)

Aronoff, M. (1976). *Word Formation in Generative Grammar*. Cambridge, Mass.: MIT Press.

Atkinson, J. M. & Drew, P. (1979). *Order in Court*. London: Macmillan.

Atlas, J., & Levinson, S. (1981). *It*-clefts, informativeness, and logical form. In Cole (ed.) (1981: 1-61).

Austin, J. L. (1975 [1962]). *How to Do Things with Words*. 2nd ed. Oxford: Clarendon Press.

(1979 [1970]). *Philosophical Papers*. 3rd ed. Oxford: Oxford University Press.

(1971) . Performative-Constative. In Searle (1971: 13 – 22).

Bar-Hillel, Y. (1954). Indexical expressions. *Mind*, **63**, 359 – 79.

(Reprinted in Bar-Hillel (1970: 69 – 88).)

(1964). *Language and Information*. Reading, Mass.: Addison-Wesley.

(1970). *Aspects of Language*. Jerusalem: The Magness Press.

Bauman, R. & Sherzer, J. (eds.) (1974). *Explorations in the Ethnography of Speaking*. Cambridge: Cambridge University Press.

Berg, J. (1991). The relevant relevance. *Journal of Pragmatics*, **16**, 411 – 25.

Bever, T. G., Katz, J. J. & Langendoen, D. T. (eds.) (1976). *An Integrated Theory of Linguistic Ability*. New York: T. Y. Crowell.

Black, M. (ed.) (1965). *Philosophy in America*. London: George Allen & Unwin Ltd.

Blakemore, D. (1988). The organization of discourse. In Newmeyer (ed.) Vol. 4, 229 – 50.

(1992) . *Understanding Utterances: An Introduction to Pragmatics*. Oxfrod: Blackwell.

Bolinger, D. (1979). Pronouns in discourse. In T. Givon (ed.) (1979:289 – 309).

Brown, G. & Yule, G. (1983). *Discourse Analysis*. Cambridge: Cambridge University Press.

Carnap, R. (1939). Foundations of logic and mathematics. In Neurath, Carnap & Morris (eds.) (1939: 139 - 214).

(1942). *Introduction to Semantics*. Cambridge, Mass.: Harvard University Press.

Carnap, R., & Bar-Hillel, Y. (1952). *An Outline of a Theory of Semantic Information* (Technical Report No. 247). Cambridge, Mass.: Research Laboratory of Electronics, MIT. (Reprinted in Y. Bar-Hillel (1964: 221 - 74).)

Carston, R. (1988). Implicature, explicature, and truth-theoretic semantics. In Kempson (ed.) (1988: 155 - 81). (Reprinted in Davis (ed.) (1991: 33 - 51).)

(1996). Metalinguistic negation and echoic use. In *Journal of Pragmatics*, **25**, 309 - 30.

(1998a). Informativeness, relevance and scalar implicature. In R. Carston & S. Uchida (eds.) (1998:179 - 236).

(1998b). Negation, 'presupposition' and the semantics/pragmatics distinction. In *Journal of Linguistics*, **34**, 309 - 50.

Carston, R. & Uchida, S. (eds.) (1998). *Relevance Theory: Applications and Implications*. Amsterdam: John Benjamins.

Chomsky, N. (1970). Deep structure, surface structure and semantic interpretation. In R. Jakobson & S. Kawamoto (eds.) *Studies in Generative and Oriental Linguistics*. Tokyo. (Reprinted in Chomsky (1972: 62 - 119).)

(1975 [1972]). *Studies on Semantics in Generative Grammar*. 2nd ed. The Hague: Mouton

(1981). *Lectures on Government and Binding*. Dordrecht: Foris.

(1982). *Some Concepts and Consequences of the Theory of Government and Binding*. Cambridge, Mass.: MIT Press.

(1986). *Knowledge of Language: Its Nature, Origin, and Use*. New York: Praeger.

(1995). *The Minimalist Program*. Cambridge, Mass.: MIT Press.

Cohen, L. J. (1964). Do illocutionary forces exist? *Philosophical Quarterly*, XIV, No. 55, 118–37. (Reprinted in Rosenberg & Travis (eds.) (1971: 580–99).)

Cole, P. (ed.) (1978). *Syntax and Semantics 9: Pragmatics*. New York: Academic Press. (ed.)

(1981). *Radical Pragmatics*. New York: Academic Press.

Cole, P. & Morgan, J. L. (eds.) (1975). *Syntax and Semantics 3: Speech Acts*. New York: Academic Press.

Comrie, B. (1976). *Aspect: an Introduction to the Study of Verbal Aspect and Related Problems*. Cambridge: Cambridge University Press.

Coulthard, M. (1985 [1977]). *An Introduction to Discourse Analysis*. 2nd ed. London: Longman.

Davis, S. (ed.) (1991). *Pragmatics: A Reader*. Oxford: Oxford University Press.

Davidson, D. & Harman, G. (eds.) (1972). *Semantics of Natural Language*. Dordrecht: Reidel.

Farmer, A. K. & Harnish, R. M. (1987). Communicative reference with pronouns. In Verschueren & Bertuccelli-Papi (eds.) (1987:547–65).

Fauconnier, G. (1975a) Pragmatic scales and logical structure. *Linguistic Inquiry*, **6**, 353–375.

(1975b) Polarity and the scale principle. *Papers from the 11 th Regional Meeting, Chicago Linguistic Society*, 188–199.

Fillmore, C. J. (1969a). Types of lexical information. In F. Kiefer (ed.) *Studies in Syntax and Semantics*. Reidel. (Reprinted in D. Steinberg & L. Jakobovits (eds.) (1971: 370 - 92).)

(1969b). Verbs of judging: an exercise in semantic description. *Papers in Linguistics*. Vol. 1, No. 1, July 1969. (Reprinted in Fillmore & Langendoen (1971: 273 - 90).)

Fillmore, C. J. & Langendoen, D. T. (eds.) (1971). *Studies in Linguistic Semantics*. New York: Holt, Rinehart and Winston.

Fisch, M. H. (1978). Peirce's general theory of signs. In Sebeok (ed.) (1978: 31 - 70).

Fox, B. (ed.) (1996). *Studies in Anaphor*. Amsterdam: John Benjamins.

Frege, G. (1892). On sense and reference. In Geach & Black (eds.) (1952: 56 - 78).

Fretheim, T. & Gundel, J. K. (eds.) (1996). *Reference and Referent Accessibility*. Amsterdam: John Benjamins.

Gazdar, G. (1979a). *Pragmatics: Implicature, Presupposition and Logical Form*. New York: Academic Press.

(1979b). A solution to the projection problem. In Oh and Dinneen (eds.) (1979: 57 - 89).

(1981) Speech act assignment. In Joshi, Webber and Sag (eds.) (1981: 64 - 83).

Gazdar, G. & Good, D. (1982). On a notion of relevance. In Smith (ed.) (1982: 88 - 100).

Geech, P. T. & Black, M. (eds.) (1952). *Translations from the Philosophical Writings of Gottlob Frege*. Oxford: Blackwell.

Giora, R. (1988). On the informativeness requirement. *Journal of Pragmatics*, **12**, 547 - 65.

(1997). Discourse coherence and theory of relevance: Stumbling blocks in search of a unified theory. In *Journal of Pragmatics*, **27**, 17 – 34.

(1998). Discourse coherence is an independent notion: a reply to Deirdre Wilson. *Journal of Pragmatics*, **29**, 75 – 86.

Givon, T. (ed.) (1979). *Syntax and Semantics 12: Discourse and Syntax*. New York: Academic Press.

Goldman-Eisler, F. (1980). Psychological mechanisms of speech production as studied through the analysis of simultaneous translation. In B. Butterworth (ed.) *Language Production*, Vol. 1: *Speech and Talk*. New York: Academic Press, pp. 143 – 54.

Goodwin, C. (1977). *Some Aspects of the Interaction of Speaker and Hearer in the Construction of the Turn at Talk in Natural Conversation*. Unpublished Ph.D. dissertation, University of Pennsylvania. (Revised version published as Goodwin (1981).)

(1981). *Conversational Organization: Interaction between Speakers and Hearers*. New York: Academic Press.

Gordon, D. & Lakoff, G. (1971). Conversational postulates. *Papers from the Seventh Regional Meeting of the Chicago Linguistic Society*, 63 – 84. (Reprinted in Cole & Morgan (eds.) (1975: 83 – 106).)

Green, G. (1975). How to get people to do things with words: the whimperative question. In Cole & Morgan (eds.) (1975: 107 – 42).

(1989). *Pragmatics and Natural Language Understanding*. Hillsdale, NJ: Erlbaum.

Grice, H. P. (1957). Meaning. *Philosophical Review*, **66**, 377 – 88. (Reprinted in Rosenberg & Travis (eds.) (1971: 436 –

44).)

(1961). The causal theory of perception. *Proceedings of the Aristotelian Society*, supp. vol. 35: 121 – 52. (Reprinted in Shwartz (ed.) (1965).)

(1968) . Utterer's meaning, sentence-meaning, and word-meaning. *Foundations of Language*, **4**, 1 – 18. (Reprinted in Searle (ed.) (1971: 54 – 70).)

(1975). Logic and conversation. In Cole & Morgan (eds.) (1975: 41 – 58).)

(1978) . Further notes on logic and conversation. In Cole (ed.) (1978: 113 – 28).

(1981). Presupposition and conversational implicature. In Cole (ed.) (1981: 183 – 98).

(1982). Meaning revisited. In Smith (ed.) (1982: 223 – 43).

(1989). *Studies in the Way of Words*. Cambridge, Mass.: Harvard University Press.

Haberland, H. & Jacob, M. (1977). Editorial: pragmatics and linguistics. *Journal of Pragmatics*. **1**, 1 – 16.

Harnish, R. M. (1976). Logical form and implicature. In Bever, Katz & Langendoen (eds.) (1976: 313 – 92). (Reprinted in Davis (ed.) (1991: 316 – 64).)

(ed.)(1994). *Basic Topics in the Philosophy of Language*. New Jersey: Prentice-Hall, Inc.

Hempel, C. G. (1960). Inductive inconsistencies. *Synthese*, **11**, 439 – 469.

Horn, L. R. (1972). *On the Semantic Properties of the Logical Operators in English*. Ph.D. dissertation, UCLA. (Distributed by Indiana University Linguistic Club, 1976.)

(1973). Greek Grice: A brief survey of proto-conversational rules in the history of logic. *Proceedings of the Ninth Regional Meeting of the Chicago Linguistic Society*, 205 – 14.

(1984) . Towards a new taxonomy for pragmatic inference: Q-based and R-based implicature. In D. Schiffrin (ed.) (1984: 11 – 42).

(1988). Pragmatic theory. In Newmeyer (ed.) Vol. 1, 113 – 145.

(1989) . *A Natural History of Negation*. Chicago: Chicago University Press.

(1991). Givens as new: when redundant affirmation isn't. In *Journal of Pragmatics*, **15**, 313 – 36.

(1992). The said and the unsaid. In *Ohio State University Working Papers in Linguistics*, **40**, 163 – 92.

(1996a). Exclusive company: *only* and the dynamics of vertical inference. *Journal of Semantics*, **13**, 1 – 40.

(1996b). Presupposition and implicature. In S. Lappin (ed.) *The Handbook of Contemporary Semantic Theory*, 299 – 319. Oxford: Blackwell.

Huang, Yan. (1990). *Lectures on Pragmatics*. Mimeo. Department of Linguistics, University of Cambridge.

(1991). A neo-Gricean pragmatic theory of anaphora. *Journal of Linguistics*, **27**, 301 – 35.

(1994). *The Syntax and Pragmatics of Anaphora: A Study with Special Reference to Chinese*. Cambridge: Cambridge University Press.

Jacobs, R. A. & Rosenbaum, P. S. (eds.) (1970). *Readings in English Transformational Grammar*. Waltham, Massachusetts:

Ginn and Company.

Jefferson, G. (1972). Side sequences. In Sudnow (1972: 294 – 338).

Jespersen, O. (1924). *The Philosophy of Grammar*. London: George Allen & Unwin LTD.

―― (1976 [1924]). *The Philosophy of Grammar*. New York: Norton.

Joshi, A. K., Weber, B. L. & Sag, I. A. (eds.) (1981). *Elements of Discourse Understanding*. Cambridge: Cambridge University Press.

Karttunen, L. (1971). Implicative verbs. *Language*, **47**, 340 – 58.

―― (1973). Presuppositions of compound sentences. *Linguistic Inquiry*, **4**, 169 – 93.

Karttunen, L. & Peters, S. (1975). Conventional implicature in Montague grammar. *Proceedings of the First Annual Meeting of the Berkeley Linguistic Society*, 266 – 78.

―― (1979). Conventional implicature. In Oh & Dinneen (eds.) (1979: 1 – 56).

Kasher, A. (ed.) (1998). Pragmatics: Critical Concepts. Vols. 1 – 6. London: Routledge.

Keenan, E. L. (1971). Two kinds of presupposition in natural language. In Fillmore and Langendoen (eds.) (1971: 45 – 54).

―― (ed.) (1975). *Formal Semantics of Natural Language*. Cambridge: Cambridge University Press.

Keenan, E. O. (1976). The universality of conversational postulates. *Language in Society*, **5**: 67 – 80. (Reprinted in A. Kasher (ed.) (1998 vol 4: 215 – 29).)

Kempson, R. M. (1975). *Presupposition and the Delimitation of*

Semantics. Cambridge: Cambridge University Press.

(1977) . *Semantic Theory*. Cambridge: Cambridge University Press.

(1979). Presupposition, opacity and ambiguity. In Oh & Dinneen (1979: 283 - 97).

(1984). Pragmatics, anaphora and logical form. In Schiffrin (1984: 1 - 10).

(1988a). Grammar and conversational principles. In Newmeyer (ed.) Vol. 2, 139 - 162.

(1988b). (ed.) *Mental Representations: the Interface Between Language and Reality*. Cambridge: Cambridge University Press.

Kempson, R. & Gabbay, D. (1998). Crossover: a unified view. In *Journal of Linguistics*, **34**, 73 - 124.

Ketner, K. L. & Kloesel C. J. W. (eds.) (1986). *Peirce, Semeiotic, and Pragmatism: Essays by Max H. Fisch*. Bloomington: Indians University Press.

Kiparsky, P. (1982). Word-formation and the lexicon. In Ingemann, F. (ed.) (1982) *Proceedings of the 1982 Mid-American Linguistic Conference*. University of Kansas.

Kiparsky, P. & Kiparsky, C. (1970). Fact. In M. Bierwisch & K. Heidolph (eds.) *Progress in Linguistics*. (Reprinted in Steinberg & Jakobovits (eds.) (1971: 345 - 69).)

Kuno, S. (1987). *Functional Syntax: Anaphora, Discourse and Empathy*. Chicago: Chicago University Press.

Lakoff, G. (1972). Linguistics and natural logic. In Davidson and Harman (eds.). (1975). Pragmatics in natural logic. In Keenan (ed.) (1975: 253 - 86).

Lakoff, R. (1995). Conversational implicature. In Verschueren,

Ostman & Blommaert (eds).

Leech, G. N. (1981 [1974]). *Semantics*. 2nd ed. Harmondsworth: Penguin.

—— (1980). *Explorations in Semantics and Pragmatics*. Amsterdam: John Benjamins.

—— (1983). *Principles of Pragmatics*. London: Longman.

Leech, G. N. & Thomas, J. (1985). Language, meaning and context. In Collinge (ed.) *An Encyclopaedia of Language*. London: Routledge.

Levinson, S. C. (1979). Pragmatics and social deixis. *Proceedings of the Fifth Annual Meeting of the Berkeley Linguistic Society*, 206–23.

—— (1983). *Pragmatics*. Cambridge: Cambridge University Press.

—— (1987a). Minimization and conversational inference. In Verschueren & Bertuccelli-Papi (eds.) (1987: 61–129). (Reprinted in A. Kasher (ed.) (1998 vol. 4: 545–612).)

—— (1987b). Pragmatics and the grammar of anaphora: a partial pragmatic reduction of binding and control phenomena. *Journal of Linguistics*, **23**, 379–434.

—— (1989) . A review of Relevance. *Journal of Linguistics*, **25**, 455–472.

—— (1991). Pragmatic reduction of the binding conditions revisited. *Journal of Linguistics*, **27**, 107–62.

Lyons, J. (1968). *An Introduction to Theoretical Linguistics*. Cambridge: Cambridge University Press.

—— (1977). *Semantics*, Vols. 1 & 2. Cambridge: Cambridge University Press.

McCawley, J. (1978). Conversational implicature and the lexicon. In

Cole (ed.) (1978: 245-59).

Marinet, A. (1962). *A Functional View of Language*. Oxford: Clarendon Press.

Mey, J. (1993). *Pragmatics: An Introduction*. Oxford: Blackwell.

Mey, J. & Talbot, M. (1988). Computation and the soul: A propos Dan Sperber and Deirdre Wilson's *Relevance*. *Journal of Pragmatics*. **12**, 743-89.

Miller, G. A. (1963). Speaking in general. Review of J. H. Greenberg (ed.) *Universals of Language*. *Contemporary Psychology*, **8**, 417-18.

Mitchell, T. F. (1978). Meaning is what you do—and how he and I interpret it: a Firthian view of pragmatics. *Die Neueren Sprachen*, **3**, 224-53.

Montague, R. (1974). *Formal Philosophy: Selected Papers*. (ed. by R. H. Thomason) New Haven: Yale University Press.

Morris, C. W. (1937). *Logical Positivism, Pragmatism and Scientific Empiricism*. Paris: Hermann et Cie.

(1938). *Foundations of the Theory of Signs*. In Morris (1971).

(1946). *Sign, Language and Behavior*. In Morris (1971).

(1971). *Writings on the General Theory of Signs*. The Hague: Mouton.

Neurath, O., Carnap, R. & Morris, C. (eds.) (1939). *International Encyclopedia of United Science*. Chicago: University of Chicago Press.

Newmeyer, F. (ed.) (1988). *Linguistics: The Cambridge Survey*. Vols. 1-4. Cambridge: Cambridge University Press.

Oh, C.-K. & Dinneen, D. A. (eds.) (1979). *Syntax and Semantics* 11: *Presupposition*. New York: Academic Press.

Palmer, F. R. (1981 [1976]) *Semantics*. 2nd ed. Cambridge: Cambridge University Press.

Peirce, C. S. (1931 - 1935). *Collected Papers*. Vols. 1 - 6. (eds. by C. Hartshorne and P. Weiss) Cambridge, Mass.: Harvard University Press.

(1958). *Collected Papers*. Vols. 7 & 8. (ed. by A. W. Burks) Cambridge, Mass.: Harvard University Press.

Quirk, R., Greenbaum, S., Leech, G. & Svartvik, J. (1985). *A Comprehensive Grammar of English Language*. London: Longman.

Richardson, J. F. & Richardson, A. W. (1990). On predicting pragmatic relations. In *Proceedings of the 16th Annual Meeting of the Berkeley Linguistic Society, Parasession on the Legacy of Grice*, 498 - 508.

Rogers, A., Wall, R. & Murphy, J. P. (eds.) (1977). *Proceedings of the Texas Conference on Performatives, Presuppositions and Implicatures*. Washington: Center for Applied Linguistics.

Rosenberg, J. F. & Travis, C. (eds.) (1971). *Readings in the Philosophy of Language*. New Jersey: Prentice-Hall, Inc.

Ross, J. R. (1970). On declarative sentences. In Jacobs and Rosenbaum (eds.) (1970: 222 - 72).

(1975). Where to do things with words. In Cole and Morgan (eds.) (1975): 233 - 56).

Russell, B. (1905). On denoting. *Mind*, **14**, 479 - 93. (Reprinted in Russell (1994).)

(1918). The philosophy of logical atomism. *The Monists*, **28**, 495 - 527. (Reprinted in Russell (1986).)

(1986). *The Collected Papers of Bertrand Russell*. Vol. 8. (ed.

by Alasdair Urquhart) London: George Allen & Unwin.

(1994). *The Collected Papers of Bertrand Russell*. Vol. 4. (ed. by Alasdair Urquhart) London: Routledge.

Sacks, H. (1967 - 1971). *Lecture Notes*. Mimeo. Department of Sociology, University of California, Irvine.

(1974). An analysis of the course of a joke's telling in conversation. In Bauman and Sherzer (1974: 337 - 53).

(MS). *Aspects of the Sequential Organization of Conversation*.

Sacks, H., Schegloff, E. A. & Jefferson, G. (1974). A simplest systematics for the organization of turn-taking in conversation. *Language*, **50**, 696 - 735. (Reprinted in A. Kasher (ed.) (1998 vol. 5: 193 - 242).)

Sadock, J. M. (1974). *Toward a Linguistic Theory of Speech Acts*. New York: Academic Press.

(1977). Aspects of linguistic pragmatics. In Rogers, Wall & Murphy (eds.) (1977: 67 - 78).

(1978). On testing for conversational implicature. In Cole (ed.) (1978: 281 - 97). (Revised version in Davis (ed.) (1991: 365 - 76).)

Sadock, J. M. (1984). Whither radical pragmatics? In D. Schiffrin (ed.) (1984:139 - 49).

(1988). Speech act distinctions in grammar. In F. J. Newmeyer (ed.)(1988:183 - 99).

Schegloff, E. A. (1972). Notes on a conversational practice: formulating place. In D. Sudnow (ed.) (1972: 75 - 119).

(1979). The relevance of repair to syntax-for-conversation. In T. Givon (ed.) (1979: 261 - 86).

(1988). Presequences and indirection. *Journal of Pragmatics*,

12, 55 – 62.

(1996). Some practices for referring to persons in talk-in-interaction: a partial sketch of a systematics. In B. Fox (ed.) (1996: 437 – 85).

Schegloff, E. A., Jefferson, G. & Sacks, H. (1977). The preference for self-correction in the organization of repair in conversation. *Language*, **53**, 361 – 82.

Schenkein, J. (ed.) (1978). *Studies in the Organization of Conversational Interaction*. New York: Academic Press.

Schiffrin, D. (ed.) (1984). *Meaning, Form, and Use in Context: Linguistic Applications*. Washington, D. C.: Georgetown University Press.

Searle, J. R. (1965). What is a speech act? In Black (ed.) (1965: 221 – 39). (Reprinted in Rosenberg & Travis (eds.) (1971: 614 – 28).)

(1968). Austin on locutionary and illocutionary acts. *Philosophical Review*, Vol. 57, No. 4. (Reprinted in Rosenberg & Travis (eds.) (1971: 262 – 75).)

(1969). *Speech Acts: An Essay in the Philosophy of Language*. Cambridge: Cambridge University Press.

(ed.) (1971). *The Philosophy of Language*. Oxford: Oxford University Press.

(1975a). A taxonomy of illocutionary acts. In K. Gunderson (ed.) *Language, Mind and Knowledge*. Minnesota Studies in the Philosophy of Science. University of Minnesota Press. (Reprinted in Searle (1979: 1 – 29).)

(1975b). Indirect speech acts. In Cole and Morgan (eds.) (1975: 59 – 82).

(1975c). Speech acts and recent linguistics. In D. Aaronson and R. W. Rieber (eds.) *Developmental Psycholinguistics and Communication Disorders*. Annals of the New York Academy of Sciences, Vol. 263. (Reprinted in Searle (1979: 162 – 79).)

(1979). *Expression and Meaning*. Cambridge: Cambridge University Press.

Searle, J. R., Kiefer, F. & Bierwisch, M. (eds.) (1980). *Speech Act Theory and Pragmatics*. Synthese Language Library, Vol. 10. Dordrecht: Reidel.

Searle et al (1992). (*On*) *Searle on Conversation*. Compiled and introduced by H. Parret & J. Verschueren. Amsterdam: John Benjamins.

Sebeok, T. (ed.) (1978). *Sight, Sound, and Sense*. Bloomington: Indiana University Press.

Shwartz, R. (ed.) (1965). *Perceiving, Sensing, and Knowing*. New York: Doubleday.

Sinclair, A. (1976). The sociolinguistic significance of the form of requests used in service encounters. Unpublished Diploma dissertation, University of Cambridge.

Sinclair, J. M. & Coulthard, R. M. (1975). *Towards an Analysis of Discourse: the English Used by Teachers and Pupils*. London: Oxford University Press.

Smith, N. V. (ed.) (1982). *Mutual Knowledge*. London: Academic Press.

(1989). *The Twitter Machine: Reflections on Language*. Oxford: Basil Blackwell.

Smith, N. V. & Wilson, D. (1979). *Modern Linguistics: the Results of Chomsky's Revolution*. Harmondsworth: Penguin.

Sperber, D. & Wilson, D. (1981). Irony and the use-mention distinction. In Cole (ed.) (1981: 295 – 318).

(1982). Mutual knowledge and relevance in theories of comprehension. In Smith (ed.) (1982: 61 – 131).

(1986) . *Relevance: Communication and Cognition*. Oxford: Blackwell.

(1998). Irony and relevance: A reply to Seto, Hamamoto and Yamanashi. In R. Carston & S. Uchida (eds.) (1998: 283 – 93).

Steinberg, D. D. & Jakobovits, L. A. (eds.) (1971). *An Interdisciplinary Reader in Philosophy, Linguistics and Psychology*. Cambridge: Cambridge University Press.

Strawson, P. F. (1950). On referring. *Mind*, **59**, 320 – 44. (Reprinted in Strawson (1971).)

(1952) . *Introduction to Logical Theory*. London: Methuen.

(1964). Intention and convention in speech acts. *Philosophical Review*, **73**, 439 – 60. (Reprinted in Searle (ed.) (1971: 23 – 38).)

(1971). *Logico-Linguistic Papers*. London: Methuen.

Sudnow, D. (ed.) (1972). *Studies in Social Interaction*. New York: Free Press.

Terasaki, A. (1976). *Pre-announcement Sequences in Conversation*. Social Science Working Paper 99. School of Social Science, University of California, Irvine

Thomas, J. (1995). *Meaning in Interaction: An Introduction to Pragmatics*. London: Longman.

Verschueren, J. (1987). Pragmatics as a theory of linguistic adaptation. In *Working Document* #1, Antwerp: International Pragmatics Association.

Verschueren, J., Ostman, J.-O. & Blommaert, J. (eds.) (1995). *Handbook of Pragmatics*. Amsterdam: John Benjamins.

Warnock, G. J. (1989). *J. L. Austin*. London: Routledge

Wilson, D. (1975). *Presuppositions and Non-Truth Conditional Semantics*. New York: academic Press.

——(1998). Discourse, coherence and relevance: A reply to Rachel Giora. *Journal of Pragmatics*, **29**, 57 – 74.

Wilson, D. & Sperber. D. (1979). Ordered entailments: an alternative to presuppositional theories. In C.-K. Oh & D. A. Dinneen (eds.) (1979:229 – 324).

——(1981). On Grice's theory of conversation. In P. Werth (ed.) (1981: 155 – 78). (Reprinted in A. Kasher (ed.) (1998 vol. 4: 347 – 68).)

——(1998). Pragmatics and time. In R. Carston & S. Uchida (eds.) (1998:1 – 22).

Zipf, G. K. (1949). *Human Behavior and the Principle of Least Effort*. Cambridge: Addison-Wesley.

程雨民 1997《语言系统及其运作》,上海外语教育出版社。

何兆熊 1989《语用学概要》,上海外语教育出版社。

何自然 1988《语用学概论》,湖南教育出版社。

胡壮麟 1995《当代语言理论与应用》,北京大学出版社。

姜望琪 1991 "True or False?"《北京大学学报(英语语言文学专刊)》第 2 期。

——1997 "Pragmatics 溯源"《北京大学学报(外国语言文学专刊)》。

李月菊 1994《人才交流会上招聘者与应聘者会话分析》,北京大学英语系硕士论文。

廖秋忠 1992《廖秋忠文集》,北京语言学院出版社。
陆俭明等　1982《现代汉语虚词例释》,商务印书馆。
吕叔湘 1984（主编）《现代汉语八百词》,商务印书馆。
钱冠连 1997《汉语文化语用学》,清华大学出版社。
宋国明 1997《句法理论概要》,中国社会科学出版社。
涂纪亮 1987《分析哲学及其在美国的发展》,中国社会科学出版社。
　　　 1988(主编)《语言哲学名著选辑》,三联书店。
徐烈炯 1988《生成语法理论》,上海外语教育出版社。
　　　 1995《语义学》,第二版,语文出版社。
赵晓泉 1996《学术讨论中的"补偏救弊"现象》,北京大学英语系硕
　　　　　士论文。
朱德熙 1982《语法讲义》,商务印书馆。